HOW TO WRITE PROPOSALS THAT PRODUCE

by
Joel P. Bowman
Bernadine P. Branchaw

Oryx Press
1992

The rare Arabian Oryx is believed to have inspired the myth of the unicorn. This desert antelope became virtually extinct in the early 1960s. At that time several groups of international conservationists arranged to have 9 animals sent to the Phoenix Zoo to be the nucleus of a captive breeding herd. Today the Oryx population is nearly 800, and over 400 have been returned to reserves in the Middle East.

Library of Congress Cataloging-in-Publication Data
Bowman, Joel P.
    How to write proposals that produce / by Joel P. Bowman, Bernadine P. Branchaw.
    p. cm.
    Includes bibliographical references and index.
    ISBN 0-89774-656-2
    1. Proposal writing in business.   2. Business presentations.
I. Branchaw, Bernadine P.   II. Title.
HF5718.5.B69   1992
658.15'224—dc20   91-3190
                                                                    CIP

Contents

List of Illustrations

Preface

Having read, written, evaluated, and analyzed many proposals, we realized that proposal writing is both an art and a science. For a proposal to be accepted, it must be not only well-written (an art), but also well-organized according to the research process of defining the problem, developing a methodology to collect and analyze data, interpreting and evaluating the findings, drawing conclusions, and making recommendations (a science).

When teaching our students, working with our academic colleagues, and consulting with practitioners in business and industry, we noticed that the existing books on proposal writing focused on the technical aspects of developing projects, finding sources of funding, and responding to requests for proposals (RFPs). No book on proposal writing focused specifically on the process of writing. Because our experience suggested that the art of producing a well-written, persuasive document was at least as problematical for proposal writers as any of the other tasks associated with developing and funding a project, we decided to write this guide.

The primary audience for *How to Write Proposals That Produce* includes practitioners in both private sector businesses and industries and those working in nonprofit institutions and government agencies. The book is not an academic text that emphasizes theory; it is a practical book for the experienced businessperson who wants field-tested techniques for effective communication. This book is also suitable for use in college classes in which students are expected to prepare proposals as part of their course requirements. It would be a useful addition to courses in report writing or courses in management or marketing requiring major projects.

The emphasis of *How to Write Proposals That Produce* is on writing techniques for internal and external proposals. The book stresses the competitive nature of proposals, the need to improve writing skills, the need for audience analysis, and the need to understand how presentation affects results. It provides a step-by-step guide to the proposal writing process, from the initial stages of planning, to outlining, to writing the first draft, to preparing the final document, to preparing materials for an oral presentation. Key points are summarized at the end of each chapter.

In Chapter 1, "The Nature of Proposals," we discuss proposal purposes, types, and forms. Chapter 2 covers the first step of the planning process: audience analysis. We believe that our coverage of audience analysis is the most thorough currently available. Chapter 3, "Strategies for Success," outlines the planning process with emphasis on the need to prepare a document that will address concerns of the audience. Chapter 4, "The Writing Process: Beginning and Revising," continues the discussion of planning, focusing on the development of checklists, outlines, and mockups to provide structure and direction for the proposal.

Chapter 5, "The Writing Process: Grammar and Style," covers the chief stumbling blocks for most writers: grammar and style. Because most writers are uncertain about the correctness of their writing, we cover the principal grammatical rules and the important elements of writing style. Chapter 6, "Special Techniques: Headings, Lists, and Tables," covers the ways to present information so that it is clear and readable. Chapter 7, "Special Techniques: Graphs and Charts," shows you how to use graphs and charts to clarify and supplement the text, including illustrations of computer-generated graphs and ways to avoid some of the problems associated with their use. Although the appearance of a proposal will not be the main criterion by which it is evaluated, appearance counts, so Chapter 8, "Format and Appearance," shows how a proposal can be formatted to improve its chances for success and provides examples of how desktop publishing equipment can enhance the appearance of a proposal. Possible proposal components—front matter (cover, title page, table of contents, and abstract); body (introduction, technical section, project management, evaluation, costs, and qualifications); and supplemental parts (appendix, bibliography, and index) are thoroughly discussed in Chapter 9, "The Finished Document."

Internal and external proposal evaluations are examined in Chapter 10, "Proposal Evaluations." Because a proposal writer may also need to prepare an oral presentation as part of the proposal process, we included Chapter 11, "Oral Presentations," which outlines the steps necessary for making an effective presentation. The chapter also discusses the preparation of visual aids.

The final chapter, Chapter 12, "Documentation," emphasizes the need for appropriate documentation in written materials. It covers such issues as plagiarism and copyright laws as well as the placement of references and appropriate forms for entries. Although it is not intended as a substitute for the style manual typically used in your business or industry, it provides sample entry forms according to three major style manuals—*Publication Manual of the American Psychological Association, Chicago Manual of Style,* and *MLA Handbook for Writers of Research Papers.*

The bibliography and the extension checklist provided in the Appendixes are also designed to aid you in your efforts to submit winning proposals.

CHAPTER 1

The Nature of Proposals

Imagine for a minute that you have a wonderful new idea for improving your manufacturing process so that your company can produce higher quality widgets at a lower cost. Testing your idea, however, will require $2,500, which is not in your current budget. Even though money is tight, you decide to send a memo to your boss about your idea, suggesting that you, your boss, and the vice president of manufacturing meet to discuss its practicality. Your memo might look something like the one displayed in Figure 1-1.

Jan 16, 19xx

To: Your Boss

From: You

BETTER WIDGETS AT LOWER COSTS

I have an idea for a new manufacturing process that would result in higher quality widgets at lower cost.

I'd like to meet with you and Bill Rodale to discuss my idea and the possibility of testing it to see if I'm right. If I am, XYZ could save more than $200,000 the first year alone through reducing the number of defective widgets and lowering manufacturing costs.

I can be available for a meeting any day next week at your convenience. Please give me a call to let me know your thinking on this.

Figure 1-1. An Informal Proposal.

Your memo is a proposal. You have something to "sell," and you have made an offer that can be accepted, rejected, or modified to meet the needs of the recipient. Your memo is also a technical document in that it suggests a possible solution to a specific problem.

The term *proposal* applies to a wide range of documents: from casual to formal, from short to long, and from general to extremely specific and detailed. Some proposals may be presented orally. In the previous example, you simply could have called your boss and told him or her about your idea and requested the meeting during the call. Virtually all proposals that may result in a significant commitment of time, money, or other limited resources, however, are eventually presented in written form.

At the simplest level, a proposal is a recommendation, plan, or suggestion offered by one party to another. As modern business has evolved, the process of preparing and reviewing proposals has become increasingly complex and increasingly essential. Almost all major projects undertaken by business and industry, governmental agencies, and non-profit organizations begin with a *request for a proposal* (RFP), a *request for procurement* (RFP), or an *invitation for bids* (IFB).* Proposals may also be solicited for minor projects, and many projects are undertaken because an individual saw a need and prepared a successful proposal. For many modern organizations, proposals are the principal sales tool—the single most important way the organization acquires customers for its products or services.

Writing successful proposals can be lucrative for the writer as well as for the writer's organization. Accepted proposals typically result in contracts to provide service, materials, supplies, or equipment that may be worth anywhere from hundreds of dollars to many millions, or in the case of some governmental contracts, perhaps even *billions* of dollars. To be successful with your proposals, you first need to ensure that you are offering competitive products or services. You also need to be able to present what you are offering in an attractive, persuasive way. The ability to write successful proposals depends on a sound understanding of what a proposal is and what it should do; a thorough knowledge of the readers and the problem they need solved; and the writing skills necessary to present information clearly, concisely, and persuasively.

DEFINITION

A written proposal is a document that offers to solve a problem for a reader or group of readers by providing specified goods and/or services at a specified cost or in exchange for something else. Typical reasons for writing proposals include the following:

- To bid on construction projects.
- To bid on technical projects (supercomputers, jet airplanes, etc.).
- To provide management consulting services.
- To develop and present training programs.
- To obtain funding for academic research.
- To obtain funding for community projects.
- To obtain approval for new policies or procedures.
- To secure advertising accounts.

---

*In general, we will use the abbreviation *RFP* to include all published requests for proposals or bids on products or services.

As a rule, proposals are competitive documents. Whether they are competing with other proposals, as is usually the case with solicited proposals, or competing with alternative ideas for a share of limited resources, proposals are essentially sales presentations with a specific decision or course of action as the desired outcome.

Although a proposal is designed to sell a concept to a specific audience, it relies on a logical presentation of facts and other evidence as its principal tool of persuasion. A good proposal is a well-written, well-developed, and well-organized technical document that states specifically what will be undertaken and why, when, how, and by whom. It also tells how much it will cost and how the results will be evaluated. In many cases, a written proposal and the subsequent letter of acceptance will constitute a legally binding contract. In other cases, a separate contract will be written incorporating elements from the proposal and any mutually agreeable additions or alterations. In brief, proposals have a sales function, a technical function, and a legal function; the writer needs to ensure that all three functions are properly handled.

A Sales Document

Because a proposal is an offer to exchange goods and/or services, it needs to be persuasive. The writer is responsible for producing the kind of document the readers will find appealing; the readers are under no special obligation to be persuaded. The readers almost always have other options that will be competing for their time and money. Your competition may be proposals from other individuals or organizations, or it may be from alternative courses of action. In either case, your proposal will need to persuade the readers that your solution to their problem would be the best.

The reasons readers reject proposals are the same as those for rejecting any persuasive appeal:

No trust:	For one reason or another, the reader does not trust you, your organization, or members of your profession in general.
No need:	The reader doesn't perceive a problem.
No desire:	The reader perceives a problem but doesn't believe that it is sufficiently important to worry about.
No urgency:	The reader perceives a problem and would like it solved but has higher priorities at the moment.
No value:	The reader perceives a problem and would like it solved but doesn't believe that the solution you propose will provide an adequate return on investment.

No belief: For one reason or another, the reader does not believe that your solution will work or that you can deliver what you promise.

To be effective, a proposal must include sufficient sales material to overcome each of these inherent negatives.

A Technical Document

Because proposals offer to do or provide something for the reader or reader's organization, the description of what will be accomplished or provided needs to be clear and complete. The writer is responsible for ensuring that the description of the product or process is sufficiently accurate to preclude misunderstandings. The kind of technical detail will, of course, differ according to the type of product or service provided, but regardless of the type, the technical specifications will be central.

A Legal Document

Because the proposal is a promise to perform certain work (usually in the form of a product or service) in exchange for a specified reward, a proposal is often a legal document, binding the writer to whatever terms are specified in it. For this reason, writers are responsible for ensuring that they (or their organizations) can deliver the product, service, or other work specified for the stipulated compensation. In many cases, the writer or the writer's company will be held to the terms and conditions specified in the proposal, including any penalties for failure to deliver the goods or services as promised by the specified date.

PROPOSAL PURPOSES

The purposes of a proposal are to persuade the potential client that:

- You are able to provide a product or service to fulfill a need or solve a problem.
- Your product or service is superior to or more cost-effective than those of your competitors.
- You have the reputation, expertise, personnel, and equipment required to do what you promise and to do it on the specified schedule.

A well-written proposal is *not* a substitute for expertise in providing a specific product or service, nor is it a substitute for credibility—the reputation you have established by your previous performance. To be successful, a proposal must begin with something worth offering. That something is almost always expertise in an area of interest to a particular client. Writing an effective proposal begins with knowing your job—knowing what you can do and how much you need to charge for it to make a desirable profit.

In most cases, many different individuals or organizations are capable of providing the same type of product or service at about the same cost, and a well-prepared proposal is often the deciding factor in who receives the contract. The purpose of the proposal is to present what you have to offer a specific audience in the best way possible. The proposal allows you to show the readers that you have a clear understanding of their problem, that you can supply the product or services that will solve that problem, and that the readers will find you or your organization a worthy business partner.

Propose a Solution to a Problem

Proposals may be either *solicited* or *unsolicited*. A solicited proposal is written in response to an RFP. The RFP will provide a description of the problem from the perspective of those requesting the proposal. In addition, it will usually set forth any specifications or special requirements believed necessary for a solution to the problem. When a homeowner wishes to remodel, perhaps by adding a room to the existing structure, he or she would specify where the room should be added, its size, the number of windows, the location of any plumbing, and so on. With complex projects, building a new military aircraft, for example, the specifications believed necessary to solve the problem may run to thousands of pages. Successful proposals indicate clearly that the writer and his or her organization are aware of and able to address each aspect of the problem specified in the RFP.

An unsolicited proposal is written to solve a problem perceived by the writer. You may notice, for example, that part of your organization's manufacturing process or a particular office procedure is less effective than it might be (as was the case in Figure 1-1). You might propose to research the problem, suggest a specific product or service that could solve the problem, or propose that the organization initiate an action to solve the problem. In such cases, before the reader will be willing to consider the proposed solution, he or she would need to be convinced that the problem actually exists and that your perception of the problem is accurate.

Regardless of whether the proposal is solicited or unsolicited, the writer will need to demonstrate that he or she understands the problem from the reader's perspective, that he or she has the expertise required to solve the problem, that the solution will benefit the reader, and that the proposed solution is better than possible alternatives.

Describe Products or Services to Meet a Need

Proposals offering products or services as solutions to problems are often called *bids*. In many cases, the readers will know exactly what they or their organizations need and specify those needs in an IFB. In such cases, the readers will be primarily concerned with your ability to meet those specifications with appropriate quality, on schedule, and for an attractive cost. In other cases, the readers may not have a clear idea of what they want or need, and it will be your job to show them that your product, service, or proposed action will solve their problem. The acceptance or rejection of a proposal frequently depends on whether the description of the product, service, or suggested action is sufficiently convincing.

Persuade the Reader to Accept an Offer

Proposals typically follow all the rules for other business reports, including the emphasis on accuracy, reliability, and objectivity. The credibility of the writer and the writer's company, after all, depends in part on the veracity and reliability of the information presented in the proposal. One of the objectives of the proposal is to persuade the readers that you and your organization will make desirable business partners. In some industries, many proposal readers and writers will know each other, at least by name and reputation. When this is the case, the credibility and reputation of the writer and his or her organization will already have been established and will influence the proposal review process.

When the writer and his or her organization are unknown to the readers, the proposal itself has the responsibility for doing the work of establishing credibility and persuading the readers. Regardless of how well reader and writer know each other, however, the principal purpose of a proposal is to persuade the reader to accept the offer. For this reason, successful proposals incorporate appropriate persuasive techniques, with the nature and amount of persuasive material being based on the relationship between the reader and writer. The nature and amount of persuasive material required will also vary from proposal to proposal depending on the complexity and cost of the product or service required. A training director in an organization, for example, may telephone a communication consultant to conduct a seminar on proposal writing for new employees. The decision on whether to hold the seminar may be based on the phone call or on a subsequent letter and sample materials. The training director might solicit additional proposals only if the materials submitted by the first consultant proved inadequate.

In other cases, a firm may solicit sealed bids for a product or service through public forums (announcements—often in the form of paid advertisements—in trade magazines, newsletters, or regional newspapers). In some cases, cost may be the main determining factor in the awarding of the contract. In other cases, however, the organization soliciting the bids will consider other issues, such as the bidder's reputation for quality and reliability, and the writer's ability to be persuasive may be the deciding factor.

TYPES OF PROPOSALS

Proposals are frequently identified according to their origin, level of formality, length and complexity, or manner of production. As mentioned previously, for example, proposals are either *solicited* or *unsolicited*, depending on whether they have been requested or have been initiated by the writer. They are also frequently identified as *internal* or *external*, based on whether they remain within the writer's organization or are prepared for an outside agency. Additionally, they may be identified by their form.

Solicited and Unsolicited

Proposals prepared in response to a request are *solicited*. Major projects are almost always described in a *Request for Proposals (RFP)* or an *Invitation for Bids (IFB)*, which are often sent directly to the organizations with the right qualifications for completing the project. The availability of the RFP or IFB may also be advertised in appropriate trade publications. The principal difference between an RFP and an IFB is that the IFB defines the product or service more specifically than the RFP, and the principal factor in determining who receives the contract will be the cost at which the required specifications can be met. IFBs can be issued for the purchase of virtually any standard item, from automobiles to ball bearings. The organization wanting to purchase the product sets the standards and evaluates the bids based on a combination of cost and quality. An organization might purchase personal computers for its clerical staff by sending an IFB to appropriate manufacturers, for example. RFPs typically allow for greater latitude in the ways problems may be solved and provide more room for negotiation in the type of product or service that will be considered acceptable. Most RFPs and IFBs require that the product or service be customized to meet certain specific needs.

RFPs may solicit *sales proposals* or *qualification proposals*, depending on how much those preparing the RFP know about what is required to solve the problem. A company might know, for example, that it needs a new minicomputer that will be used primarily to perform database functions. In such a case, the company can simply request proposals from appropriate manufacturers, specifying the use to which the new computer would be put, the current required capacity, anticipated capacity, the kind of connectivity required, and so on. Because minicomputers are available in a wide variety of configurations, the company winning the contract would need to customize the equipment to meet the specific needs of the purchasing organization, and no two companies would specify quite the same equipment in the same configuration.

If the company isn't sure how best to solve its computing problems, on the other hand, it might solicit qualification proposals from computer consultants describing the type of problems that need to be addressed and requesting information about the consultants' qualifications to recommend a computer system that would best meet the organization's needs. In such a case, the organization soliciting the proposal is primarily interested in the qualifications of those submitting proposals as evidenced by previous successes with similar problems and a demonstrated understanding of the current problem and possible solutions.

A number of resources are available to help organizations locate appropriate RFPs and IFBs. Many libraries will help with computerized searches. Many federal agencies, such as the National Institutes of Health and the National Science Foundation, publish lists of projects and areas of research eligible for grants, and advertisements may appear in *The Wall Street Journal* and local newspapers as well.

Figure 1-2 lists some of the more common sources of RFPs, IFBs, and advertisements of availability. This list is not meant to be exhaustive. The listings here will direct you to additional listings. Note also that in many cases the sources will contain considerable overlap.

Annual Register of Grant Support, 25th ed., National Register Publishing Company, Wilmette, IL: 1991.

Catalog of Federal Domestic Assistance, 25th ed., General Service Administration, Washington, DC: 1991.

Commerce Business Daily, Commerce Department, Washington, DC: 1992.

DIALOG OnDisc® The GRANTS Database™, Dialog Information Services, Inc., 3460 Hillview Avenue, Palo Alto, CA: 1992.

Directory of Research Grants 1992, The Oryx Press, 4041 N. Central at Indian School Rd., Phoenix, AZ: 1992.

Federal Assistance Monitor, CD Publications, 8204 Fenton Street, Silver Springs, MD: 1992.

Federal Grants and Contracts Weekly: Project Opportunities in Research, Training and Services, Capitol Publications, PO Box 1453, Alexandria, VA: 1992.

Federal Register, National Archives and Records Administration, Washington, DC: 1992.

The Foundation Center's User-Friendly Guide: A Grantseeker's Guide to Resources, 2nd ed., Judith B. Margolin, ed., The Foundation Center, 79 5th Avenue, New York, NY: 1992.

Figure 1-2. Sources of RFPs and IFBs.

Foundation Directory, 14th ed., The Foundation Center, 79 5th Avenue, New York, NY: 1992.

Foundation Fundamentals, 4th ed., Judith B. Margolin, ed., The Foundation Center, 79 5th Avenue, New York, NY: 1992.

Foundation Grants Index, 20th ed., The Foundation Center, 79 5th Avenue, New York, NY: 1992.

The Grant Advisor, The Grant Advisor, P.O. Box 3553, Arlington, VA: 1992.

Grantsmanship Center News, The Grantsmanship Center, 1031 South Grand Avenue, Los Angeles, CA: 1992.

Research Monitor News, National Information Service, Washington, DC: 1992.

SPIN (Sponsored Programs Information Network), The Research Foundation of SUNY, Albany, NY. FAX: (518) 434-7150, BITNET: RSPIN@SYNCENVM.

Taft Corporate Giving Directory, Taft Group, Rockville, MD: 1971.

Taft Foundation Reporter, Taft Group, Rockville, MD: 1971.

Figure 1-2. Sources of RFPs and IFBs (continued).

Unsolicited proposals are prepared by individuals who perceive problems that need solving. The problem may be internal (within the writer's own company) or external (in another organization). Although unsolicited proposals rarely involve issues of the complexity of those delineated by RFPs, they are often more difficult to write because the target audience—the reader or readers who will make the decision—may not be aware of the problem, and, in fact, the audience may be at least partially responsible for having created the situation the writer is viewing as a "problem." For this reason, unsolicited proposals typically need to be more persuasive than solicited proposals, beginning by convincing the reader that a problem does exist and overcoming any initial resistance to changing current practices and procedures.

Solicited proposals have the advantage of being expected and desired. They also typically have the disadvantage of having greater and more obvious competition than unsolicited proposals. While unsolicited proposals do not usually compete with other offers to solve the same problem, the reader does not expect and may not desire them. They will need to compete for the reader's attention as well as for the limited resources that may be available within the organization.

Internal and External

Internal proposals are quite simply those that remain within the writer's organization. They are typically directed to a specific individual, department, or functional area, and they range in formality from handwritten suggestion box entries to lengthy, printed and bound reports. They may be brief suggestions submitted to an immediate supervisor, or a departmental project designed to persuade the Chief Executive Officer (CEO) to authorize the development of a new product line.

An external proposal, on the other hand, is a marketing tool designed to persuade a prospective customer to purchase products or services from the submitting company. Although some internal proposals may be lengthy and formal, external proposals are usually longer and more formal than those that stay within the company. Many external proposals are costly to prepare owing to the kind and quantity of research, concept development, and proposal preparation that may be required. For this reason, the first and most important task in planning an external proposal is *screening*. An organization needs to determine whether the time, money, and effort that will go into preparing the proposal are likely to be worth it. An organization should not necessarily bid on every project for which it might be qualified and will probably do better by focusing on those few RFPs for which it is uniquely qualified.

Forms of Proposals

Proposals also range in formality, from extremely informal suggestions presented orally or in brief memos (such as that in Figure 1-1) to the extremely formal. The most formal proposals are ordinarily printed and bound and are often presented in conjunction with a formal oral presentation. In general, the formality of proposals increases as the complexity and costs of the project increase. Competing organizations are required to invest more time and resources in planning and preparation to compete for the reward of winning the contract.

The length of proposals also typically increases as the complexity and costs of the project increase. As the money an organization is going to commit to a project multiplies, those responsible for the decision desire increasingly greater detail. The manner of production also changes correspondingly. Short, informal reports are usually produced by one individual and submitted in memo or letter format. Lengthy, formal proposals are almost always a group effort, with each member of the team being responsible for his or her area of expertise, and the final product is often printed and bound.

Over the years, a variety of names have been used to classify proposals according to their form or appearance. Short, relatively informal proposals presented in letter or memo format, for example, are often called *letter proposals* and *memo proposals*, respectively. Long, formal proposals requiring heavy investment in preparation may be termed *major* or *detailed*, while brief proposals are called *minor* or *brief*.

Proposals prepared by one person may be referred to as *individual proposals*, while those requiring a team effort are referred to as *team proposals*. When one individual is able to undertake a project, that person usually assumes responsibility for planning, organizing, and preparing the proposal. When the project is complex and requires the skills of a number of specialists, most organizations assemble a proposal team, usually assigning one individual to coordinate activities and manage the development of the proposal. The team would consist of specialists from such departments as engineering, design, legal, logistics, manufacturing, marketing, personnel, and purchasing.

While the terms used to classify proposals will vary from organization to organization, their purposes and the strategies used to achieve them remain the same. Successful proposals persuade the reader that the writer and the writer's company can provide the most cost-effective solution to a specific problem. The remainder of this book is designed to show you how to present your qualifications for solving problems in the best way possible.

KEY POINTS FROM CHAPTER 1

The key points from Chapter 1 are the following:

1. A proposal is an offer to solve a problem for a reader or group of readers by providing specified goods and/or services at a specified cost or in exchange for something else.
2. Proposals have sales, technical, and legal functions.
3. Proposals may be solicited or unsolicited. Solicited proposals are written in response to a *request for proposals* (RFP). Unsolicited proposals are submitted to offer a solution to a problem perceived by the writer.
4. Proposals offering products or services to meet a need are often called *bids*.
5. The nature and amount of persuasive material required will vary from proposal to proposal based on how well the reader and writer know each other and the complexity and cost of the product or service required.
6. Proposals may be identified according to their origin (solicited or unsolicited, internal or external), level of formality (formal or informal), length and complexity (long or short, major or minor, brief or detailed), or manner of production or appearance (individual or team, letter or memo).

CHAPTER 2

Audience

The audiences for proposals vary almost as much as the types of proposals do. Internal audiences, members of your own organization, for example, will have a different perspective of your suggestions than will external audiences. Because they usually know you, your capabilities, or your job function and because they are familiar with your organizational environment, they already have a great deal of information that will influence their attitude toward your proposal. External audiences, on the other hand, may know virtually nothing about you or your organization, so they must depend entirely on the information you present to understand and evaluate what you propose.

The same is true of your analysis of the audience. You may have a clear conception of the likes, dislikes, and biases of those within your own organization for whom you may prepare proposals but know virtually nothing about those in an external organization who will be responsible for reading and evaluating your proposal. In general, the more you know—or can find out—about your audience, the better off you will be. Proposals are typically accepted or rejected based on three principal factors:

- The reader's perception of the concept presented by the writer.
- The reader's perception of the writer's technical competence.
- The reader's perception of the writer and the writer's organization as desirable business partners.

Note that each of the three factors is dominated by the word *perception*. What the reader perceives becomes the reality by which each proposal is evaluated. Your organization may, in fact, be the best qualified to undertake a particular project, but if your proposal is carelessly prepared, it may give the readers the impression that your organization is careless with everything it does.

TYPES OF READERS

As is true for all business communication, proposals are delivered to a specific audience to achieve a specific purpose. To be successful, you will need to adapt your message to the interests and desires of those people who form your audience. One of your first concerns when writing the proposal is to identify and analyze the background and needs of your audience.

In analyzing your audience, you may need to consider both *demographic* and *psychographic* factors. Demographics include such factors as age, sex, income, political and religious preferences, ethnic background or affiliation, educational level, and other traits common to groups of people. Psychographic factors include values, needs, opinions, beliefs, and perceptions. A knowledge of these factors can help you anticipate what your readers will consider important as they evaluate the proposals they receive.

Your audience may include both technical and nontechnical readers. You will need to address both groups. Your audience may also include those whose principal concern will be the *results* and those whose principal concern will be *costs*; those who like to try new things and those who resist new ideas. In general, you will need to consider the following questions:

- Who is the real audience?
- What does the reader already know?
- What does the reader want to know?
- What does the reader *not* want to know?
- What does the reader perceive?

Who Is the Real Audience?

The person (or persons) who can make a decision or take action as a result of your proposal constitutes your real audience. If the person to whom you are writing has the authority to act on your proposal, you can be concerned with him or her only. In many cases, however, your first reader may have the authority to reject your idea but will not have the authority to approve it. Or perhaps your proposal will be evaluated by a team selected for that purpose. Your proposal should include whatever information is necessary to have each person who receives it take the appropriate action, as well as the information required to ensure that the right person sees it. From this perspective, your audience can be divided into three distinct categories:

Primary audience:	The person or persons who can make decisions or act on the proposal.
Secondary audience:	Those who will be affected by the decision or action taken.
Intermediate audience:	Those who review and route the proposal.

In general, individual readers tend to focus on their own areas of interest and specialization. Those with technical expertise tend to focus on technical details; those whose backgrounds are in accountancy or finance may focus on budgetary and financial matters; and those who work in personnel may focus primarily on the way people will be influenced as a result of the proposal. Although good decision makers will attempt to take all factors into account, they can't help but be influenced by the way in which the proposal addresses their own areas of expertise.

Who will be influenced if your proposal is accepted? Will your proposal have a negative impact on anybody in the client organization? Who will benefit? Will your proposal have legal ramifications and require evaluation by an attorney? Answers to these questions are crucial. Remember, too, that proposals which seem good and logical from your point of view, may not seem that way to the readers. A new MBA, for example, thought that he had discovered a way to save his company more than $100,000 a year by changing vendors for certain computer supplies and submitted a proposal without considering that the proposal was essentially a criticism of his manager and the others who had negotiated the current contract. In another case, a consultant recommended the elimination of a department as a way to reduce expenses without having learned that the department had been established by the organization's CEO, who had appointed his niece head of the department.

Because your proposals will always be read by individuals who have vested interests and preconceptions about what will constitute an acceptable solution, the more you can find out about your audience, the better. If the proposal is solicited, check the RFP. Does the language used in the RFP suggest a particular orientation? Are certain *value* words used repeatedly? If the RFP stresses costs, for example, the proposal should emphasize costs in relation to the return on the investment. If the RFP repeatedly solicits information about the impact on personnel, the proposal should echo that concern.

Does the RFP provide a phone number and the name of a contact person? If the contract is important to you or your organization, it's worth at least one phone call to discover in greater detail what criteria might be used in evaluating the proposals. Remember, however, that others will also be calling and that you are beginning the process of selling yourself with the call. Do your homework first, and be thoroughly familiar with the RFP and your organization's ability to solve the reader's problem. Use the phone call as a means of adding to your knowledge of the audience and *not* as a substitute for reading the RFP carefully.

What Does the Reader Already Know?

Are your readers already familiar with you, your organization, and your product or service? What are their primary interests? When you know your readers well, you have a fairly good idea of what they will know already and what information you will have to provide. When you don't know your readers, you will have to estimate the extent of their knowledge on the basis of what you do know about them. The critical questions are the following:

- Are your readers already familiar with you, your company, or your product or service?
- Are your readers familiar with business concepts and terminology?
- Are your readers familiar with any technical matters you need to include?

When your reader is unlikely to be familiar with your subject matter, take extra time to explain. A reader who doesn't understand what you are talking about is not likely to take action based on your proposal. Not long ago, a friend of ours who owns a small company was approached by representatives of a multinational corporation who wanted him to distribute one of their company's products. When he visited the corporate offices to discuss the proposal, he was met by three corporate executives and six attorneys. They asked him where his attorney was. His response was, "I don't need an attorney. If I can't understand it, I'm not signing it." Most proposal readers, regardless of how many attorneys they employ, feel the same way. They won't agree to anything they don't understand.

When your reader is already familiar with the topic, you may omit obvious details. There are times, however, when you can't be sure whether the reader understands your topic, or when you need to remind your reader of something he or she already knows. In those cases, subordinate information the reader may or should know to some other, more important point.

Not this: It's December, and Christmas will soon be here.
[Emphasizes something the reader doubtless knows.]

But this: Because Christmas sales are so important to your store, now is the best time. . . . [Emphasizes what the reader should do.]

For more information about proper emphasis and subordination, see Chapter 5.

What Does the Reader Want to Know?

Not all readers desire the same—or the same amount of—information. Some managers want a complete and thorough analysis in every report they receive. Others want only the writer's recommendation and the briefest of explanations. In general, the greater the costs (or risks) and the greater the potential gains, the more support you will need to provide. A manager may make a $5,000 investment on the basis of a one-page memo, but for an investment of $500,000, the same manager might require a six-month study and several hundred pages of documentation.

In most cases, readers will want something in between. Unless you know from previous experience that your reader has a preference for extremely brief or extremely thorough messages, or unless you have a length specification in the RFP, you should strike a balance, leaning toward providing more information as the costs associated with your proposal increase. With internal audiences you will have a better opportunity to learn how much detail is desired. If your first proposal is rejected, you can find out why, change your approach, and try again. With external audiences, you may have just the one opportunity.

Regardless of their personal interests, however, all readers, will want answers to the following questions:

- What should I do?
- What will I gain?
- What will it cost?

Because no reader will make a decision without the answers to those questions, your message will need to provide clear answers along with whatever support is required to demonstrate the validity of those answers. Your readers will always want to know if you have a clear understanding of the problem. In many cases, the readers will know exactly what they would like to have done and will specify that in the RFP. In other cases, the readers may not understand the problem or know exactly what they want. In either case, you will need to show that you understand the problem and know how to go about solving it.

What Does the Reader *Not* Want to Know?

Just as readers have different opinions about what they *should* be told, they also have different opinions about what they should *not* be told. Audience analysis helps determine what to *exclude* as well as what to *include*. Again, follow all the guidelines given in the request for a proposal. Some RFPs explicitly ask for all the details, all the criteria, and all the alternatives. If that is the case, be sure to provide everything requested. Is the RFP itself replete with detail, some of which would be obvious to all those qualified to submit? That may indicate the reader's own fondness for detail. In the case of ambiguous RFPs or unsolicited proposals, concentrate on stating clearly those things necessary for your reader to make the best decision possible. In general, it is better to err on the side of too much information than on the side of too little.

What Does the Reader Perceive?

Because the success of a proposal depends on the degree to which it meets the reader's needs and desires, writers should develop an appreciation for the reader's perception of the problem and proposal evaluation process. One of the most common failings of business reports in general and proposals in particular is that the writer focuses primarily on his or her own concerns rather than those of the readers. Focusing on the reader's concerns is often called the *you-viewpoint* or the *you-attitude*.

The you-attitude is fundamental to all effective business communication, and it is especially important in proposals because they are specifically designed to address the reader's problems and concerns. Compare the following problem statements:

Writer's Viewpoint: The Personnel Department at XYZ Corporation has a problem. I don't have a computer terminal and can't do my job well. Because I process Health and Dental Report Forms, I need to enter claims and changes of status in the computer. I have to share a terminal with Rosiland Knaus, who needs the terminal to process payroll records. Because payroll is more important than health and dental records, I often have to go from department to department trying to find a terminal not being used so that I can enter the claims and changes in status, and sometimes I am late in getting the data entered, and we receive complaints from employees who don't receive their reimbursements on time.

Reader's Viewpoint: The Personnel Department at XYZ Corporation has a problem. Health and dental records are not always processed on time, and employees are complaining that they are not receiving their insurance reimbursements promptly. As a result, employees frequently take time off work to check on the status of their claims and requests for changes in status. This inefficiency could be eliminated by the addition of a computer terminal in Personnel. With a computer terminal, I could ensure that the Health and Dental Report Forms were processed promptly upon receipt, and thus decrease the number of employees needing to take time off from work to check on the status of their claims.

Note that the presentation from the writer's viewpoint sounds like a "personal problem," whereas the reader's viewpoint focuses on the way in which the organization is affected. Because the you-viewpoint is such an important concept, we will cover it more fully in Chapter 5.

In addition to considering the situation from the perspective of those who will read the proposal, you will also need to be concerned with the perceptual orientation of your readers. We mentioned previously the ways in which differing technical backgrounds and job functions might influence the reader's concerns and perceptions. Certain personality factors will also play a role in determining perceptual orientation, and you will be more successful when you can discover those factors and use them in preparing your proposal.

PERSONAL PROFILES

For the purposes of your communication with them, you may think of readers as falling into one of four basic categories: *achiever, communicator, specialist,* or *perfectionist.* While each person has a combination of traits from these basic personality types, people tend to employ the same sets of behaviors on a regular basis. Although people are not absolutely consistent in the way they behave, most are sufficiently consistent to be predictable. When confronted by a problem, for example, some people would tend to check to see what had been done in the past. Others might seek advice from those who have had similar experiences. Still others might simply try a variety of possible solutions.

In general, people repeat the patterns of behavior that have worked for them in the past. These patterns determine the four basic personality types, which have the following characteristics:

Achiever.
- Task oriented.
- Sees life as a competition and wants to win.
- Enjoys and seeks challenges.
- Values variety and change.
- Makes decisions quickly on the basis of minimum data.
- Prefers hierarchical relationships and likes being in charge.
- Good at finding solutions to problems.
- Desires results even at the expense of breaking rules or creating conflict.

Communicator.
- People oriented.
- Enjoys cooperation, working with and through others.
- Wants to be the center of attention and be popular.
- Values spontaneity. Makes decisions by consulting others.
- Prefers democratic relationships in which decisions are made by consensus.
- Dislikes conflict.
- Desires an effective group process more than a specific result.
- Willing to break rules to achieve popularity or maintain group cohesiveness.

Specialist.

- Detail oriented. Likes to plan work and relationships and maintain predictable patterns of behavior.
- Values safety and long-term relationships.
- Enjoys being part of a team.
- Good at following guidelines and instructions.
- Good analytical skills.
- Makes decisions by checking against lists of criteria.
- Desires to achieve and maintain group harmony through following accepted procedures.
- Hesitates to break rules under any circumstances.

Perfectionist.
- Rule oriented.
- Enjoys tasks requiring critical, objective thinking.
- Checks for accuracy and for compliance with guidelines.
- Works slowly and carefully.
- Values correctness and has a strict moral code.
- Makes decisions only after gathering all the evidence and weighing the advantages and disadvantages.
- Good analytical skills.
- Prefers hierarchical relationships.
- Wants completed work to comply with stated requirements and will create conflict to achieve compliance with guidelines or moral standards.

Communication Styles

Because the basic personality types interact with the environment in different ways, they have different modes of communicating. When you can, take the individual's personality type into account. Although the following communication guidelines apply primarily in face-to-face situations, many of them are appropriate for proposals and other written communication.

With the Achiever

Be brief and specific. Avoid comments that the Achiever will consider a waste of time. Talk about results first and procedures second. Let the Achiever know the purpose of your communication before presenting detailed information. Focus on the problem first. Discuss personal matters *after* the problem is solved and only when you are sure that the Achiever is ready to take a break from working. In discussions, present the most important facts first, and arrange things in a logical order. Ask *what* questions:

- What would you like to see happen?
- What obstacles might stand in the way?

Present alternatives so that the Achiever can make his or her own decision. Avoid telling the Achiever what to do. If you disagree, focus on the facts. If you agree, focus on the results. Avoid "empathy" remarks ("I hear you," "Let me share something with you," "I'm really with you on this one"). When communicating in person, leave when finished. In proposals and other written documents, be concise to avoid giving Achievers the impression that you are wasting their time.

With the Communicator

Plan to spend some time socializing. Speak in terms of what the subject of discussion means to people. Ask for opinions and feelings. Allow the Communicator to respond and contribute his or her own ideas. Don't interrupt. Listen for clues about how the subject coincides with the Communicator's own plans. Show that you understand the Communicator by paraphrasing his or her ideas.

Be responsive to the personal aspects of the relationship. Make special arrangements for serious discussions. When possible, conduct business in a social context—take the Communicator out to lunch or dinner if you wish to be persuasive. Ask *who* questions:

- Whom could we count on to help with this?
- Who would be influenced by this?

Avoid presenting too many details. The Communicator is more interested in hearing what others (especially important others) have said than in the specific, objective facts. Be clear about who should do what next—repeat agreements about responsibilities for follow-up actions. Because conversation is important to a Communicator, make an effort to discuss the proposal with him or her either in person or on the phone before submitting it. Encourage him or her to discuss your previous projects with others, and provide appropriate contact names and phone numbers.

With the Specialist

Begin with small talk. Personal comments help break the ice. Find areas of common interest. Show the Specialist that you trust him or her. Be the first to volunteer personal information. Draw personal information from the Specialist slowly and show that you are interested in his or her goals. Avoid saying anything threatening, and if you disagree with the Specialist, look for signs of hurt feelings. Let the Specialist know that you appreciate his or her contributions.

Present new ideas slowly. Don't be a bully (Achiever) or try to overwhelm with superficial razzle-dazzle (Communicator). Show that any change will help minimize risks. Don't attempt to force a quick decision. Ask *how* questions:

- How do you think that would influence you and others in your department?
- How could we avoid that difficulty?

Show that you have weighed the risks against the benefits and that you are trying to minimize the risks and maximize the benefits. Provide personal assurances—then keep your promises. Personal trust is extremely important to a Specialist. Because Specialists resist change, be especially careful to show how your proposal is an extension of existing policies and procedures rather than a radical new approach. Indicate in step-by-step fashion how the new product, service, or procedure can be integrated with current systems. Also, remember that some businesses and industries, such as banking and the pharmaceutical industries, follow what is essentially a Specialist behavioral pattern in spite of the behavioral pattern of the individual responsible for the RFP, so you may need to take the general communication style of the business into account as well as appealing to the tendencies of the contact person.

With the Perfectionist

Be well prepared—know the facts and figures before you begin. Don't waste time beating around the bush. Use notes to keep yourself organized. Stick to the facts—leave personalities out of it. Avoid surprising the Perfectionist with changes or unexpected remarks. Discuss one subject at a time. Examine differences of opinion objectively. Show the Perfectionist that you have analyzed the situation thoroughly and that you expect him or her to do the same.

Use accepted rules and procedures as authority. Use reliable sources only—the testimony of others will likely be dismissed as "hearsay." Be direct, but don't be pushy. Ask questions about the facts:

- Have I overlooked any important details?
- Has this approach been tried before?

Allow the Perfectionist time to evaluate your information and to confirm your accuracy before making a decision. Show that you appreciate the Perfectionist's ability to weigh the evidence and to make an objective decision. If you agree, be sure to follow through. If the discussion was important, provide the Perfectionist with a summary, including a step-by-step schedule for implementing any required action.

When preparing proposals for someone you believe to be a Perfectionist, be sure to provide all the documentation required to support your proposal. He or she will be concerned more with the details than with the vision or results of your plan. The Perfectionist in particular will be concerned with the thoroughness of your analysis and the completeness of your plan. The aerospace industry and other businesses and industries making heavy use of mechanical parts and electronic components that must work right the first time and every time will share the Perfectionist's concerns for detail and accuracy, regardless of the individual communication style of the contact person for the RFP.

METAPROGRAMS

In addition to the basic personality types and communication styles, people use a series of behavioral strategies that influence their behavior. These behavioral strategies are often called *metaprograms* because they operate across contexts (in a wide variety of situations) and function much like a computer program that produces a predictable result each time it is run. The principal metaprograms are *Action, Direction, Source, Conduct, Response, Scope, Cognitive Style,* and *Confirmation*. Each of these categories has extremes of polar opposites. Most people are, of course, somewhere between the two extremes, choosing one pattern of behavior or the other depending on the situation or context.

The *Action* Metaprogram

The action metaprogram governs whether an individual is primarily an *initiator* or a *responder*. Initiators have a bias for action and are motivated by situations in which they can act and have the initiative. They do not like to wait for others to act and are frequently accused of failing to "look before they leap." Responders, on the other hand, prefer to analyze a situation thoroughly and are most comfortable when they can wait until others initiate the action and then respond to what others have done. Initiators enjoy starting new projects and may have several projects going at once. Responders, on the other hand, are slow to begin projects and often analyze and plan without taking action. Typical language used by such individuals would include the following:

Initiator:	I completed. . . . Let's go out to dinner tonight.
Responder:	It was completed. . . . Would you like to go out to dinner tonight?

The *Direction* Metaprogram

The direction metaprogram governs whether an individual is primarily motivated to *move toward* desired objectives or to *move away from* unpleasant consequences. Those who are motivated to move *toward* the desirable tend to set, and work to achieve, specific goals. They think and talk in terms of what will be gained. People who move *away from* the undesirable are motivated primarily by avoiding loss. They think and talk in terms of dangers and risks to avoid. They typically do not set goals but rather react to what they perceive as dangers in the environment. Typical language used by such individuals would include the following:

Toward: We can earn 38 percent profit! We could increase our market share by advertising.

Away from: We could easily lose our investment. Advertising is expensive, and we can't be sure that it would work. We'll lose market share if we don't increase our advertising.

The *Source* Metaprogram

The source metaprogram governs whether an individual relies on his or her own judgment or on the judgments of others. Those with an *internal* source or frame of reference need to decide for themselves. What others say is treated as information, which the individual then evaluates according to his or her personal standards. Individuals with an extremely strong internal frame of reference will resist following instructions given by others. Those with an *external* source or frame of reference, on the other hand, prefer to receive direction from others and frequently look to others to make decisions and to provide standards for conduct. Those with an internal frame of reference tend to ignore feedback they receive from others, while those with an external frame typically seek feedback from others and use that information to determine future behavior. Typical language used by such individuals would include the following:

Internal I decided. . . . I recognized. . . . I think. . . . I feel. . . .

External: My boss said. . . . The article said that. . . . What do you think? How would you feel about that?

The *Conduct* Metaprogram

The conduct metaprogram governs whether an individual tends to be a rule follower or a rule breaker and whether he or she thinks primarily in terms of procedures to be followed or alternative ways of doing things. *Rule followers* stick to developed and tested procedures. They have great respect for existing procedures. *Rule breakers* are motivated by developing options and alternatives. They typically need to discover for themselves whether an existing rule or procedure is valid and tend to respect a rule or procedure only if breaking it will clearly produce a negative result. Typical language used by such individuals would include the following:

Rule follower: The Owner's Manual says. . . .
Rule breaker: What difference does it make as long as it works?

The *Response* Metaprogram

The response metaprogram governs whether an individual tends to *match* or *mismatch* information presented by others. Matchers look for and desire sameness. They prefer to have their environment, including their relationships, remain the same, and they tend to enjoy working for the same organization for a long time. In conversation, they tend to look for and emphasize points of agreement. Mismatchers, on the other hand, look for differences and enjoy change. In conversation, they will look for and emphasize differences and exceptions to the rule. Typical language used by such individuals would include the following:

Matchers: I agree. . . . You're right. . . . I see what you mean. . . .
They have a lot in common.
Mismatchers: Yes, but. . . . You're wrong. . . . You failed to consider.
. . . They are completely different.

The *Scope* Metaprogram

The scope metaprogram governs whether an individual tends to focus on the big picture or on specific details. The *global* person is interested in the overall concept and is typically bored with details, whereas the *specific* person prefers details and may have difficulty grasping the overview. The global person prefers to receive information about and make decisions based on the big picture, leaving the details of execution to others. The global person is more interested in the final result than in the steps required to achieve the result. The specific person prefers to think first about the specific details and to approach results in a sequential, step-by-step fashion. For the specific person, it is important that each detail be correct and in place before moving on to the next detail or step. Typical language used by such individuals would include the following:

Global: Envision the result. . . . Let me give you an overview. . . .
Specific: The first step will be. . . . The picture is not clear to me. . . .

The *Cognitive Style* Metaprogram

The cognitive style metaprogram determines whether an individual is governed primarily by the analytical or the creative impulse. *Thinking people* tend to be analytical and critical. They tend to lack empathy for others and are more concerned with the task and the result than with the effects the task or result will have on others. Feeling people tend to be creative, accepting, and spontaneous. They are concerned about feelings and relationships and place a priority in knowing how changes will affect others. Typical language used by such individuals would include the following:

Thinking: Let's think about this logically. The rational thing to do. Sally has a good head on her shoulders.

Feeling: How do you all feel about this? John would be really hurt. Sally's heart is in the right place.

The *Confirmation* Metaprogram

The confirmation metaprogram governs the way in which people become convinced about the truth. This metaprogram has two parts: the sensory mode and the pattern. The sensory mode determines how the individual needs to receive the information before becoming convinced. Some people—*visuals*—need to *see* something before they are convinced; some people—*auditories*—need to *hear* about it from others; and some— *kinesthetics*—need to develop a *feeling* as a result of direct experience. Typical language used by such individuals would include the following:

Visual: I know Becky is good because I've seen her work.

Auditory: I know Becky is good because Raul told me so.

Kinesthetic: I know Becky is good because I've worked with her before.

The pattern governs how often the person needs to receive information before becoming convinced. For some, once is enough. For others, each situation is new and requires new evidence. In this culture, approximately 40 percent of the population is primarily visual; 20 percent is primarily auditory, and 40 percent is primarily kinesthetic.

Figure 2-1 illustrates the ways in which the basic personality types and metaprograms relate to each other. In general, people will tend to favor a specific hemisphere, top or bottom, left or right, and have their greatest conflicts with those who favor the opposite hemisphere. For more information about Personal Profiles, write to Dr. Joel P. Bowman, Director, Communication Unlimited, 2317 Outlook Street, Kalamazoo, MI 49001.

SENSORY MODES AND INFORMATION PROCESSING

Just as different people have different styles of interacting with the environment, they also tend to process information differently, as the confirmation metaprogram suggests. All of us use the same five senses— visual, auditory, olfactory, gustatory, and touch—to gather information

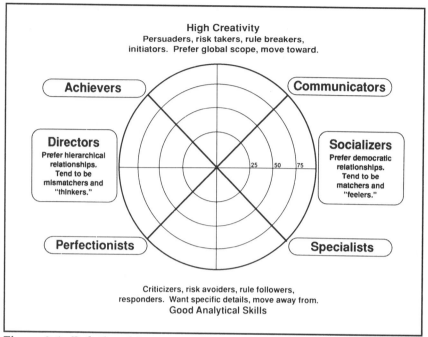

Figure 2-1. Relationships among Personality Types and Metaprograms.

from the environment. Unless one of these senses is deficient as a result of an accident, injury, or illness, they are active all the time, processing the information available to them. Of the information available to us, however, we are able to pay close attention to only a portion of it. Because we are unable to attend to everything, in the process of receiving information we *delete, generalize,* and *distort.* We tend, for example, to focus on the portion of the information that seems most important to us at the time, deleting from our conscious awareness information that seems less important. This process of deletion is known as *abstraction.* We also generalize, treating the unknown as known and making general assumptions based on one or two specific examples. We also tend to distort the information available to us, altering it so that it corresponds with our preconceptions, wishes, or fears.

Although people have and use all their senses all the time, each person has a favored sense or *representational system* on which he or she tends to rely most often for processing information. Some people favor the visual sense; others favor the auditory sense; and still others favor the kinesthetic grouping of senses—smell, taste, and touch. The kinesthetic grouping also includes the emotions. While all people use all three systems all the time, each person is most comfortable processing information in one of the systems. As mentioned previously, in this culture approximately 40 percent of the population is primarily visual; 20 percent is primarily auditory, and 40 percent is primarily kinesthetic.

People reveal their favored representational system with the words and phrases they use. The same idea can usually be expressed in any of the three systems:

I see what you mean.
I hear what you are saying.
I am comfortable with your decision.

While you should avoid drawing specific conclusions based on an individual's use of one or two stock phrases, the language a person uses repeatedly provides an important clue to the way. in which he or she processes information. In conversation, you will be more successful in your communication if you *match* the other person's mode of processing information. The same is true in written communication. Check the RFP for visual, auditory, and kinesthetic language. Figure 2-2 provides an alphabetized list of vocabulary words common to the three main representational systems.

If the RFP indicates a bias for one of the representational systems, your proposal should reflect the same bias. If the RFP is well-balanced in its use of such vocabulary, your proposal should also be well-balanced. When you can show your readers that you think the way they do by emphasizing the criteria they value and by using the vocabulary with which they are most comfortable, you will increase your chances of obtaining a favorable response.

While there is no guarantee that you will be able to discover everything you might like to know about your audience, you can learn a great deal by studying the RFP or IFB for language indicating values, degree of technical expertise, personality type, metaprograms, and sensory modalities. Conversation, whether by phone or in person, can provide additional clues about how the reader will process information and help you present your proposal in the most appealing way.

If you are familiar with other personality sorters, such as the well-known Myers-Briggs test for temperament types, for example, you can also use that information about your probable readers to help you communicate in the most effective way. Regardless of the theory of personality you prefer to use, the key to success is to be alert to the differences between your concerns and the way in which you process information and those of your audience so that you can adjust to meet their needs.

Remember, too, that effective communication requires appropriate follow-through. Buyers' remorse can occur in business and industry just as it does at the consumer level. Use these communication strategies in an ethical way, taking the audience's desired goals and outcomes into account. Match *values* as well as vocabulary, and afford your reader the respect he or she deserves.

Visual	Auditory	Kinesthetic
clarify	accent	concrete
cloud	alarm	consider
depict	amplify	contact
distinguish	ask	crash
envision	attune	feel
expose	clear	finger
flash	click	flat
focused	compose	grab
foggy	deaf	grasp
glimpse	dissonance	grope
graphic	growl	handle
hazy	harmonize	impact
illustrate	hear	irritate
imagine	listen	move
look	muffle	rub
outlook	note	scrape
paint	overtones	sharpen
perspective	question	smash
picture	rattle	solid
preview	resonate	stir
reveal	say	strike
screen	screech	stroke
see	shout	suffer
shortsighted	silence	tap
show	sound	throw
sparkling	static	tickle
spectacle	tune	touch
twinkle	utter	unbudging
view	voice	unfeeling

Figure 2-2. The Vocabulary of the Representational Systems.

KEY POINTS FROM CHAPTER 2

The key points from Chapter 2 are the following:

1. Each proposal should be adapted to the needs and desires of a specific audience.
2. Proposals are typically accepted or rejected based on the audience's perception of the writer's concept, technical competence, and desirability as a business partner.
3. Proposal writers need to consider both *demographic* and *psychographic* factors when analyzing their audience.
4. The *primary* audience for a proposal is the person or persons who can make decisions or act on the proposal. The *secondary* audience consists of those who will be affected by the decision or action taken. The *intermediate* audience is those who review and route the proposal, often with the authority to disapprove the proposal but not to approve it.
5. Proposals need to consider the varying degrees of technical expertise and interest of their readers, ensuring that the proposal can be understood by readers with less expertise without belaboring points that would be obvious to those with technical competence.
6. Proposals should emphasize the readers' perspective and stress the values and criteria specified or implied in the RFP.
7. When possible, writers should adapt the language used in proposals to match the communication strategies of the four basic personality types: *achievers, communicators, specialists,* and *perfectionists.*
8. When possible, writers should adapt the language used in proposals to match the readers' behavioral metaprograms.
9. In processing information, people delete, distort, and generalize and tend to rely on one sensory modality more than the others. Proposal writers should attempt to match the vocabulary of the favored representational systems as used in the RFP.
10. Writers should study the RFP for indications of values and criteria, personality type, metaprograms, and sensory modalities used in processing information.

CHAPTER 3

Strategies for Success

Goal-directed behavior is typically best achieved by using a *strategy*, a set procedure designed to ensure a desired result. Those who consistently write successful proposals have a strategy for doing so. The fundamental components of this strategy are *planning, maintaining a customer orientation, blending outcomes,* and *following directions.* Our presentation of these elements seems to suggest that each of them is a separate step to be performed in a particular order, but this is not exactly true. The process is recursive.

As you plan, you will think in terms of the customers' orientation and their desired outcomes, and you will consistently use the RFP or other available directions as a source for planning and for understanding the customer. You will probably also begin writing at least portions of your draft at this point, even if only in the form of checklists and notes that you intend to use later. As you begin the actual process of writing the draft, you will continue to refer to materials developed during the planning process; and once the proposal is complete, you will check it against the RFP and other planning documents before putting it in the mail.

PLANNING

A common saying in all branches of the military is that "If you fail to plan, you are planning to fail." The saying is particularly true for complex operations. Although the amount and kind of planning required will certainly vary from proposal to proposal as the complexity and costs of the project increase, careful planning is a must. Planning typically includes the following steps: *reviewing the requirements; identifying the problem, purpose, and audience; establishing a schedule; estimating the costs; preparing a draft; planning for production requirements;* and *planning the presentation package.*

Reviewing the Requirements

Whether the proposal is solicited or unsolicited, writers need to be sure that the requirements are clear, that the desired objective is feasible, and that the project is well-suited to the qualifications of their organizations. Because one of the most common failings of proposals is their unresponsiveness to the client's needs as specified in the RFP, the planning procedure always begins with a thorough review of the RFP or other sources of information about the problem and the client's needs.

The first decision, of course, is whether to submit a proposal or bid on the project at all. That decision should be made as quickly—and as inexpensively—as possible. In many cases, proposal writers will waste time (and lose credibility) by calling the issuing organization to request information contained in the RFP. RFPs and IFBs are often lengthy and difficult to read, but there is no substitute for reading them thoroughly— sentence by sentence and often even word by word—checking for the requirements of *what* the reader wants and for indications of *why* the reader wants it. Before you call to fill in any missing pieces, make sure that the information you seek is not included somewhere in the RFP or IFB, perhaps in small print in an appendix. Once the decision to submit has been made, you may still need additional information to proceed with serious planning, but the *bid/no bid* decision should be made quickly based on the feasibility of the project for your organization.

In reviewing the requirements in the RFP or, for unsolicited proposals, the requirements inherent in the situation, what the reader wants will be specified as *material specifications.* Why the reader wants it are the associated values or the *criteria of fulfillment.* An RFP or IFB, for example, might specify a certain size and grade of tire on automobiles to be purchased for use by the organization's field representatives. That would be the material specification. To be taken seriously, any proposal would need to meet that specification. The proposals that will be considered the most seriously will also address the criteria or value behind the material specification: economy, higher gas mileage, safety, durability, and so on. Because criteria of fulfillment are more difficult to determine than the material specifications, fewer proposal writers address them, so those who do are more likely to succeed. Search the entire document carefully for words and phrases that indicate particular values: *customer service, development, difficulties, economy, globalism, harmonious, human resources, improved, limits, long-term goals, potential, practical, problems, quality, quick results, scientific, scientific advancement, user-friendly,* and other words that convey values or criteria.

Identifying the Problem, Purpose, and Audience

The problem, purpose, and audience are the three central issues in planning any successful proposal. If even one of these is defined incorrectly, the proposal cannot succeed. The proposal writer needs to know exactly what is required to solve the reader's problem, and to know this, the writer also must know the reader's purpose. An IFB for office furniture, for example, might specify 100 desks and "matching" office chairs. Unless the proposal writer also knows where, how, and by whom the desks and chairs will be used, he or she will not be able to prepare an effective proposal. If the purpose is not clear from the RFP or IFB, call.

The question of audience analysis is addressed in Chapter 2. While many of those who prepare RFPs and IFBs will be sufficiently experienced to specify everything they desire in clear and unambiguous terms, many will not. A person not familiar with preparing IFBs might specify the dimensions of the desks without stating whether a shelf for a computer keyboard was required or whether the quality and appearance of the desks were critical issues. Should the chairs all have arms? How adjustable do they need to be? Those experienced in the preparation of RFPs and IFBs will typically provide complete specifications and sufficient rationale so that you will be able to determine how you can best meet their needs. When the RFP or IFB is incomplete, however, you have the added task of helping the client organization determine the products or services that will best solve the problem.

Establishing a Schedule

In planning a proposal, the writer typically needs to consider *two* schedules: The schedule by which the proposal itself will be produced, and the schedule by which the work will be completed if the proposal is accepted. The proposal is, after all, a project that usually has a specific deadline and interdependent components requiring completion, often by different people at different times.

While scheduling simple projects is usually a matter of telling two or three people what they are to do and when they need to have it accomplished, scheduling the work involved for a major proposal typically requires a calendar of events, a Gantt chart, or some other kind of visual reminder so that the project of producing the proposal can remain on schedule. Most organizations will find project management software a worthwhile investment, but a spreadsheet or even a "tables" function in a word processing program can be used to prepare an effective Gantt chart. Figure 3-1 illustrates a general schedule for the production of a proposal. Note that the manager of the proposal writing team scheduled the completion of the proposal two weeks before the proposal deadline.

In establishing a schedule for completing the proposal, you have two known dates: the date on which you can begin work on the proposal and the deadline—the date the proposal is due. The time in between needs to be allocated realistically, and you will doubtless find that your skill at estimating time requirements for various tasks will improve with practice.

The specific amount of time required for any given task will naturally vary depending on the organization, the nature of its products or services, and the individuals involved.

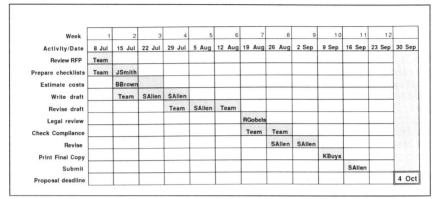

Week	1	2	3	4	5	6	7	8	9	10	11	12	
Activity/Date	8 Jul	15 Jul	22 Jul	29 Jul	5 Aug	12 Aug	19 Aug	26 Aug	2 Sep	9 Sep	16 Sep	23 Sep	30 Sep
Review RFP	Team												
Prepare checklists	Team	JSmith											
Estimate costs		BBrown											
Write draft			Team	SAllen	SAllen								
Revise draft					Team	SAllen	Team						
Legal review							RGobels						
Check Compliance								Team	Team				
Revise									SAllen	SAllen			
Print Final Copy										KBuys			
Submit											SAllen		
Proposal deadline													4 Oct

Figure 3-1. Sample Schedule for Proposal Production.

Estimating the Costs

Although cost is usually not the only factor in determining the winning proposal, it is almost always an important factor. Everyone wants to save money when and wherever possible, and in cases where two organizations can provide essentially the same products or services, the organization that can do so at a lower cost will usually win the contract.

Estimating costs, however, is not always easy, and the person with overall responsibility for writing the report may not be the best person for doing the estimating. If the estimated cost is too high, the proposal may be summarily dismissed. If it is too low, the writer and his or her organization could suffer financially. For this reason, the task of estimating costs is best left to the individual or team members with the most experience at providing such estimates.

In estimating costs, consider both the direct costs of supplying specific goods or services (materials and other tangibles) and indirect costs (overhead and other intangibles). If you are a consultant proposing a training program, for example, you need to know not only what your presentation time is worth but also how much it will cost you to produce any materials you distribute to those who attend your program.

Preparing a Draft

The complexity and costs of the project typically influence the process of writing and revising the proposal. Whereas a short proposal prepared by one individual may be completed in a matter of hours or days, complex team projects may require that different individuals write different sections, which may be revised several times before being combined for further revision to ensure uniformity of style.

Drafts should be dated and clearly marked as drafts. Unless drafts are dated, it is easy to lose track of which version is the most recent, and unless each page of a draft is marked as such, draft material may be submitted in place of the final version accidentally. Drafts prepared with word processing programs can easily include the word *draft* and the date in a header or footer, and PostScript® printers can place the word *draft* on each page of a document so that it can't possibly be overlooked.

Planning for Production Requirements

The level of formality will often dictate the way in which the proposal is produced. If the proposal is informal and short, it may simply be word processed. Longer, more formal proposals may be produced in-house, using desktop publishing equipment and software. Using a microcomputer or workstation, desktop publishing software, and a high-quality laser printer can save an organization money in production costs, but using such equipment and software effectively requires training and practice. In addition to the cost savings, such equipment offers the additional advantage of providing greater control over production.

Formal proposals that need to be printed and bound have more stringent production requirements and require greater lead time for final production. Printers do not always attach the same importance to your deadlines as you do, and once you have delivered your materials to a print shop, you have essentially lost control over the production of the document. If you have not worked with the print shop previously, and if the proposal is important to you, check the printer's reputation carefully so that you can leave your materials with confidence.

Planning the Presentation Package

Because the reader's perception of the writer's organization and its ability to complete the project in a desirable way is influenced by the form in which the proposal is presented, the presentation package requires careful attention to ensure its suitability for the problem, purpose, and audience. In many cases, the proposal itself will be all the reader has to go by in determining whether your organization is the best qualified to undertake the project. Appearance does count. A proposal that does not *look* professional will suffer in comparison with those that do, regardless of the content. Although governmental agencies and larger organizations have specific evaluation procedures, the differences between the winning proposal and the others are often more psychological than substantive.

In other cases, the two or three organizations submitting the best proposals may be invited to present their materials orally. This presentation is essentially a combination sales presentation and problem-solving meeting. Oral presentations are covered in Chapter 11. An oral presentation provides members of both organizations the opportunity to understand each other better and to ensure that each organization can meet its objectives. The kind of meeting and the number of people involved will influence the nature of the presentation. Will all those attending the meeting from the client organization have read the proposal? What kind of handout package will be required to supplement or highlight information in the proposal? What kind and how many visual aids would be most appropriate (videotape, slides, overhead transparencies, flip charts, models, samples of previous work, and so on)? Who should do the actual presenting? Will specialists in technical areas be required to provide an adequate explanation? If so, do they have well-developed presentation skills? If you know that an oral presentation is likely, these are all questions that need to be addressed well in advance. To be successful, oral presentations require planning and rehearsal.

MAINTAINING CUSTOMER ORIENTATION

While you are planning, remember that the single most important strategy to help ensure a successful proposal is to maintain a *customer orientation*. Have you ever been in a store where the salesclerks were too busy talking with each other to help you find what you needed? Or have you ever talked with sales representatives who thought that they knew your business better than you do? If so, you know how offensive an inappropriate sales technique can be.

Proposals can offend in essentially the same way if the writer loses track of the customers' orientation. Before accepting your proposal, your readers will need to believe that you understand and can solve the problem as *they* perceive it. In Chapter 2, we discussed this basic concept as the *you-attitude* or *you-viewpoint*. Basically, you need to be sure of what your customers want, and you need to know what criteria they will use to determine whether they have received it. The only ways to discover how your readers perceive the problem are by studying the RFP or IFB and by asking questions. If the customers desire to institute a training program to increase employee self-esteem, for example, how do they know that the current level of self-esteem is inadequate? How will they know if your training program has improved it? Make sure that you understand their concerns before you begin serious planning.

Customer orientation consists of more than your understanding of the reader's problem. Your writing style, proposal organization, and presentation of graphical and statistical data also demonstrate your attitude toward the reader and become an influencing factor in the reader's perception of your proposal. Readers always appreciate clear and concise writing and also appreciate having the proposal organized for easy reading. Chapters 4 and 5 present specific techniques for organizing proposals and for developing a clear, concise writing style.

In general, use the active voice to avoid confusion about who is responsible for critical actions.

Not this: At the time of installation, it will be determined whether employees. . .

But this: At the time of installation, we will determine whether employees. . .

When possible, use positive language rather than negative language. The human brain does not always process negative language appropriately, and even when the meaning is clear, the mental effort required to process a negative sentence is greater than that required to process a sentence expressing the same concept using positive language. What happens, for example, when you read the following sentence: *Do not think of purple elephants.* If you are like most people, you did exactly what you were asked *not* to do. The same thing happens in most cases where negative language is used:

The dog is not chasing the cat. [What *are* the cat and dog doing?]

Do not eat the cake in the refrigerator. [Do you make an image of a cake in a refrigerator? Which is more compelling, your image of the cake or the word *not?*]

Also, use the standard order of subject-verb-object for most of your sentences, and remember that long sentences (those more than about 20 words) and long paragraphs (those more than about 8 lines in single-spaced material and about 15 lines in double-spaced documents) are more difficult to read than short sentences and short paragraphs. Too many short sentences and too many short paragraphs, on the other hand, will make your material seem choppy. See Chapter 4 for additional suggestions.

Additionally, provide your readers the courtesy of calculating all mathematical problems, even when such calculations seem obvious to you. Scientists, engineers, and financial managers may, of course, check all your figures, but readers with general managerial backgrounds (and the decision maker may be among them) will appreciate your courtesy in supplying the information.

BLENDING OUTCOMES

Previously we mentioned the bid/no bid decision. In general, this decision should be based on the "fit" between your organization and the client organization. Proposals should always be submitted from a win-win standpoint: Both your organization and the client's organization should benefit as a result of the project. When that is not the case, a no-bid decision is probably in your long-term best interests.

In the long run, your success will depend on the relationships you build with others. Whenever you are selling someone a product or service (or offering to sell, as is the case with a proposal), think about the kind of relationship you want to build. Are you interested in repeat business? Are you interested in referrals? Do you desire positive word-of-mouth advertising? For most people in most organizations, the answers to these questions are "yes." If you persuade the readers to purchase something that won't really meet their needs, you will lose the chance to sell them additional products or services in the future. If you agree to a price without a sufficient profit margin for yourself, you won't be in business long. Blending outcomes guarantees that both your organization and the client's organization will be satisfied with the results.

Seemingly incompatible outcomes, which often occur in product negotiations, can frequently be resolved by changing the reader's *frame of reference*. If the customers are concerned about cost, for example, you may be able to change their frame of reference by "chunking up" to a higher criteria, such as value or quality. When you can't meet the price your competition offers, for example, you will need to show how your product or service will prove a better investment, help your customers make a better impression on their customers, or—for those readers who are motivated by moving away from negative possibilities—avoid waste. Even when the readers are persuaded by the lower cost on their first purchase, they may prefer more quality the second time around. Not long ago, a major Midwestern pharmaceutical company purchased thousands of fine line felt-tip pens from the vendor quoting the lowest price. The inexpensive pens proved a mistake, however, as approximately 40 percent of them had defective tips and had to be discarded with little or no use. The next time around, the company paid much closer attention to vendors offering a good combination of price and quality. The pens purchased the second time around cost more but saved money in the long run.

Blending outcomes requires a clear conception of the benefits your product or service offers your customers and your readers' criteria of fulfillment. When you know what your product or service will do for your customers and you know how to state that in terms your readers will find appealing, your proposals will be much more successful. In general, when you discuss the features and benefits of your product or service, emphasize the benefit.

Not this   Our office furniture has a 20-year warranty.
But this: The 20-year warranty on our furniture guarantees your investment and lasting satisfaction.

Not this: Our microcomputers come with DOS 5.5 and Windows.

But this: Because our microcomputers come with DOS 5.5 and Windows already installed, installation is quick and easy.

FOLLOWING DIRECTIONS

Most RFPs and IFBs provide a number of specific directions for sections to include, topics to cover, and formats to follow. Each of these directions needs to be followed to the letter. The two most common reasons cited for rejecting proposals are that (1) the proposal wasn't received by the deadline, and (2) the instructions weren't followed.

A governmental agency or major corporation may receive hundreds of proposals for any one project. Those faced with the task of sorting through the proposals are naturally going to eliminate as many as possible as quickly as possible. They will assume that lateness and failure to follow directions are indicative of a general lack of attention to detail that would carry over to work on the project itself.

In following the directions, make sure to use the vocabulary of the RFP. If the RFP tells you to include a section on *Administration*, for example, be sure to entitle the section *Administration*, in spite of the fact that you may call that category of information *Project Management*. A reader scanning through your proposal quickly is not going to make a special effort to see what you have done with the information to be included in *Administration*, and your proposal may be disqualified on that basis alone.

Consider every direction an absolute. If the RFP states that proposals "shall not exceed 15 pages," do not exceed 15 pages. If the RFP says that proposals need to be double spaced, do not use space and a half. If the RFP says that the margins need to be 2 inches, leave 2-inch margins. Sometimes an RFP will provide a rationale for an unusual direction, but often they do not. In some cases, as is true with length, for example, you can surmise the intent behind the direction with some degree of assurance. In other cases, as might seem the case with 2-inch margins, you might be inclined to assume an error in the RFP. In such cases, call.

KEY POINTS FROM CHAPTER 3

The key points from Chapter 3 are the following:

1. A strategy is a set procedure designed to ensure a desired result.
2. A successful strategy for proposal writing includes the following components: planning, maintaining a customer orientation, blending outcomes, and following directions.

3. The amount and kind of planning will vary from proposal to proposal but typically includes the following steps: reviewing the requirements; identifying the problem, purpose, and audience; establishing a schedule; estimating the costs; preparing a draft; planning for production requirements; and planning the presentation package.
4. Maintaining a customer orientation is the single most important strategy for developing successful proposals.
5. In general, positive language communicates more quickly and more clearly than negative language.
6. Proposals should always be submitted from a win-win standpoint. Blend outcomes so that both your organization and the client's organization benefit.
7. The two most common reasons cited for rejecting proposals are that (a) the proposal wasn't received by the deadline, and (b) the instructions weren't followed. Make sure that you follow all the directions provided in the RFP or IFB.
8. Use the same vocabulary as that used in the RFP or IFB.

CHAPTER 4

The Writing Process: Beginning and Revising

As mentioned in the previous chapter, the process of writing actually begins during the planning phase. Even before you make the bid/no-bid decision, you will need to take notes on the critical aspects of the RFP or IFB, and these notes will eventually become a part of the draft of your proposal. Once an organization has decided to bid, the writing process typically begins with the development of checklists.

Checklists provide structure and direction for the proposal. Outlines and mockups that will eventually become the draft of the proposal develop naturally as the checklists are completed. This step-by-step process helps ensure that the writing proceeds in a logical, timely manner.

DEVELOPING CHECKLISTS

Many RFPs and IFBs are complex documents, with page after page of specifications, explanations, and proposal requirements. Because it is easy to overlook details that may prove critical, the first step in the writing process is to develop conformance checklists that will serve as guides to planning and completing the proposal.

Depending on the nature of the project, you may wish to develop three or more separate checklists. Typical categories of checklists include conformance, specifications, and criteria or values.

Conformance Checklists

Conformance checklists are designed to ensure that you have complied with the proposal requirements specified in the RFP. Many government agencies and large organizations supply checklists as an aid for proposal writers. If such a checklist is provided, it should, of course, be used. You will probably do well to compare it with the actual requirements stated in the proposal itself to ensure that those who prepared the checklist didn't overlook anything. Typical entries for conformance checklists include the following:

❑ **Deadline.** When is the completed proposal due? If you miss this, nothing else will matter.

❑ **Required forms.** When specific forms (cover sheets, background information on those who will be involved with the project, the submitting organization, and so on) are required, the name of the form, its number (if applicable), and its placement should be noted.

❑ **Required signatures.** Most proposals need to be signed by individuals authorized to make decisions for the submitting organization and perhaps by the intended project manager as well.

❑ **Required topics.** Most RFPs and IFBs specify a list of topics and the order in which those topics should be covered. List those topics, using the vocabulary of the RFP, and include a description of the details that should be covered as part of the discussion of each topic.

❑ **Table of contents.** The formats for long proposals generally require a table of contents. If the nature of the work requires a number of graphic aids (graphs, charts, illustrations, or tables), separate tables may be required for those.

❑ **Abstract.** Many proposals require a separate abstract or executive summary. Check to see whether the RFP or IFB specifies a *summarizing abstract* or a *descriptive abstract*. (See Chapter 9.) If neither is specified, use a summarizing abstract or, for long proposals, an executive summary.

❑ **Price list, budget, or other financial details.** Most RFPs or IFBs will specify how the client organization desires to see any financial details. Provide the information in that form—if they request the price by the gross and you normally price your product by the hundredweight, make sure that you base your bid on your cost by the gross.

❑ **Documentation or other references.** Research projects in particular will require a bibliography of pertinent literature. Other projects may require other kinds of demonstrations of appropriate research and problem familiarity.

❑ **Descriptions of equipment and facilities.** Many projects require special equipment and facilities. When this is true, RFPs and IFBs typically request information about the proposing organization's access to such equipment or facilities.

❑ **Vitae of senior personnel.** Especially when specific expertise is required for completion of the project, the vitae of the project manager and other senior personnel may be required. Research projects may require a separate listing of the recent publications of those involved in the project.

❏ **Previous relationship with organization.** Governmental agencies in particular will want a history of your business relationship with the agency.

❏ **Required supplements.** If the project involves specialized knowledge or research on human or animal subjects, appropriate authorizations will need to be included. Required licenses, special certifications, or bonding; animal-care statements; human subjects certification; environmental impact statements; language fluency; and a wide variety of other supplemental information may be required.

❏ **Proposal length.** Many RFPs and IFBs limit the length of the entire proposal or certain sections of it. Make sure that any stated lengths are noted exactly, and then be sure to adhere to them. In some cases, you may be able to apply for an exception, in which case you may need to include a statement justifying the variance or a form authorizing the variance.

❏ **Cover letter.** Some RFPs will provide a required cover sheet. Others may request a letter of transmittal including a summary of the proposed activities. Make sure that the letter, cover sheet, and envelope all include the correct name and address of the individual or department responsible for receiving and processing the proposals.

❏ **Copies.** Check to see how many copies are specified. Note also how many of the copies require original signatures.

Study the RFP closely to ensure that nothing is overlooked. Be sure to note specifically any deviations from requirements and provide the appropriate rationale, as Figure 4-1 indicates:

3.3.1.3.6	**Backup Rings**
	Deviation Requested:
	In some cases where envelope and weight can be substantially reduced, capstrips are proposed as anti-extrusion devices, rather than backup rings. This will not be done on external seals. Refer also to comment on Paragraph 3.2.1.1.1.8.
3.3.1.3.9	**Plugs**
	Deviation Requested:
	Standard ST7M141 does not allow oversize plugs normally used for salvage. CFM has no objection to implementing the specification but will require approval for use of oversize plugs for salvage purposes.

Figure 4-1. Deviation Requests.

The best checklists are developed based on the RFP and the special requirements of your own business or industry. The checklists included in the Appendix B will provide additional suggestions. Although designed primarily for proposals submitted to governmental agencies, most of the items apply regardless of the type of proposal being planned.

Supplemental Checklists

In addition to a conformance checklist, you may also need separate checklists for materials specifications or product requirements. In many proposal writing situations, a values checklist, designed to help you track value words or the reader's criteria of fulfillment, would also be beneficial. To develop such a checklist, simply keep track of value words and the context in which they are used. You might, for example, use a photocopy of the RFP or IFB and a highlighter and mark each value word and note its location. Value words do not occur in an RFP by accident; they reveal the concepts of greatest importance to those who prepared the RFP.

The following words, for example, all indicate values or concerns. You may wish to compile your own list based on the common concerns in your business or industry before you attempt to locate value words in an RFP.

aesthetics	beauty
commitment	economy
efficiency	elegance
human resources	personnel
profits	quality
savings	specialized
training	warranty

Checkmark Space

As you develop your checklists, allow space—with appropriate lines or boxes—that will permit you to check off items as you comply with them. Figure 4-2 illustrates two examples of checklist formats.

PREPARING MOCKUPS

Once you have listed all the tasks or items specified in the RFP or IFB in your conformance checklist and prepared other appropriate checklists, you are ready to prepare a mockup—a representation—of your completed document. Preparing a mockup allows you to do some brainstorming on the appropriate content and accompanying graphics.

Job	Person Responsible	Due Date	Completed	Date
1	Albertson, Timothy	Jan 10	❏	_____
2	Burton, Richard	Jan 20	❏	_____
3	Carerra, Roberta	Jan 30	❏	_____
4	Dahl, Henrietta	Feb 5	❏	_____
5	Embertson, Jules	Feb 15	❏	_____

Completed	Specification
_____	Checking for safety
_____	Starting
_____	Stopping
_____	Turning
_____	Signaling
_____	Performing maintenance

Figure 4-2. Checklists Allowing Checkmark Space.

Mockups typically begin as *thumbnails* (or small-scale representations) of the pages allocated to each section showing space allocated for the content and graphics for major sections. Thumbnails help in the planning process by allowing you to see the overall section or the complete proposal so that you can determine how to best present the information in the space available. Once the thumbnails have provided you with an overview, full-scale mockups are created on full-size blank pages. Full-scale mockups of the proposal allow you to plan more specifically how much text can be allocated for each section. Again, the process is recursive. With each progressive mockup, more detail is added until the first draft is complete.

For team proposals, thumbnails and full-page mockups serve the additional functions of helping to coordinate team activities and of allowing team members to share information and ideas before the actual writing process begins. The mockups can be posted (on a wall or on storyboards) so that team members can periodically review each other's ideas throughout the planning process. Such reviews help ensure that the final proposal will be coherent, consistent, and complete. Figure 4-3 illustrates sample mockups.

WRITING THE DRAFT

As you have gone through the process of planning, analyzing the audience, and preparing the appropriate checklists and mockups, you have, in fact, already begun writing the proposal. The next step is to organize the materials you have already gathered. Once you have determined the overall organization, you can turn your attention to the actual words, sentences, and paragraphs required to fill in the details.

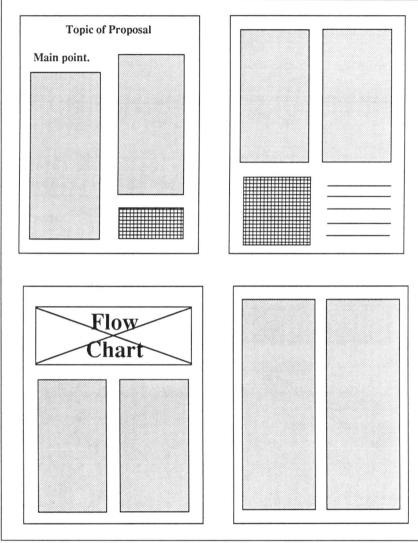

Figure 4-3. Sample Mockups.

Organization

In many cases, the problem of organization will solve itself because the RFP or IFB will specify that specific topics be covered in a specific order. When that is the case, be absolutely sure to use the topics and organizational pattern required by the RFP. When solicited proposals do not specify a particular structure, you may use the generic organizational structure recommended for unsolicited proposals, with appropriate modifications based on the nature of the project involved.

When you do not have specific guidelines for preparing the proposal, include the following elements:

- A summarizing introduction
- A detailed problem statement
- A statement of methodology
- A project management statement
- A statement of your qualifications

A Summarizing Introduction

Because the summarizing introduction may be the only section your audience reads, you need to demonstrate that you thoroughly understand what the problem is and have the expertise to solve it. Provide the reader with an overview of your project stating your proposed solution and the benefits to the audience.

A Detailed Problem Statement

Define the problem clearly and accurately. Demonstrate to your reader that you understand what the problem is. State what you and the reader will have to do to solve the problem, and what difficulties you will encounter as you work to solve the problem.

A Statement of Methodology

Because your reader will want to know how you are going to go about solving the problem, you need to provide a detailed description of what you plan to do. You might wish to include how a similar problem was solved previously by you or by others. Primary and secondary research may help convince your reader that you have the ability to solve the problem. Present the results of your research in this section, and present the documentation and other supporting details in an appendix.

A Project Management Statement

A project management statement provides your reader with information about what you will be doing, when you will be doing it, how you will be doing it, and how much it all will cost. The reader will want the specifics—names, dates, lists of supplies, materials, equipment needed. Clarify who will be report to whom and when. State how progress will be measured and what the evaluation criteria will be.

A Statement of Your Qualifications

Your reader will want to know how you are qualified to solve the problem. What are your credentials? Have you solved similar problems before and for whom? Did you meet your deadlines? Did you do what you said you would do? Can you provide references? Answers to these and similar questions will help establish your credibility with an audience not already familiar with the quality of your work. Most RFPs will also require you to submit an updated resume of yourself and all key personnel who will be working on the project.

Words

Because the goal of all communication is the transfer of meaning from the mind of the sender to the mind of the receiver, the words we use to convey meaning are critical. As the basic building block of language, words constitute individual units of meaning. The problem is that two people might assign different meanings to the same word. What, for example, is an *economical* automobile? Is it one with *high* gas mileage (what's *high* gas mileage?), or is it one with a *low* sticker price? What about an *inexpensive* automobile? To what extent does your annual income influence your perception of *inexpensive*?

Because different individuals may interpret words in different ways, writers need to be especially careful with word selection. In face-to-face communication, participants have the opportunity to ask questions: "When you say *inexpensive*, about how much did you have in mind, Mr. Smith?" Written communication does not afford that opportunity. If you are careless with word usage, you probably will not have the opportunity to explain what you really meant. To communicate clearly follow these suggestions:

1. **Use short, familiar words.** In general, short, familiar words communicate more quickly than long, unfamiliar words. In some cases, however, the long word will be more familiar or more exact, and some short words are too vague to communicate clearly.

Not This	But This
ameliorate	improve
consummate	complete
effectuate	do
enhance	increase
facilitate	help
herewith	here
institute	start
interrogate	ask
perceive	see
subsequent	after

2. **Use specific words rather than general words.** In general, specific words communicate more clearly than general words. Tell the reader exactly what you want to have happen. Whenever you expect something from your reader, let the reader know precisely what you expect. Whenever you promise something, let the reader know exactly what you are offering. Anything not specified is subject to interpretation.

Specific	General
Newsweek	magazine
George Bush	person
New York City	place
29 April	soon
15 percent increase	increase
down jacket	jacket
five 6' long pipes	several pipes
58	many
5 percent	a lot

3. **Avoid being overly specific.** Although specific words convey a clearer image than general words, being too specific sounds pompous. Does it have to be a Mercedes Benz, or will any car do? Does it have to be a Yellow Cab, or will any taxi do?

4. **Use concrete words rather than abstract words.** Concrete words help the reader form a mental image of the people, places, items, or actions that you intend. For example, a concrete term for computers might be Macintosh IIfx or IBM OS/2. The test for a concrete word is whether you can see it, smell it, taste it, hear it, or feel it. Abstract words can't be seen, smelled, tasted, heard, or felt. Abstract words name general conditions, qualities, or concepts, such as freedom, justice, cooperation.

Concrete	Abstract
Room 1170	Place
A 13-watt compact fluorescent bulb	Light
Alice Williams	Person
The New York Times	The paper
ABC, NBC, and CBS	The media

Concrete and abstract are, of course, relative terms. Few words are *absolutely* concrete or *absolutely* abstract. Most words are concrete or abstract only in relation to other words. This concept is usually referred to as the *ladder of abstraction*. The following example is not complete, and the "steps" on the ladder would change from context to context.

Most Abstract	Life form
	A human being
	A U.S. citizen
	A voter
	A woman
	A middle-aged woman
	A 40-year-old woman
	An executive
	A woman executive
	A member of the Williams family
	A Williams woman
	Alice Williams
Most Concrete	Alice Williams, 1 January 19xx

5. **Avoid redundancies, expletives, and other wordy expressions.** A redundancy is an expression that says the same thing twice, such as the expression *baby puppies* (all puppies are "babies") or *widow of the late* John Smith (if she's a widow, he's "late"). Expletives are unnecessary words added as filler. Sentences beginning with *there is, there are, it is,* and *in order* are the most common offenders.

Not this: *There are* some proposal writers *who* always do well.
But this: Some proposal writers always do well.
Not this: We have met the requirements *that are* specified in the RFP.
But this: We have met the requirements specified in the RFP.

Common redundancies, expletives, and wordy expressions include the following:

advanced planning	in order
attached hereto	located on
bad disaster	necessary requirements
basic fundamentals	new innovation
cancel out	past experience
clean up	qualified expert
close down	refer back
due to the fact that	reiterate again
each and everyone	repeat again

6. **Avoid jargon.** Jargon includes "businessese" and "legalese" as well as expressions common to a wide variety of technical professions. When you are writing to a technical audience, you may find that jargon common to your profession is the most appropriate way to express certain ideas. Architects, engineers, and research scientists, for example, have all developed a specialized common vocabulary. An architect writing a proposal for consideration by other architects would do well to use the language of the profession. For a more general audience, however, the same language might be inappropriate. In all cases, avoid expressions based on outdated legal language and formulaic business expressions.

> As per our contract (We have completed)
> As per your request (Here is)
> At the present time (Now, currently)
> Do not hesitate to call me (Please call when)
> Enclosed herewith please find (The enclosed brochure)
> Feel free to contact me at your earliest convenience (Please call soon)
> I remain yours most sincerely (Sincerely)
> In the final analysis (The results are)
> It has been brought to my attention (Thank you for calling to let me know   Thank you for writing)
> Thanking you in advance   (I would appreciate your consideration)

7. **Avoid clichés.** Expressions wear out from overuse. When an expression has reached the stage of being a cliché, it has lost its impact. Select a fresher, stronger way of expressing the same idea. If you put your *nose to the grindstone* or *burn the midnight oil,* you can probably add to the following list of clichés.

busy as a bee	last but not least
by leaps and bounds	pretty as a picture
clear as crystal	slow but sure
in this day and age	strong as an ox

8. **Avoid Latin and other foreign expressions.** In most cases, use English. Some scientific applications will require Greek or Latin constructions, and other occupations occasionally make effective use of French or other foreign expressions. When foreign expressions are appropriate for your occupation, by all means use them. Unless you are certain of their appropriateness, however, you should avoid them. Many writers, for example, use the Latin

abbreviations *i.e.* (*id est*, that is) and *e.g.* (*exempli gratia*, for example) incorrectly, and even when used correctly, foreign expressions frequently sound pompous.

ergo	per se
ex post	pro forma
fait accompli	raison d'•être
forte	tête-a-tête
ipso facto	via
per	vis-à-vis

9. **Avoid sexist language.** Language that suggests that certain work is suitable for members of one sex only or that otherwise implies that one sex is inferior to another is sexist. If you use the masculine pronoun *he* to refer to *a manager* and the feminine pronoun *she* to refer to *a secretary*, for example, you are using sexist language. Many common expressions are now considered sexist, so proofread your document carefully to ensure that sexist terms have been replaced with their equivalent gender neutral terms.

businessman (businessperson)	foreman (supervisor)
cameraman (camera operator)	man hours (work hours)
chairman (chairperson)	manpower (help, workers)
draftsman (drafter)	to man (work, run, operate)

10. **Use the right word at the right time.** Make the relationships between your ideas clear and explicit. Link ideas together by repeating key terms, showing cause-effect relationships, comparing or contrasting ideas, or demonstrating chronological or spatial relationships.

   a. Repeat key words, phrases, and ideas to provide logical transition from sentence to sentence. To avoid sounding monotonous, use pronouns and synonyms to stand for key words.

   b. Show cause and effect relationships so that your reader can develop a good understanding of why things happened the way they did (or will happen the way you predict). *Because, therefore, thus*, and *then* all indicate a cause-effect relationship between events. Before you use this form of transition, make sure that the one event really did cause the other and not merely precede it in time.

Not this: Because it was morning, I woke up.
But this: Because the sunlight coming through the open blinds disturbed my sleep, I woke up.

   c. Compare and contrast ideas to show your reader the relationships between them. When one thing is *like* another in certain respects, describing those similarities for your reader will help him or her understand the points you are trying to make. Be sure to describe significant differences as well as the similarities to avoid misleading your reader into believing that the two items or concepts are identical.

   d. Indicate chronological and spatial relationships when those are important so that your reader can form a clear mental picture of what is happening.

     (1) The meeting began promptly at 9; it adjourned at 10.
     (2) Turn left at the first light. Go 1.5 miles and turn right.

11. **Use action verbs.** Action verbs help make your writing clear and specific. They tell the reader exactly who is (was, will be) responsible for performing which action. Passive constructions and nominalizations (verbs turned into nouns: *demonstrate* into *demonstration*) frequently omit the person or thing responsible for performing the action and are therefore more difficult to understand.

Not this: A 42 percent savings *was achieved* by . . .
But this: We *achieved* a 42 percent savings by . . .
Not this: The *decision was made.*
But this: We *decided.*

The following are common action verbs:

accomplished	eliminated	performed
achieved	evaluated	planned
completed	financed	provided
constructed	implemented	recommended
created	invented	reviewed
distributed	managed	supervised

Use *be* (*is, are, was, were*), *do* (*did, done*), *make,* and *take* verbs sparingly. They can be weak, wordy, and lifeless. Use verbs that give punch to your writing. Note the difference between the following weak expressions and their stronger equivalents:

Weak	**Strong**
a reduction is necessary	we must reduce
be careful when investing	invest carefully
did	planned, organized
make a recommendation	recommend

make an appearance	appear
put on a demonstration	demonstrate
take a look	see
take into consideration	consider

Sentences

A sentence is a group of words that expresses a complete thought. As a unit of composition, sentences come in four basic types—simple, compound, complex, and compound-complex—depending on the arrangement of phrases and clauses. The main thing to remember is that good writing employs variety. A document consisting of all simple sentences would sound simplistic and choppy. On the other hand, a document containing only compound-complex sentences would sound stilted and be difficult to read.

Use sentence types to control emphasis and subordination throughout your proposal. In general, short, simple sentences have impact. Put important ideas in them. Explanations and ideas of lesser importance can be placed in longer, compound or compound-complex sentences. Use the subordinate clause in a complex sentence to subordinate information you would prefer to have your reader gloss over:

Not this: We are unable to meet the price you desire. Our quality, however, is much higher than that specified in the RFP. [Two independent clauses give equal weight to both ideas.]

But this: Although our price is slightly higher than desired, our quality exceeds the minimum specified in the RFP by more than 80 percent. [The concept of "higher price" is subordinated to—made less important than—the concept of "higher quality."]

The following list presents a brief review of sentence types:

1. **Simple sentences contain only one independent clause.**
   a. Darlene prepared the report.
   b. Darlene and John prepared the report.
   c. Darlene prepared the report and made the presentation.
   d. At the annual meeting in Detroit, Michigan, Darlene presented the findings of her research.
2. **Compound sentences contain two or more independent clauses.**
   a. Terry conducted a historical study, and Linda conducted an experimental study.
   b. The requestor discussed the project with management, and the supervisor discussed the project with the company's attorney.

3. **Complex sentences contain one independent clause and at least one dependent clause.**
   a. Whereas the first chapter had only 15 pages, the second chapter had 35 pages.
   b. The opening paragraph, which contained the topic sentence, contained the problem statement and purpose.
   c. Proposals were requested after the president gave an overview of the project.
4. **Compound-complex sentences contain two or more independent clauses and at least one dependent clause.**
   a. Before they made their presentation, Mr. Townsend toured the first floor of the new building, and Ms. VanHoestra toured the second floor.
   b. After they attended a seminar on proposal writing, Jerry submitted a proposal to the United States government, and Harriet submitted one to her state government.

Paragraphs

A paragraph is a unit of thought in writing. While it may consist of only one sentence, it is usually a series of sentences about a single topic. That topic is usually expressed in one sentence, the *topic* sentence, that expresses the main idea of the paragraph. Additional sentences in the paragraph provide supporting details, evidence, examples, and explanations for that main idea.

Unity and Coherence

Readers expect paragraphs to be unified and coherent. To maintain unity in the paragraph, relate all sentences to the development and support of the topic sentence. The topic sentence establishes expectations in the reader, and the rest of the paragraph needs to satisfy those expectations. Eliminate all sentences that do not support or explain the main idea of the paragraph. A unified paragraph also has coherence, with each sentence being related in a logical way to the sentence that precedes it. To maintain coherence, clarify the relationships among ideas. Each sentence in the paragraph builds on the previous sentence. To link sentences in the paragraph use transitional expressions, such as the following:

Addition:	and, also, in addition, next, first, finally, last, furthermore
Comparison:	likewise, similarly, not only . . . but also, in comparison
Contrast:	but, yet, however, although, nonetheless, while, though
Result:	therefore, accordingly, consequently thus, then, as a result

| Sequence: | first, second, finally, moreover, also, next, then, after |
| Summary: | in short, in other words, that is, briefly, in sum |

Organization and Structure

The placement of the topic sentence determines the organizational pattern for the paragraph. The two basic organizational patterns for ordering sentences in a paragraph are *deductive* and *inductive*. Other organizational patterns that may be used to develop the paragraph are chronological , spatial, and problem-to-solution.

1. **Deductive.** The most common organizational pattern for the development of paragraphs is the deductive order. In deductive order, the topic sentence states the recommendation or general conclusion and is placed early in the paragraph, frequently first. The rest of the sentences in the paragraph provide the supporting details, facts, and explanations on how the writer arrived at the recommendation or conclusion. The advantage of deductive order is that it is direct; the reader knows the recommendation or other main point immediately. When you know that your reader will be receptive to your recommendation, use the deductive order.

2. **Inductive.** Inductive order is the reverse of the deductive pattern. With inductive order, the topic sentence typically states the problem at the beginning of the paragraph. The sentences that follow provide the facts, explanations, and possible solutions. The paragraph ends with a conclusion or recommendation. Inductive order may also begin with a series of known facts about a subject that accumulate to a logical conclusion, with the topic sentence presenting that conclusion at the end of the paragraph. Inductive order develops the main idea more slowly than deductive order, but it is usually more persuasive when you know that your reader may resent or resist the conclusion or recommendation.

3. **Chronological.** When you need to present information in a time sequence, the best pattern is chronological. In this pattern, the topic sentence states the beginning point in a process or sequence; the following sentences report the items, details, or events arranged in the order in which they occurred or should occur. Chronological order typically uses time references (*first, second, third*, and so on) as transitions.

4. **Spatial.** When your subject is a physical item, then you would choose to use the spatial order to describe it. For example, you might describe it from left to right, top to bottom, or inside to outside. Spatial order may be used to describe a new building by giving the dimensions (height, width, length, depth), directions (north, south, east, west), relationships (higher, lower, above, below), and proportions (larger, smaller).

5. **Problem-to-Solution.** The problem-to-solution order applies the inductive order of presentation. The topic sentence states the problem, and the supporting sentences provide the solution. Most proposals follow the problem-to-solution order. The topic sentence defines a specific problem; the supporting sentences offer possible solutions and then recommend a solution.

REVISING

We mentioned previously that writing is a recursive process. The process of revision is an essential step between the conception of the project and the completion of the proposal. The common saying, "Hard writing makes easy reading," is essentially correct. Writers put in time and effort so that their readers won't have to. Those who review proposals don't want to work any harder than necessary at the task, and they appreciate it when the writers have clearly made an effort to ensure a readable document.

No two writers approach the task of revising in quite the same way. Some prefer to work with outlines and short notes to themselves until the final proposal is virtually complete. Others prefer to write each draft as though it could be final. Some prefer to work in short bursts, writing for half an hour or an hour, taking a break, and then returning to the task. Others prefer to do the bulk of their writing in one sitting, regardless of how long it might take.

With experience, you will find the procedure that works best for you, the one that allows you to produce your best quality work in the least amount of time. The principal things to remember are that to produce anything, you must start someplace, and that anything you do produce can be changed. "Rough drafts" are supposed to be rough. They are "polished" in the course of revision. How much revision is required will, of course, depend on the length and complexity of the proposal and the audience for whom it is intended. The time you have available to work with the materials will also be a consideration. No matter how much time and effort you put into it, no proposal will ever be perfect. One more revision will almost certainly result in one more improvement. At some point, however, you need to ask whether one more revision will be cost-effective: Will the improvement that may result be worth the investment in time and resources?

When the proposal is important to you, let your work sit for a day or two between revisions. If possible, have an outside reader with a background similar to that of the intended audience read your material and provide feedback. Take his or her comments seriously. If it is a team project, everyone on the team should read the materials being prepared by the others, and one or more readers from outside the team should be recruited as well. Larger organizations typically have a required review process before the proposal will be allowed to go forward. By all means, take advantage of the expertise of those who review proposals on a regular basis, and you may wish to consider enlisting an additional review as well.

When readers' opinions conflict, recognize that something probably needs changing even if the readers don't agree on what it is. Look for the underlying cause of their difficulty, which may have occurred one or more paragraphs before the place where they commented. Check your topic sentences. Are they clear and arranged in a logical order? Check your support sentences. Does each contribute appropriately? Even experienced readers rarely look back to see where they originally began having difficulty; they simply comment at the point they recognize that they are uncomfortable with what you are saying. This is especially true when two or more readers have conflicting opinions about what needs to be done to improve a piece of writing.

The objectives of revising are to ensure that the proposal meets the requirements of the RFP or IFB; to correct errors in fact, spelling, grammar, and style; and to improve the clarity and coherence of the document as a whole. When you are satisfied that the proposal meets the requirements of the RFP or IFB and that the document as a whole correctly addresses the concerns of its intended audience, you may still wish to edit to improve the writing style.

Editing the style of writing is especially important if different individuals have prepared various sections of the report. The final writing style should be reasonably uniform from section to section, so it is usually best to have one individual do the final editing. In addition to editing to ensure clarity and correctness, you may need to revise to condense or expand material, to rearrange it for greater effectiveness, or to improve its style or tone.

Condense

Many proposals must adhere to strict limits on length. Even when the RFP or IFB does not specify a length, however, virtually all readers appreciate concise writing. Condense by eliminating as many of the following as possible:

1. **Expletives.** Expletives (*it is, there is/are, to be, in order*) are often indicative of sloppy writing. If you are using a word processor, do a global search for common expletives and rewrite sentences appropriately.

   Not this: *In order* to accomplish our objectives
   But this: To accomplish our objectives

2. **Redundancies.** The most common redundancies are tautologies—two words that express the same concept (*personal friends, necessary requirements, the color red, qualified expert, reiterate again, widow woman*). Retain the word that expresses the appropriate concept best.

   Not this: We have met the *necessary* requirements.
   But this: We have met the requirements.

3. **Passive voice.** Passive voice (*it was concluded that, it was determined*) is typically more difficult to understand than active voice because it tends to disguise the person performing the action, and the reader will often need to convert the sentence into an active construction before fully comprehending it.

   Not this: It was decided to use a steel I-beam because of the length of the span.
   But this: The engineer recommended a steel I-beam because of the length of the span.

4. **Repetitions.** In addition to eliminating common redundancies, watch for and eliminate more general types of unnecessary repetitions (*thank you again, to repeat again, help to provide assistance, let me again remind you*). Check to see if you begin and end your paragraphs with virtually identical sentences. Do one or more of your support sentences convey the same concept? Have you asked several consecutive rhetorical questions when one would have been sufficient?

Expand

When space permits, you may wish to expand your proposal by adding information in the following categories:

1. **Reader benefits.** In any persuasive situation, the reader will respond favorably when he or she is convinced that the benefits of acting will outweigh the costs. Make sure that the benefits are clear. In the case of solicited proposals, the reader or readers already want what they have requested, so your principal task will be to show them the benefits of selecting your organization to perform the work. For unsolicited proposals, you may need to persuade your audience of the desirability of the action as well as the benefits of having you or your organization perform it.

2. **Specific details.** In most cases, specific details communicate more clearly than the general. *Next Wednesday by noon* is an easier concept to grasp than *soon*. As you revise, check for vague language and be more specific where possible. In some cases, however, increased

specificity serves no purpose. Consider the difference between telling someone that you'll meet them at 8:57 a.m. to discuss the proposal and telling him or her that your most recent TV commercial will air at 8:57 a.m. In the one case, the specificity is superfluous; in the other, it is essential.

3. **Explanations.** The kind and amount of explanation required depend on the audience. Who will be involved in the decision-making process? What does each person who will review your proposal need to know to decide in your favor? In some cases, an additional sentence or two of explanation can make the difference between understanding and reacting favorably to a recommendation and missing the point completely.

   Not this: Although some companies omit the XYZ, we have included one in our bid.

   But this: Although some companies omit the XYZ, we have included one in our bid because the XYZ has been shown to double the useful life of the product.

4. **Future possibilities.** In some cases, the current proposal might not be as important as future proposals and the long-term relationship you would like to establish with the reader and his or her organization. Don't make promises you can't keep, and ensure that you keep every promise you do make. If the RFP contains stipulations that you believe are not in the best interests of the client organization, let the client know. If the client elects to proceed with the project and employs one of your competitors, he or she will eventually discover that your analysis and recommendation were correct. Long-term credibility is almost always worth more than a short-term contract.

Rearrange

As you revise your materials, it's important to look beyond the correctness and appropriateness of individual sentences and paragraphs and to look at the arrangement of ideas. If the proposal is solicited, check to make sure that the sections are arranged in the order specified in the RFP. If the proposal is unsolicited, make sure that the materials are structured logically and appropriate for your intended audience and purpose. In general, keep related ideas close together, and review transitions from topic to topic. Make sure that the relationship between adjacent concepts is clear.

Improve

One of the principal purposes of revision should be to make the proposal more appealing to its intended audience. Check the document to ensure that it properly emphasizes positive concepts and subordinates the negative without misleading the reader into thinking that difficulties will be more easily overcome than will actually be possible. Negative sentences are more difficult to understand and remember than positive sentences, so change as many negative sentences into positive constructions as possible.

Not this:	The data from our previous efforts have not been ignored.
But this:	We have considered the data from our previous efforts.

Increase the forcefulness of your writing by checking the essential *subject-verb-object* positions in your sentences to ensure that the subject and objects are key concepts and that the verbs are action verbs in active voice. Change nominalizations back into verbs.

Not this:	We made a decision
But this:	We decided
Not this:	The assistance rendered by you in preparation of this document is appreciated.
But this:	Thank you for your help.

OVERCOMING WRITER'S BLOCK

When people procrastinate writing, they may be experiencing writer's block. Everyone who writes has experienced writer's block at one time or another, but writer's block is especially critical for proposal writers because proposals almost always have a specific deadline. Those who would write proposals do not often have the luxury of giving in to writer's block.

The four major causes of writer's block are insufficient preparation, fear of rejection, fear of producing an imperfect document, and fear of making a wrong decision. The only cure for insufficient preparation is, of course, more preparation. Some people, however, use additional preparation as an excuse to put off the process of writing. When additional preparation will not sufficiently increase your confidence in your proposed course of action, consider that something else may be responsible for your writer's block. If you worry about rejection, remember that rejection of the proposal is not the rejection of you as a person or of your organization. A rejection may be, in fact, important feedback about the quality of your proposals or your competitiveness as an organization. You can use a rejection as a basis for improving. If your proposal is rejected, do your best to discover why, change your approach, and try again.

Writing is a process that demands reviewing, revising, and rewriting. The most important step in writing is to begin: Commit your initial thoughts to paper (or computer disk) without worrying about grammar or the organizational structure. Write first, then revise. Expecting the first draft to be perfect is unrealistic. The function of the first draft is to commit ideas to paper where they can be studied, analyzed, and changed as necessary. Grammar and style can be corrected along the way. Although the next chapter provides a brief overview of grammar and style, those who write on a regular basis need an English handbook (for rules on punctuation, capitalization, use of numbers, and other problems of language and mechanics) and comprehensive style guides. Familiarity breeds confidence. The more familiar you are with the fundamentals of English usage, the less time you will spend worrying about correctness.

You may recall from Chapter 2 that some people require much more information than others before they are willing to make a decision. If you are comfortable with your decisions only when you have completed *all* the research—*twice*—and determined that no other information about the project is available anywhere in this galaxy, you will need to learn to live with a certain level of uncertainty and begin the process of writing while research continues. Regardless of how much research you do, you will never know everything there is to know about a project, and if you wait until you do, the proposal will never be written.

Try to determine beforehand what level of confidence you need in your decisions before they are acceptable. This will obviously vary based on the nature of the project. Scientific and engineering applications, for example, usually require a higher level of certainty than would a proposal to conduct communication training seminars. Begin working on the sections in which you have the highest levels of confidence, and fill in areas of uncertainty as more information becomes available.

KEY POINTS FROM CHAPTER 4

The key points from Chapter 4 are the following:

1. The process of writing actually begins during the planning phase.
2. Checklists help ensure that no details are overlooked inadvertently.
3. Conformance checklists are designed to ensure that the proposal complies with all the requirements specified in the RFP.
4. Specifications checklists help ensure that all materials meet stated requirements.
5. Values checklists help the writer recognize and address the client's main values or criteria of fulfillment.
6. Mockups help proposal writers plan content and graphic support.
7. Solicited proposals are typically organized according to requirements stated in the RFP or IFB.
8. Unsolicited proposals use the following pattern: *summarizing introduction, detailed problem statement, statement of methodology, project management statement,* and *statement of qualifications.*

9. Proposal writers need to select words, phrases, and sentences carefully to avoid being misinterpreted.
10. Paragraphs may be structured deductively, inductively, chronologically, spatially, or from problem-to-solution.
11. The process of writing is recursive. Sentences, paragraphs, and sections may be condensed, expanded, rearranged, and improved to ensure that the final document is as effective as it can be.
12. Writer's block can usually be overcome by recognizing that the process of writing demands reviewing, revising, and rewriting.

CHAPTER 5

The Writing Process: Grammar and Style

If you prepare proposals on a regular basis and that preparation constitutes one of your major job responsibilities, you are essentially a professional writer. Even if writing proposals and other business documents is only a small part of what you do, because those documents contribute to your success and to the financial well-being of your organization, you have a vested interest in performing the task as well as possible.

Writing well—and writing quickly and easily for that matter—requires a good grounding in grammar and style. The overview we present here is not intended to serve as a substitute for one or more English handbooks and guides to style. Professionals in every area have their own tools of the trade. Those whose income depends on the success of their written documents should consider English handbooks, dictionaries, thesauruses, and guides to effective style among their tools of the trade. The more you know, the better off you will be. Writing, however, like many things in life, is subject to Pareto's Law: 20 percent of the rules cover 80 percent of the difficulties writers encounter. The following sections on grammar and style concentrate on that 20 percent.

GRAMMAR

The rules of grammar describe the way language works. For groups of words to be understood as sentences, the relationships among them have to follow certain principles. If, for example, we change the relationship of the words in the first sentence of this paragraph so that it reads, *Grammar language works of rules the way the describe*, it becomes clear that the relationship among words is as important to the meaning of a sentence as are the words themselves. The following are the most important rules governing those relationships.

Agreement

The term *agreement* is used to refer to the grammatical relationship between subjects and verbs and between pronouns and their antecedents.

Subject and Verb Agreement

Subjects and verbs must agree in number [singular or plural]. Singular subjects must have singular verbs. Plural subjects must have plural verbs.

Mark is writing the proposal. [Singular]
Mark and Tom are writing the proposal. [Plural—compound subject]

- Intervening words do not influence the agreement between a verb and its subject.
  Each of them *is* writing a portion of the proposal. [*Each* is the singular subject.]
  Neither of them *is* writing the proposal. [*Neither* is the singular subject.]
- *As well as* and *along with* do not form compound [plural] subjects.
  Mark, as well as Tom, is writing the proposal. [Mark is the subject.]
- Singular subjects joined by *or, either/or, neither/nor,* or *not only/but also* require a singular verb.
  Mark *or* Tom is writing the proposal. [Only one of them will do the writing.]
- When two subjects are joined by *or* and one of them is singular and the other is plural, the verb agrees with the closer subject.
  The associates or *Mark* is writing the proposal.
  Mark or his associates *are* writing the proposal.
- Collective nouns used as subjects may be either singular or plural. They usually take singular verbs because the group is acting together as one unit. A collective noun takes a plural verb when the members act individually.
  The *team* of engineers *is* being honored tonight. [The team is being honored as a group.]
  The *team* of engineers *were* talking among themselves. [Team is thought of as a group of individuals.]

Pronoun and Antecedent Agreement

Pronouns and their antecedents must agree in number [singular or plural], person [first, second, or third], and gender [masculine, feminine, or neuter].

I wanted *my* copy of the proposal. [First person, singular]
You wanted *your* copy of the proposal. [Second person, singular or plural]
He/she wanted *his/her* copy of the proposal. [Third person, singular]
We wanted a copy of *our* proposal. [First person, plural]
They wanted a copy of *their* proposal. [Third person, plural]
Charles wrote *his* version of the specifications. [Masculine]
Karen wrote *her* version of the specifications. [Feminine]
The *request* for proposal specified *its* requirements. [Neuter]

- Indefinite antecedents require singular pronouns. Each, either, neither, one, anyone, everyone, someone, somebody, a person, an individual are always singular.

  Not this: *Each* person is required to do *their* share. [Faulty agreement]

  But this: *Each* person is required to do *his or her* share. [Correct]

  Not this: A *manager* is required to do *their* share. [Faulty agreement]

  Not this: A *manager* is required to do *his* share. [To assume that a manager is male is sexist, and many readers find sexist language offensive.]

  But this: A *manager* is required to do *his or her* share. [Correct]

  Or this: *Managers* are required to do *their* share. [Correct]

- Collective nouns used as antecedents may be either singular or plural depending on whether the group is acting as a group or individually. The *team* of engineers received its award. [*Team* is thought of as one unit.]
  The *team* of engineers went home and told their spouses about the award. [*Team* is thought of as a group of individuals.]

Pronoun Case

The case of a pronoun shows its grammatical function in the sentence. English has three cases, the *subjective* (also called the *nominative*), the *objective* (also called the *accusative*), and the *possessive* (also called the *genitive*).

- Pronouns in the subjective case serve as subjects or subject complements.
  Who [subject] is responsible? It is *I*.[Subject complement]
- Pronouns in the objective case serve as objects of verbs or objects of prepositions.
  Give the assignment to *him*.[Object of the verb *give*]
  We gave the party for *her*. [Object of the preposition *for*]
- Pronouns in the possessive case show ownership or relationship.
  His assignment was to complete the project by Monday.

Errors occur for each of these uses. Watch in particular for the following problems:

Not this: *Me* and Jason will write the report. [Objective case used incorrectly.]

But this: Jason and *I* will write the report.

Not this: Between you and *I*, Shirley will be named to head the project team. [Subjective case used incorrectly.]

But this:	Between you and *me*, Shirley will be named to head the project team.
Not this:	*You* receiving the award is a major accomplishment. [Objective case used incorrectly.]
But this:	*Your* receiving the award is a major accomplishment.

Shifts

A shift is an unnecessary change in person, point of view, or verb tense. In some cases, a shift in person results in faulty agreement between a pronoun and its antecedent.

Not this:	A *person* who buys a *house* commits *themselves* to a substantial financial obligation. [Shift from singular to plural]
But this:	A *person* who buys a *house* commits *him-* or *herself* to a substantial financial obligation. [Singular person throughout]
Or this:	*People* who buy *houses* commit *themselves* to substantial financial obligations. [Plural throughout]

One of the most common shifts is the use of *you* to refer both to the reader and as a substitute for *one, a person,* or *people* in general. The best rule to follow in proposals and business documents in general is to use the second person, *you,* only when you specifically mean your reader or readers.

| Not this: | As *you* read this proposal for the ABC Security System, ask *yourself* why *you* would engage in shoplifting [The first two pronouns clearly refer to the reader. The third probably refers to an indefinite person, *one.*] |
| But this: | As *you* read this proposal for the ABC Security System, ask *yourself* why *anyone* would engage in shoplifting . . . |

Shifts in verb tense can also be confusing. Verbs in successive clauses do not need to be in the same tense, but the progression of verb tenses should make sense.

| Not this: | We *have constructed* nearly 100 bridges and *are* responsible for designing 50 more. [Are the designs complete, in process, or planned for the future?] |
| But this: | We have constructed nearly 100 bridges and have been responsible for designing 50 more. |

Run-on Sentences

Two independent clauses [clauses that can stand by themselves as complete sentences] must be separated by a period, a semicolon, or a comma and a conjunction. When they are not, a run-on sentence results.

Not this:	The engineers approved the proposal the director did not.
But this:	The engineers approved the proposal. The director did not.
Or this:	The engineers approved the proposal; the director did not.
Or this:	The engineers approved the proposal, but the director did not.

A common error is the use of a conjunctive adverb [*accordingly, consequently, however, moreover, nevertheless, therefore,* and so on] as though it were a coordinating conjunction [*and, or, but, for, nor, so,* and *yet*].

Not this:	We will bid on Project A, however we will not bid on B.
But this:	We will bid on Project A; however, we will not bid on B.
Or this:	We will bid on Project A; we will not, however, bid on B.

Comma Splice

When two independent clauses are joined by a comma only, the result is usually referred to as a *comma splice.*

Not this:	The engineers approved the proposal, the director did not.
But this:	The engineers approved the proposal. The director did not.

Mismodification

Misplaced modifiers modify the wrong word, phrase, or clause. A *dangling modifier* has no word, phrase, or clause that it can logically modify. Avoid mismodification by placing the modifier close to the word, phrase, or clause that it modifies.

Not this:	The carpenter has a hammer talking to the engineer. [The hammer seems to be doing the talking.]
But this:	The carpenter talking to the engineer has a hammer.

Not this: Entering the room, the light went out. [The light cannot logically be entering the room, so the phrase "Entering the room" is *dangling.*]

But this: When he entered the room, the light went out.

Faulty Parallelism

Like ideas should be expressed with the same grammatical construction. Parallel structure is required of items in a series or list or when comparing ideas, contrasting ideas, or coordinating ideas, as with the correlative conjunctions (*both/and, either/or, neither/nor,* and *not only/but also*).

Not this: The manager's duties included planning, organizing, controlling, and to direct personnel.

But this: The manager's duties included planning, organizing, controlling, and directing.

Not this: Please purchase a computer, a printer, a desk, and see if you can buy a chair as well.

But this: Please purchase a computer, a printer, a desk, and a chair.

Not this: I will *either* write the proposal *or* John will.

But this: *Either* I will write the proposal *or* John will.

Or this: I will *either* write the proposal *or* ask John to write it.

Not this: We not only purchased a computer but a laser printer too.

But this: We purchased not only a computer but also a laser printer.

Note that if you have a series of items in list [whether numbered or unnumbered], the items should be parallel—the same part of speech or the same type of phrase or clause. If the first item in the list is a question, for example, all the items should be questions. If the first item is an adverbial phrase, all the items should be adverbial phrases.

Not this	**But this**
1. We defined our purpose.	1. Define purpose.
2. Who is our audience.	2. Analyze audience.
3. What should we do?	3. Determine methodology.
4. Discuss findings.	4. Discuss findings.
5. Our conclusions.	5. Draw conclusions.
6. Finally, recommendations.	6. Make recommendations.

Faulty Predication

The subject of the sentence must be able to perform the action specified by the predicate. Many common phrases that would be perfectly acceptable in conversation or informal usage are not acceptable in formal writing. Behavior that requires a choice or a decision, for example, must be performed by an agent capable of deciding. In such sentences, if the subject of the sentence could be replaced by the pronoun *it*, then check for faulty predication.

Not this:	The company invests its money wisely. [Only people can choose investments.]
But this:	The company's controller invests the company's money wisely.
Not this:	Management decided to develop a new line of products. [Only people can decide.]
But this:	The managers decided to develop a new line of products.
Not this:	This machine prefers to warm up slowly. [Machines don't have preferences.]
But this:	Allow this machine to warm up slowly.

Punctuation

Punctuation marks clarify writing and help the reader to understand the meaning of sentences. The common marks of punctuation that cause difficulty are the comma, the semicolon, the colon, and the underscore.

Comma

The comma is used to separate or set off elements in a sentence. It functions much the same in writing as a short pause does in speaking. Confusion may result when required commas are omitted and when unnecessary commas are included. The following are the most common rules of comma usage:

1. Use a comma to separate three or more items in a series.
   Proposals require your knowledge, analysis, and creative imagination.
2. Use a comma to separate two independent clauses joined by a conjunction [*and, but, or, for, nor, yet,* or *so*] in a compound sentence.
   Some clients know what the problem is, but other clients expect the consultant to identify the problem.
3. Use a comma after introductory words, phrases, or clauses.
   Incidentally, we have the material you requested.
   Yes, we have the material you ordered.

Hearing the news from his colleague, Brian notified his supervisor.
In the spring of next year, we'll begin construction of the building.
While you were in the meeting, I took several phone messages for you.

4. Use a comma to separate nouns of direct address, appositives, and parenthetical and other nonessential expressions.
   Yes, Mr. Adams, I'll be happy to prepare the report.
   Ms. Adelson, our supervisor, called the meeting for 9 a.m.
   The proposal, however, needs proofreading.
   The proposal writer, needing more information, wrote to the director.

Semicolon

Semicolons are stronger separators than commas.

1. Use a semicolon to separate independent clauses not joined by a conjunction.
   The main purpose of the proposal is to persuade; it is a sales presentation.
2. Use a semicolon before transitional expressions other than coordinating conjunctions that join independent clauses. Follow the expression with a comma.
   We have completed the proposal; however, we have not had a chance to proofread it.
3. Use a semicolon to separate items in a series when any of these items contain commas.
   The company has plants in Gary, Indiana; Detroit, Michigan; and Chicago, Illinois.

Colon

Colons are typically used to introduce lists and extended quotations. They may also be used to separate elements [such as volume numbers and issue numbers] in some forms of documentation and to separate independent clauses when the second clause amplifies the meaning of the first.

My analysis of the problem suggests the following courses of action:
On the occasion of his inauguration, Lincoln had the following to say:

Colons should *not* be used to separate a verb and its object or a preposition and its object. Make sure that the element that precedes the colon is a complete sentence.

Not this: The most important of these are: I-beams, rivets, and welding equipment.

But this: The most important of these are I-beams, rivets, and welding equipment.

Or this: The most important of these are the following: I-beams, rivets, and welding equipment.

Underscore

The underscore is used to emphasize or set off words when italics are not available. In handwritten or typed documents, the underscore is used where italics would be used in printed or word processed documents. When you are using equipment capable of italicized print, use italics rather than the underscore.

1. Use underscores for titles of books, magazines, newspapers, movies, titles of TV series, and similar published works.
   In the May 1 issue of *The Wall Street Journal* Johnson reviewed Ted Barkel's book *How to Write a Winning Proposal.*
2. Use an underscore to emphasize words used as words or expressions used as expressions.
   Use *an* before a word starting with a vowel and *a* for all other words.

Capitalization

Capital letters serve as signals to the reader about sentence patterns, names, titles, and other proper nouns and adjectives. If you question whether a word should be capitalized, check a dictionary. Words normally capitalized will be entered in the dictionary with the initial letter capitalized. The following are the most common rules for capitalization:

1. Capitalize the days of the week, months of the year, and holidays.
   On Friday, December 24, we'll close the office at noon so we can enjoy the Christmas holidays.
2. Capitalize titles of specific academic courses but not names of subjects except proper nouns and their derivatives in those titles.
   Ms. Englebright taught several American history courses, Latin, and Geography 210.
3. Capitalize degrees when they are used after an individual's name but not when they are used as general terms.
   Shirley Haggerty, Ph.D., received her doctorate from Michigan State University, her master's degree from Ohio State University, and her bachelor's degree from Indiana University.
4. Capitalize proper nouns and adjectives.
   Karl Haenicke, who was born in Seattle, Washington, speaks German and French fluently.

Numbers

The rules for the use of figures are by no means universal. The two most common rules are known as the "rule of ten" and the "rule of one hundred." The "rule of ten" essentially says that the numbers one through ten should be spelled out and that 11 and above should be expressed in figures. According to the "rule of one hundred," the numbers one through one hundred are spelled out, and the numbers 101 and above are expressed as figures. In general, modern usage favors the "rule of ten," but some organizations and industries still prefer the older rule. Whichever of these general rules you follow, there are exceptions. The most common additional rules are the following:

1. Use figures for numbers used with abbreviations.
   We were to use only No. 2 pencils for our drawings.
   The meeting started at 9 a.m. and finished at 2 p.m.
2. Use a figure for one number and spell out the other when two adjacent numbers modify the same noun. Use a figure for the larger number and spell out the shorter number.
   Sue prepared five 10-page reports for the director.
   Please purchase ten 29-cent stamps for me.
3. Spell out numbers that begin a sentence. When the number cannot be written in one or two words, rewrite the sentence to avoid having the number at the beginning.
   Five reams of 20-pound paper will be sufficient.
   We received 296 registrations for the convention.
4. Spell out indefinite numbers and amounts.
   We expect about five hundred people.
   A few thousand people were expected.
5. Express amounts of money in figures. Omit the decimal and zeros when expressing whole amounts of money. Spell out indefinite amounts of money. Use figures and words for large amounts of money.
   Joan had $5; Jim had $10.
   We needed several thousand dollars for a down payment on the house.
   The Browns won 10 million in the lottery.
6. Use figures for numbers referred to as numbers.
   Place a 2 in the appropriate box on your sheet.
7. Spell out numbers 1 through 10 [or 1 through 100]. Use figures for numbers over 10 [or over 100].
   Of the five applicants, only two were selected for interviews.
   Our firm received 16 request for proposals. [Rule of ten]
8. Use figures to express percentages. Except in tables and lists, spell out the word percent.
   Over 25 percent of the customers responded to our questionnaire.
9. Use figures for expressing ratios and proportions.
   The responses were 2 to 1 in our favor.
10. Use figures for weights, dimensions, and other measurements.
    The board measured 8 feet and 6 inches.
    We have 30 pounds of small nails available.
11. Use figures to express periods of time.
    Payment on our 15-year mortgage is due in 10 days.

We attended a 3-day conference.
The conference lasted 3 days.
12. Spell out ordinals that can be written in one or two words. Hyphenate all compound cardinal numbers between 21 and 99.
This is the first time that we are submitting a bid.
Forty-five of us plan to attend the reunion.

STYLE

Writing can, of course, be grammatically correct and still not be effective. The factors that influence the way writing communicates are usually referred to as *style*. An effective writing style is one that communicates quickly, clearly, and in an interesting way. For this reason, the matter of style comes back to the central questions about audience: what is interesting to one person may not be at all interesting to another. If you are interested in the stock market, for example, you will enjoy reading a detailed analysis of the latest transactions. If you are not, you would consider having to read such a document punishment. The same is true for virtually any subject. Part of what constitutes effective style is determined by the audience and their attitudes toward the subject.

No matter how interested they are in your subject, however, the audience will be affected by how you present your information. Fortunately, the most important principles behind an effective writing style are few and relatively simple. Make a conscious effort to check your proposals for the seven elements of effective writing—*clarity, conciseness, courtesy, confidence, conversational tone, completeness,* and *correctness.*

Clarity

Your first and most important obligation to your reader is to write a message he or she can understand. A clear message transfers your thoughts to your readers without misunderstanding. A clear message is one that can be understood the *first* time. Because clarity saves your readers time, it also encourages them to react favorably to your message. To achieve clarity

1. **Keep sentences short.** Shorter sentences—17 to 20 words on the average—are easier to understand than complex sentences. Using all short sentences, however, can make your writing choppy and monotonous.

2. **Maintain paragraph unity.** Each paragraph should contain just one topic sentence to express the main idea. Additional sentences in the paragraph provide support and explanations for that main idea.

3. **Improve readability.** Consider your audience when preparing your proposal. What is the reading level of your audience? Even well-educated readers appreciate material written so that it can be grasped quickly and easily. Select words you are fairly certain your readers will know and understand. Use the standard order of subject-verb-object for most sentences. Paragraph for readability— shorter paragraphs are easier to read than long ones, especially in single-spaced material. In single-spaced material, once a paragraph is longer than about 8 lines (lines, *not* sentences), readers may overlook material in the middle.

4. **Provide examples and illustrations to help clarify your main ideas.** Depending on the kind of product or service you are proposing, many of your readers will need to *see* your concept before they will be able to appreciate it. Use appropriate graphs, charts, drawings, photographs, and other illustrations to help clarify your idea. (See Chapter 7.)

5. **Use appropriate special techniques.** Headings, lists, and tabulations will also help you to present complex information in an easy-to-read document. White space, boldface, underscores, various typefaces, and type sizes will also help you prepare a document that will be easy for your reader to read. (See Chapter 6.)

Conciseness

When you say what needs to be said in the fewest words, you are being concise. Brevity and conciseness are not quite the same. A brief message is simply short; a concise message is also complete. Each word and each sentence should accomplish something for you, whether it is conveying information or establishing tone. To achieve conciseness

1. **Avoid redundancies.** Redundancies are wordy expressions. Instead of saying *square in shape,* just say *square.* Instead of saying *refer back,* just say *refer.*

Not this	But this
month of April	April
check in the amount of 10	check for 10
qualified expert	expert
needless to say	[Omit—if it is needless to say, don't say it.]

2. **Avoid expletives.** Expletives are unnecessary words and phrases. They do not contribute to the meaning of a sentence. Recast the sentence to eliminate the expletive.

Not this: [There are] some engineers who do well.
But this: Some engineers do well.

Not this: [It is] recommended that we purchase Model X.
But this: We recommend purchasing Model X.

Not this: [In order] to replace the value . . .
But this: To replace the value . . .

Not this: The main boiler is [located] on the first floor.
But this: The main boiler is on the first floor.

Not this: He seems [to be] confident.
But this: He seems confident.

3. **Remove deadwood constructions.** For example

Not this	But this
due to the fact that	because
at this point in time	now
the reason why is because	the reason is that
regardless of the fact that	although

4. **Use action verbs rather than nouns, infinitive phrases (*to make, to put*), or weak verbs, such as *to be, to have, to do,* or *to make*.**

Not this	But this
to put on a demonstration	demonstrate
to make a proposal	propose
to make a recommendation	recommend
to make a decision	decide

Not this: The salesperson put on a demonstration of the new computer.

But this: The salesperson demonstrated the new computer.

Not this: He seems [to be] confident.
But this: He seems confident.

Specific action verbs include the following:

accomplish	operate
analyze	organize
calculate	outline
conduct	perform
construct	prepare
create	produce
develop	provide
equip	purchase

generate   reduce
improve   select
manage   train

5. **Use possessives rather than "of" phrases.**

Not this	But this
tools of the carpenter	the carpenter's tools
the voice of the supervisor	the supervisor's voice
the hands of the engineer	the engineer's hands

Note that in most cases inanimate objects are not capable of possession and require the "of" construction.

Not this: the car's door [The car does not "own" the door.]
But this: the door of the car
Or this: the car door

6. **Change unnecessary *who, which*, and *that* clauses into modifiers.**

Not this: The engineer who is energetic designed this model.
But this: The energetic engineer designed this model.
Not this: The design that won an award is the one we selected
But this: The award-winning design was the one we selected.
Not this: James Fox, who was the son of a carpenter, created some practical designs.
But this: James Fox, the son of a carpenter, created some practical designs.
Not this: They purchased equipment that is made of steel.
But this: They purchased steel equipment.

7. **Avoid tagging *-izes* to the ends of words.**

Not this	But this
utilize	use
prioritize	rank
visualize	see
finalize	complete
initialize	initial
materialize	appear

8. **Use active voice.** In most business writing, active voice is preferable to passive voice because it is clearer and more forceful. In active voice the subject performs the action. In passive voice the subject receives the action. Passive voice always contains a form of the verb *to be (is, are, was, were, been, being)* plus the past participle of the verb (usually an *-ed, n,* or *t* ending—*received, torn, dealt*). The preposition *by* is implied or stated.

Active voice: The engineer drafted a design. [The subject of the sentence—*engineer*—is the doer of the action. The object of the sentence—*design*—receives the action.]

Passive voice: The design was drafted by the engineer. [The subject of the sentence—*design*—receives the action. Was is a form of the verb to be. *Drafted* is the past participle of the verb *draft*. The preposition by is stated.]

Passive voice: The design was drafted. [Whoever drafted the design is implied rather than stated.]

One of the problems with passive voice is known as lost performative. In the sentence, The design was drafted, for example, the doer of the action—the performer—is "lost" or deleted from the sentence. Readers must decide for themselves who performed the action. In most cases, readers need to know who performed the action. This aspect of passive voice can be used effectively, however, when the reader has made a mistake:

Active voice: You failed to complete page 2 of the checklist.

Passive voice: Page 2 of the checklist should be completed before the draft is submitted for review.

Eliminating passive voice also eliminates grammatical errors, such as dangling modifiers, that creep into passive sentence constructions.

Not this: By following instructions, the motor was assembled. [The motor didn't follow the instructions. Eliminate the passive voice, and you also eliminate the dangling modifier.]

But this: By following instructions, we assembled the motor. [Active voice precludes the dangling modifier.]

Courtesy

A courteous message takes the reader's feelings and point of view into consideration. Examine everything you write from your reader's point of view. What will your reader think about your message? How will your message make your reader feel? Put your reader's problems first. Think—and write—in terms of how your reader will benefit by agreeing with you or from doing what you ask. How will your reader benefit from your message? In business writing, courtesy is often called the *you-attitude*, the *you-viewpoint*, or the *reader viewpoint*.

1. **Focus on *you* instead of *I* and *we*.** Take the reader's point of view into consideration and not the writer's. Put your reader's problems first. Anticipate the reader's needs and questions and offer explanations and answers.

We-viewpoint:	We are happy to have your order. We shipped it this morning.
You-viewpoint:	You will receive your order by May 12; we sent it by Express Truckers this morning.

We-viewpoint:	I need to have your calculations no later than Tuesday.
You-viewpoint:	Receiving your calculations by Tuesday will enable me to meet our departmental deadline.

2. **Treat your reader as an equal.** Courtesy depends on the writer not only understanding the reader's viewpoint, but also assuming that the writer and reader will be able to cooperate as equals. Business relationships are interdependent. Feel neither superior nor inferior to your reader because you are actually working together as a team. The basic assumption of a courteous message is that writer and reader are both reasonable people with good intentions of meeting each other's objectives.

3. **Say *please*, *thank you*, and *may I*.** Saying *please* and *thank you* when appropriate helps create a polite and courteous tone in your writing.
   May I please have the information by March 15 so that I can prepare my report for the Board of Directors meeting on March 30.
   Thank you for telling me about the problem you have been having with the motor.
   I appreciate all the work you have done on this proposal.
   May I recommend an alternative solution to you.

4. **Be tactful, thoughtful, considerate, and empathic of your reader.** Avoid tactless words that may offend your reader. Use language that helps the reader feel good about your proposal. Rather than simply *telling* your readers how they will benefit from your proposal, *show* them. Avoid blanket statements that the reader has to accept on faith. Provide specific illustrations to support your claims.

Not this:	You will benefit from our training program.
But this:	Our training program will enable you to reduce your training costs by 40 percent.

5. **Avoid lecturing the reader.** No one likes to be told that he or she should or must do something. Recognize that readers do have a choice. They are free to choose an alternative course of action. You lecture your reader when you use the following words:

you must	you need to
you should	you ought to
it's imperative that you	

6. **Be concise but not terse or brusque.** Being concise means that you say what needs to be said. Being terse or brusque means that your message is too pithy, abruptly concise, curt, or blunt. You can hurt your reader's feelings when you are too much to the point. Take the time to provide explanations and reasons.

7. **Avoid discriminatory language.** Many readers find sexist language offensive. Use gender neutral language when the sex of those being referred to is unknown.

Not this	But this
businessman	businessperson
chairman	chairperson
draftsman	draft person or drafter
fireman	fire fighter
flagman	flagger
maintenance man	maintenance worker
man hours	work hours
man the machine	operate, run, work the machine
manpower	personnel, help
policeman	police officer
spokesman	spokesperson
workman	worker

8. **Respond to your reader's request promptly.** The longer it takes you to respond to a reader's letter or memo, the more likely you are to lose that person's goodwill. When responding to a proposal, be sure that you observe the deadline. In general, correspondence deserves a response within 48 hours.

Confidence

Your proposals will be more successful when you show confidence in yourself, confidence in your reader, and confidence in your proposal. Confidence is also called *positive tone.* As mentioned previously, negative language is typically more difficult to understand than positive language (*the dog is not chasing the cat*), and it also tends to create a negative attitude in the minds of those reading it. For these reasons, attempt to express ideas using positive language and with a positive attitude.

Assume that your readers will do what is right unless you have absolute proof that they will not, and assume that your readers are capable of overcoming obstacles. Always give the readers the benefit of the doubt.

1. **Concentrate on the positive.** Subordinate problems and negative factors. Say what you can and will do, not what you cannot or will not do.

Not this:	We cannot comply with your request to deliver the goods by Friday.
But this:	Because we are already committed to our production schedule, the earliest we can deliver your goods will be on Monday.
Not this:	We cannot match the price you quoted for the computers.
But this:	Although the unit price on our computers is higher than you requested, we back our product with a full year of on-site service.

2. **Eliminate negative words and phrases.** Your choice of words indicates to your reader how you feel about yourself and your ability to get a job done. Avoid negative words and phrases, such as

claim	no
difficult	regret
don't	unfortunately
forgot	We are at a loss to understand
inferior	won't
mistake	You forgot [failed, neglected, claim]
misunderstood	You must [should, ought, need]
never	

3. **Show confidence in your proposal.** Avoid expressions that suggest uncertainty.

I hope	If [you want, have further questions]
I trust	Why not

Not this:	I hope that you'll like our product.
But this:	Our product offers the following advantages
Not this:	Why not give our product a try?
But this:	To try our product for 30 days, simply complete the form at the back of the brochure
Not this:	If you have further questions, please call.
But this:	Please call me when I can be of further assistance.

4. **Avoid overconfidence.** Overconfidence leads to presumptuousness, which is a violation of courtesy. Do not presume that your readers will act or think in a particular way just because you want them to.

Not this:	To confirm your order simply check the box on the enclosed reply card [when the reader has not placed an order yet].
But this:	To order, simply check the box on the enclosed reply card.
Not this:	Our product is the only way you can save . . .

But this: Our product offers these demonstrated savings

Conversational Tone

Your writing style should be an extension of your personality, and your messages should read much the same way you would talk to your reader if you were communicating face-to-face rather than by mail. The best writing sounds natural to the ear. Use natural, conversational, unpretentious words.

1. **Avoid jargon.** Jargon clutters a proposal and makes the writer sound insincere. Except when you are using technical language to communicate with a technical audience, jargon may confuse or annoy your reader. Unless you are absolutely certain that your audience will understand technical or business jargon, avoid it.

2. **Avoid clichés.** Clichés are overused, trite expressions. While a cliché may be used for good effect from time to time [may *hit the nail on the head*], a few go a long way.

3. **Put variety in your writing.** Vary your words and your sentence beginnings. Begin sentences with nouns, adjectives, adverbs, modifiers, phrases, or clauses to achieve variation and avoid monotony. Vary sentence structures and lengths. Use simple, compound, complex, and compound-complex sentences. Use patterns for emphasis, as in Caeser's famous report: "I came; I saw; I conquered." Patterns that are too uniform for too long, however, tend to distract the reader from your main point. Also vary paragraph length. Too many long paragraphs are difficult to read; too many short paragraphs give the document a choppy appearance.

4. **Control emphasis and subordination by placement, proportion, language, and mechanics.**

   a. **Placement.** Where you place an idea in a message influences the amount of attention a reader will pay to it. The beginnings or endings of sentences receive the most emphasis. The opening and closing paragraphs usually receive the most attention.
      Least emphatic: We recognized that *a merger* was the only possible solution.
      More emphatic: *A merger* was the only possible solution.
      Most emphatic: The only solution possible is this: *merge*.

   b. **Proportion.** How much space you give an idea indicates your degree of concern. Take extra time and space to explain the ideas that are most important to you and your reader. Study the RFP and note whether the concepts that seem central to you are the ones emphasized in the RFP. If the client organization seems more or less concerned about a particular issue than you are, it may be worth a phone call to make sure that you understand the client's position correctly.

c. **Language.** Sentences are more emphatic when they are about people doing things. They are less emphatic when they have ideas as subjects. Nouns should be concrete and specific, and verbs should be in the active voice for greater emphasis. Remember that some ideas should be subordinated rather than emphasized. Negative information, for example, may be subordinated by using abstract, general words, and passive voice.

d. **Mechanics.** You can also emphasize important ideas by using *italics* or <u>underscoring</u>, using CAPITAL letters, using **boldface**, using color, putting key ideas in a numbered list, and surrounding main points with extra white space. You may also change the typeface and the size for emphasis.

5. **Visualize your reader as you write.** Employ the you-attitude. Put yourself in your reader's position. What is best for the reader? What benefits can you offer the reader? Be interested in your reader. Blend outcomes so that your proposal truly represents a win-win solution for both you and your reader.

Completeness

Your message is complete when you have presented all the information requested and you have achieved the reader's goodwill. Examine your proposal to make sure that you have covered everything you intended to cover. Prepare checklists of what is required by the RFP, and then check off the items as you complete them.

1. **Provide all the facts and details required in the RFP.** If you leave something out, your proposal will not be considered. When relevant, supply additional information that may be helpful to the reader. Your readers may not know what questions to ask you; they can merely tell you what the problem is.

2. **Ask or answer all questions.** When you are initiating correspondence, be sure to ask specifically for everything you want. If you don't ask for it, the reader may overlook it; and if your request is too general, the reader may not know what to provide.

    Not this: Please send me any information you have on the Olson Fund.

    But this: Please send me the application form for the Olson Fund.

When you are responding, supply all the required information. To the extent required by the situation, include the specifics, the examples, the explanations, the dates, the statistics, and the test results. Also, when appropriate, answer questions your reader should have asked but didn't. If you don't have an answer for a question, say so. Ignoring the question or omitting information may indicate that you overlooked the question or that you have something to hide. At best, the reader may view this as carelessness and, at worst, dishonesty.

3. **Check for the five Ws—*who, what, when, where,* and *why.*** Sometimes you may need to answer *how* also.

   • *Who* will do *what* next?
   • *When* and *where* will events take place?
   • *Why* did the problem occur, and *how* can it be corrected?

Correctness

Correct messages contain accurate facts, figures, and statements in addition to having correct spelling, grammar, mechanics, and language usage. Freedom from superficial errors is a nonverbal message that tells your reader that you are an intelligent, careful person who pays attention to details.

1. **Proofread carefully for misspelled words, names, titles.** One misspelled word can cause a reader to react unfavorably to your proposal. Misspellings are typically interpreted as carelessness. If you are careless with your spelling, then the logical assumption is that you will be careless in other areas too. Spell checkers can find most errors, but they can't detect errors in homonyms, such as *hear, here; there, their; to, two, too,* and the like.

2. **Use proper grammar.** Make your subjects and verbs agree and make your pronouns and antecedents agree. Avoid faulty predication. Make sure all your lists and items in a series are parallel in construction. Remove dangling modifiers. Avoid shifts in person.

3. **Use correct punctuation and capitalization.** When in doubt, look it up. While it is unlikely that a proposal will be rejected because of an error in punctuation or capitalization, a single omitted comma, or the use of an unnecessary comma, may bias a critical reader against the proposal. While not all authorities agree about all matters of usage, when in doubt, it's better to check than to guess.

4. **Use words properly.** If you have a question about the correct usage of a particular word, look it up. Be especially careful with words often confused. Do you mean *affect* or *effect*? Are you *anxious*, or are you *eager*? When do you *imply*, and when do you *infer*? Sometimes similar words have different meanings.

   Not this: We have worked continuously on this proposal since January. [Implies no time off for eating, sleeping, and other activities.]

   But this: We have worked continually on this proposal since January. [We took time off to eat and sleep.]

   When in doubt, check a dictionary or a style manual.

5. **Proofread the entire proposal.** In addition to checking for errors in grammar and mechanics, double check the accuracy of all figures and dates. Numbers can easily be transposed. Recalculate totals. Ensure that decimals are in the correct place. It is easy to overlook errors in figures in columns and tables. Be sure to check each entry to ensure that it is correct.

KEY POINTS FROM CHAPTER 5

The key points from Chapter 5 are the following:

1. Writing well—and writing quickly and easily—requires a good grounding in grammar and style.
2. The rules of grammar describe the way language works, and violations of those rules often cause confusion.
3. The most common problems of usage are lack of agreement, shifts, run-on sentences and comma splices, mismodification, faulty parallel construction, and faulty predication.
4. When in doubt, check a dictionary or English handbook and guide to style.
5. The principal components of style are clarity, conciseness, courtesy, confidence, conversational tone, completeness, and correctness.

CHAPTER 6

Special Techniques: Headings, Lists, and Tables

Proposals, like other reports, employ a variety of special techniques, such as headings, lists, and graphic aids, to present complex information to the reader in an orderly and logical manner. In general, the longer and more formal the proposal, the more such techniques will be required to help organize material and to emphasize key points. This chapter will cover headings, lists, and tables. Graphic aids are covered in Chapter 7.

HEADINGS

A heading is a group of words set off from the text that identifies the content following it, making it easy for a reader to locate important material. A good heading is both brief—one to eight words—and specific, clarifying the topic and saying something important about it at the same time.

Not this:	Office Automation
But this:	Recent Developments in Office Automation
Not this:	Telephone Usage
But this:	Telephone Use Up 60 Percent

Unless it would already be obvious, headings serve their purposes best when they actually say something *about* the material that follows rather than simply state its topic. In some cases, of course, the content will be expected by or well-known to the reader, and briefer headings would be preferred, such as those used in some standard internal proposal forms justifying new purchases. Note also whether the RFP or IFB specifies the headings to be used. If so, use those headings exactly as they are stated in the RFP or IFB.

In general, headings should not be complete sentences because sentences are too wordy to focus the reader's attention on the topic. The exception to this rule is a series of short questions.

    I.   What Is It?
   II. How Does It Work?
  III. How Much Does It Cost?

Unless the headings are questions, they do not require end punctuation. To help headings stand out and make them more readable, surround them with plenty of white space. The amount of white space will vary depending on the relative importance of the heading, with the most important headings being set off by the most white space.

Use headings as an aid to readability. A heading that states *Reasons for Using Computers* establishes the expectation in a reader that a list of reasons will follow. Satisfy such expectations explicitly. Make your reasons (or whatever topic the heading implies) clear and easy to find. Headings should be designed to help the reader find information quickly and easily by dividing the pages of material into clearly identified blocks so that the reader can develop a sense of the purpose of each block and the overall plan of the proposal. Most people find solid pages of text without headings or other visual interruptions difficult to read.

Purposes

The main purpose of a heading is to tell the reader the topic of discussion that follows. Headings serve as introductions to what you are going to present and discuss. Headings also serve as a guide for the writer. When you develop your outline, you are essentially developing the headings for your proposal. Main entries on the outline become the main headings of the proposal; subentries become subheadings.

The headings will, in turn, become the entries for the table of contents. For this reason, it is important to begin with a well-developed outline, and to ensure that changes you make while writing are reflected in the outline as well as in the draft of your document. Headings follow all the rules of outlining (such as *no single subdivisions should occur*), so the outline, list of headings, and table of contents should all show the same entries at the same levels and in the same order.

Appearance and Format

The appearance and format of headings may vary from one organization to another and from one creative designer to another. To differentiate the various levels of headings, you can use capitalization, underlining, and page position—centered, flush with the left or right margin, or indented. With word processors you have many more options, including different typefaces, styles, and sizes.

Typefaces

Typeface refers to the style or shape of the letters. The two major categories of typefaces are serif and sans serif.(See examples and additional explanation in Chapter 8.) Serif type is typically used in the body of proposals and other business and technical documents because the serifs are an aid to readability, serving to guide the reader's eye along a line of text. Sans serif type is best used for headings and other headlines, and it works well when reverse print (white print on a black background) is required.

Type Styles

Each typeface is available in a variety of styles or *fonts*, modifications of the original typeface. Some of the different type styles are

plain

bold

italics

ＯＵＴＬＩＮＥ

SHADOW

The bulk of the text should, of course, be in a plain style so that the other type styles have the contrast required to perform their function. Bold type styles are used for emphasis and frequently for headings and subheadings. Italics are used to emphasize titles, to set off specific words and phrases, and for captions. The outline and shadow type styles are used for diversion and to make a point really stand out. They are more appropriate for use in materials that might accompany the proposal, such as brochures or flyers, rather than in the proposal itself.

Type Size

Type size is the measurement of the type. Type is measured in points (72 points is equal to one inch). With modern word processing equipment, type size can vary according to your desires. For document writing, 10- or 12-point type, depending on the typeface, is common. Although modern word processing equipment is capable of printing small type sizes (typically down to 4 points), material that requires a type size smaller than 10 points will need to be typeset and printed to ensure legibility. Note also that typefaces of the same point size may vary in length so that different typefaces of the same point size will result in unequal line lengths.

Times: This is a sample of 12-point type. 1, 2, 3

Helvetica: This is a sample of 12-point type. 1, 2, 3

For more information on typography, see Chapter 8.

Guidelines for Use

No matter what format you use for your headings, be consistent. Main headings, typically called *first-level* or *first-degree* headings, should be the same typeface and type size; headings of the second level should be the same typeface and type size, and so forth. Different typefaces may be used for the various levels of headings, but they should be compatible with the type used in the text.

Headings follow the same rules used for outlining. Headings, for example, must be parallel in grammatical construction. All the main headings, which correspond to the Roman numerals in traditional outlining form, must use the same grammatical structure. If the first main heading is a question, all the main headings should be questions. If the first main heading is a noun phrase, all the main headings should be noun phrases. Subheadings should be parallel with the other subheadings in the same section. The subheadings in a section do not need to be grammatically parallel with the main headings, nor do they need to be parallel with subheadings in other sections. Figure 6-1 illustrates the importance of parallelism in heading use.

Faulty Parallelism

I.   Recent Developments in Office Automation

    A. New Computer Systems

    B. What's New in Telephone Services?

    C. Using the New Printers

II. Planning for Upgrading Current Equipment

    A. Our Current Equipment

    B. Inefficiencies Caused by Outdated Equipment Growing

III. How Much Would Upgrading Cost?

    A. Costs of Computer Equipment.

    B. Installing the New Telephone Services

    C. New Printers Are Expensive.

    D. What About Training?

Parallel and Logical

I.   What's New in Office Automation?

    A. New Computer Systems

    B. New Printing Equipment

    C. New Telephone Services

II. Does Upgrading Make Sense?

    A. Increasing Repair Costs

    B. Increasing Costs of Inefficiencies

III. How Much Would Upgrading Cost?

    A. New Computer Equipment

    B. New Printing Equipment

    C. New Telephone Services

    D. Training

Figure 6-1. Parallelism in Headings.

Although no standard format has been officially adopted for a system of headings, the following are the most important guidelines for the use of headings.

1. Headings in solid capital letters are superior (in hierarchy) to headings that include lowercase letters.
2. Centered headings are superior to headings on the margin.
3. Headings that stand on a line alone are superior to those that run into the line of text.
4. Larger type sizes should be used for more important headings. Avoid using a typeface for subheadings that is larger than the main headings.
5. Headings in solid capital letters are not underscored, but headings using capitals and lowercase letters may be underscored to increase their visibility.
6. Boldfaced headings should not be underscored because the underscore reduces readability.
7. No two headings should appear without intervening text. Because no subdivision can be equal to the main division of which it is a part, the main division must include information about all the subdivisions included within it. The most common error here is to use a main heading immediately following the title of the proposal.
8. The proposal title must be in a form clearly superior to those used for all the headings in the proposal.
9. Single subdivisions should not occur. If you divide a topic, at least two subdivisions will occur, and you must discuss *all* the subtopics that result from the division. If you do not want to discuss some of the subtopics, narrow your topic to exclude those subdivisions.
10. Whatever forms are used, the same system must be used consistently throughout the proposal. For example, headings of the same level should all have the same position, same combination of capital and lowercase letters, same typeface, and same type size.
11. The whole of each division must equal the sum of its parts. The entire topic, for example, must be covered by the material covered in the main divisions. Select topics that accurately indicate the material you wish to cover.
12. The headings in the text use the same wording as that used in the table of contents

Levels of Headings

Although many proposals are long and complex enough to require five levels of headings, most will use only three levels of divisions and subdivisions. If your proposal is so long and complex that five levels of heading are inadequate, treat each major division as a separate chapter or

perhaps even as a separate volume, with each division having its own title.
As mentioned previously, the five levels of headings follow the same
pattern as your outline:

I. Main Topic—First Level Heading
   A. Subtopic—Second Level Heading
   B. Subtopic—Second Level Heading
      1. Sub-subtopic—Third Level Heading
         a. Sub-subsubtopic—Fourth Level Heading
            (1) Sub-sub-sub-subtopic—Fifth Level Heading
            (2) Sub-sub-sub-subtopic
         b. Sub-sub-subtopic
      2. Sub-subtopic

II. Second Main Topic

Figure 6-2 illustrates one standard physical presentation of headings
prepared for a proposal using five levels of headings. Note that most
proposals do *not* require five levels of headings. Two or three levels of
headings usually suffice for proposals up to 15 or 20 pages long. The main
principle, regardless of the number of levels of headings, is that the form
and appearance of the headings need to clarify their relative importance.
Figures 6-3, 6-4, and 6-5 illustrate alternative heading styles for shorter
proposals.

TITLE OF PROPOSAL

The title of proposals should be centered, boldfaced, and keyed
in all capitals. Use a larger type size for the title than for any of the
headings. If you can't use a larger font, you may use S P A C E D
C A P I T A L   L E T T E R S for the title, leaving a space between each
letter and three spaces between words. Proposals prepared on a
typewriter may use underlining in place of boldface, but headings in
solid capital letters or boldface should *not* be underscored. Provide
more white space above the heading of the highest level. The typeface
may also be different from that used in the text. Titles of two or more
lines should be double spaced and keyed in inverted pyramid style,
that is the longest line is first followed by increasingly shorter lines.

Figure 6-2. Standard Hierarchy of Headings.

FIRST-LEVEL HEADINGS

When five levels of headings are required, first-level headings are typically centered, boldfaced, and keyed in all capitals. The type size should be smaller than that used for the title, but it may be larger than that used for subheadings. In long proposals, headings of this type may indicate section headings and would appear on a new page. For double-spaced material, you may follow the traditional typewritten format and use a five-space paragraph indention, or, if you are using word processing equipment, you may follow the typesetting standard and block paragraphs following headings. Single-spaced material should always have blocked paragraphs.

Second-Level Headings

Second-level headings are centered, boldfaced, and keyed in capital and lowercase letters. Capitalize the first word and all others except articles (a, an, the) conjunctions (and, but, or) and prepositions with three letters or fewer (to, of, for). Most proposals use headings of this type to indicate major divisions. Subdivided sections must have at least two subdivisions of relatively equal importance.

Third-Level Headings

Third-level headings are boldfaced and keyed in capital and lower-case letters at the left margin. When you are preparing a document that has only one level of heading, this is an appropriate heading to use as it is highly visible without being obtrusive.

Fourth-Level Headings. Fourth-level headings are an integral part of the paragraph, separated from the first sentence by a period. They are boldfaced and keyed in capital and lowercase letters at the left margin with a double-space above. This form of heading is sometimes called a run-in head. If your document has just one level of heading and is short on space, this is a logical heading form to use.

Fifth-level headings are an integral part of the first sentence of the paragraph. The first few words of the sentence are boldfaced or underscored. Only the initial word is capitalized, unless other words are proper nouns or proper adjectives. Because the heading should contain significant information, the sentence should be written so that the first few words clearly indicate the main topic of the paragraph. This form of heading is also called a run-in head.

Figure 6-2. Standard Hierarchy of Headings (continued)

PROPOSAL TITLE

Many of the proposals you will write will require only three levels of headings. The proposal title may be solid capital letters, centered, and boldfaced. This title is in Helvetica, a *sans serif* typeface, and the text is Times, a *serif* typeface. The title, the headings, and the text in this example are all 12-point type.

First Main Heading

Your main headings can use a combination of capital and lowercase letters and be centered and boldfaced. The headings, like the title, are in Helvetica.

First Subheading

The subheadings look the same as the main headings, except that they appear on the margin. This combination of headings and text provides a traditional appearance.

Figure 6-3. Alternate Heading Forms.

LISTS

Like headings, lists are another way to call attention to important points in a proposal. When you use a list, you call attention to each fact in two ways: separately and as part of a whole. Lists are especially useful for showing the steps required in a process, the factors in a situation, or the parts of a whole. Whenever you use a list, provide it with the same kind of introduction as you would use for a graphic aid: Tell your readers that they are about to encounter a list and what they will find in it. The introduction to the list should be a complete sentence, which may be concluded with a colon. Avoid using a colon to end a sentence fragment.

Not this:	My reasons are:
But this:	I have reached these conclusions for the following reasons:
Or this:	The following reasons support my conclusions:
Or this:	My reasons are as follows:

Proposal Title

Modern word processing and page-layout equipment and software make it possible for you to create a wide variety of alternatives to the formats developed for manual typewriters. This title is right justified and set in 24-point Cooper Black. The text is set in 12-point Garamond.

First Main Heading

Main headings and subheadings can both be left justified as long as their size indicates their relative importance. In this case, the main heading is in 14-point type.

Subheading

The subheading is set in 12-point type. Note that the size difference makes it easy to tell by looking which heading is more important.

Figure 6-4. Nontraditional Heading Forms.

When the items in the list complete the introductory clause, no punctuation is required to separate the introduction and the list:

My reasons are
1. It is good for business.
2. It is good for our employees.
3. It is good for the environment.

As is true for headings, all items in a list must be grammatically parallel. If the first item is a question, all the items should be questions. If the first item is a declarative sentence, all items should be declarative sentences. Lack of parallelism in lists is essentially faulty logic, as Figure 6-6 illustrates.

Italicized Headings

Italicized headings can be effective in short proposals requiring fast action. Because italic typefaces are more difficult to read than plain typefaces, however, they are inappropriate for use as headings in long documents. Italicized headings also make the proposal seem informal, which may not always be appropriate.

Caption Headings

Caption headings, which appear on the left margin opposite the text, are also useful for shorter documents with only one or two levels of heading. Because the text is presented in short lines, documents using caption headings are easy to read. This format is especially useful for short proposals in memo format. In such cases, the title of the proposal is the subject line of the memo.

Virtually any effect that a typesetter can achieve can be duplicated with modern word processing and page-layout equipment and software. Learning the requirements of good design, however, requires time. Unless you have a professional graphic designer on your team, you will do well to stick to reasonably traditional heading forms.

Figure 6-5. Additional Alternatives for Headings.

Lists can be either numbered or unnumbered. Numbering the items in a list implies a hierarchy, with 1 coming before 2 in one way or another: order of importance, chronological order, spatial order, or some other logical order. Use an unnumbered list when you wish to stress all the items equally. Use a *bullet* or other marker to make each item stand out. Any of the following markers can be used for unnumbered lists:

Faulty Parallelism

We should institute an on-going communication training program for the following reasons:

1. The number of customer complaints about service has been increasing.
2. A good investment.
3. Increased cooperation and improved productivity.
4. How could it be implemented?

Parallel and Logical

We should institute an on-going communication training program for the following reasons:

1. Customer complaints about service have been increasing.
2. Low-cost training can produce major savings.
3. Increased cooperation will improve productivity.
4. Implementation would be easy.

Figure 6-6. Importance of Parallelism in Lists.

--   two hyphens (use only if your word processor can't produce an *em* dash)

—   a dash (called *em* because it is as long as an *m* in the same typeface)

*   an asterisk (use only if your word processor can't produce a bullet)

°   a degree symbol

▲   a triangle

...   a series of periods

❐   an outline box

▧   a solid box

●   a bullet

⮕   an arrow

❈   a decorative figure (for special occasions only)

Lists can also be boxed, screened, or boxed and screened to highlight or separate the listed information.

TABLES

Tables are used to present data arranged systematically in rows and columns so that the reader can easily make comparisons, see relationships, detect inconsistencies, and interpret the information. When data are presented in prose form, a reader may have difficulty in understanding their purpose, especially when the data contain complex qualitative and quantitative information. Because tables are more visually appealing than a solid block of prose containing many figures, the reader is most apt to look at the table first and then go back to read the prose.

Tables have the advantage of being subject to less distortion than the graphic aids that sometimes replace them. In a table, the actual data are presented as figures, so the reader is not likely to misinterpret such factors as rates of increase or decrease, which sometimes occurs when the same data are presented in graphic form. See Chapter 7 for more information about distortion in graphic aids.

Types of Tables

Tables can be informal or formal. Informal tables generally are short and simple and presented as an integral part of the paragraph. They present data in columns and rows with white space around them for emphasis. Informal tables are not numbered, titled, framed, or included in the list of illustrations. Formal tables present complex data in ruled columns and rows. They are numbered, titled, framed, and included in the list of illustrations. Formal tables are also referenced within the written text.

Parts of a Table

A formal table consists of the following parts:

I. Heading
   A. Table Number
   B. Table Title

II. Body
   A. Stub
      1. Stub Head
      2. Stub Item
   B. Spanner Head
      1. Column Head
      2. Column Head
   C. Field
      1. Rows
      2. Columns
   D. Notations
      1. Source
      2. Footnotes

The main heading of a formal table consists of the table number and table title. When it is necessary to identify the source of the data, an asterisk is placed at the end of the title or subtitle referring the reader to a footnote, which is placed in the notation section of the table. Each column and each row is identified by a heading.

The first column on the left is the *stub* column. Its heading is referred to as the *stub head*. A stub is a title for a row of (horizontal) data. Should a stub column contain substubs, then the substubs are indented two or three spaces to show that they are subordinate to the stub item. A spanner head is one that extends over several column heads. A column head is a title to a vertical column. A headnote is an explanatory note or comment. Its full citation is given in the footnote. The actual data found in the rows and columns are the *field*. The notations at the end of the table contain the source of information and other footnotes. Figure 6-7 illustrates the layout and identification of parts of a formal table.

Heading	Table Number		Table Title	
		Subtitle		
		Headnote*		
Body	Stub	Column	Spanner Head	
	Stub/Head**	Head	Column Head	Column Head
	Stub Item			
	Stub Item			
	Substub			
	Substub		Field: rows and columns	
	Stub Item			
	Stub Item			
	Stub Item			
	Stub Item			
Notations	Source: Primary data			
	* Footnote			
	** Footnote			

Figure 6-7. Layout and Identification of a Formal Table.

KEY POINTS FROM CHAPTER 6

The key points from Chapter 6 are the following:

1. Proposals, like other reports, employ headings, lists, graphic aids, and other special techniques to help present complex information in an organized, logical way.

2. Headings are used to break up the text so that the reader can locate important material quickly and easily.

3. A good heading is brief and specific, clarifying the topic and saying something important about it.

4. If the RFP or IFB specifies headings, be sure to use the specified headings.

5. Modern word processing equipment allows writers more options in the presentation of headings than was possible with older equipment. The basic rules, however, still apply.

6. Numbered and unnumbered lists can help draw attention to important points. Numbering a list implies a sequence or hierarchy. Lists may be boxed, screened, or boxed and screened for greater emphasis.

7. Tables are used to present data arranged systematically in rows and columns so that the reader can easily make comparisons, see relationships, detect inconsistencies, and interpret the information. Tables are less likely to be misinterpreted than are the graphic aids that frequently replace them.

8. Tables may be formal or informal. Formal tables are set off from the text by a title and frame. The columns and rows are typically ruled to indicate separate categories of information. Informal tables present columns and rows of information as an integral part of the paragraph.

CHAPTER 7

Special Techniques: Graphs and Charts

Because proposals typically present complex information and need to do so in a way that is both clear and persuasive, they often employ graphic aids. Graphic aids dramatize what the writer wants the reader to see. Because this culture places so much emphasis on the visual representation system (see Chapter 2), for most readers a picture really will be worth a thousand words. The words are necessary to express ideas completely, but the pictures help the reader quickly grasp the meaning of the information.

FUNDAMENTALS

Words are, of course, the primary means of presenting information in the proposal; graphic aids are secondary, designed to illustrate and support. Graphic aids supplement and enhance the text and should not function as a substitute for it. Graphic aids need to be self-explanatory and independent. Just as the text must be complete without the help of graphic aids so, too, must the graphic aid tell the whole story without the help of the written word. The text does not, however, need to duplicate all the details of the graphic aid.

Although the terms *figures, illustrations, graphs,* and *charts* are often used interchangeably, they are not identical in meaning. *Figure* is the broadest category. All graphic aids other than tables (see Chapter 6) are figures. The term *illustration* is usually used to refer to a drawing or pictorial representation, such as a drawing of a mechanical part, or a photograph. *Graphs* are visual representations of plotted data, and charts are illustrations not plotted on an X and Y axis. Charts typically show flows of authority (organizational chart), data (flow chart), electricity (schematic), or tasks and time (Gantt chart, PERT chart).

Before using a graphic aid to illustrate a concept, the proposal writer needs to ask three questions:

1. What is my purpose for using a graphic aid?
   a. Summarize information
   b. Depict trends, changes, or comparisons over time
   c. Show simple comparisons, especially in quantity

    d. Depict parts of a whole
    e. Use pictures or symbols to represent data
    f. Show external or internal features
2. What kind of graphic aid will best achieve my purpose?
    a. Tables—informal or formal
    b. Figures—line, bar, or pie graphs; PERT or Gantt charts; picto-grams; photographs; diagrams; organizational charts; flow charts; maps; printouts; drawings
3. Who is my audience, and what does he or she need or want to know?
    a. Primary audience
    b. Secondary audience
    c. Audience's knowledge and limitations

Figures are not substitutes for tables. Tables give exact values, and figures provide illustrations of values. Tables are precise and accurate and do not lend themselves to misinterpretation in the way that figures can. Unless figures are prepared carefully, they may—intentionally or uninten-tionally—mislead the reader. A wide variety of charting and presentation software is available to help writers produce effective, presentation-quality graphs and charts based on a set of given data. In most cases, the writer simply needs to enter the appropriate data and then specify the desired graph or chart. As helpful as these programs are, however, they will not automatically produce the graphs and charts correctly. For many charts, the data will need to be sorted or arranged in a particular order for the resulting graph or chart to be drawn correctly. Check your graphs and charts carefully to ensure that all pertinent information is visible and correctly placed.

GRAPHS

The five most common graphs are the bar, line, pie, pictograph (any graph using drawings or pictures to represent data), and scatter.

Bar Graphs

Bar graphs are best for showing comparisons. Units of measurement, such as dollars or amounts, are placed on the vertical (Y) axis, which begins at zero. The horizontal (X) axis usually shows time increments. All bars should be the same width, and the spaces between the bars should be the same width but smaller than the width of the bars. Bars can run vertically—for measuring height, weights, monetary units—or horizontally—for indi-cating time and length. Vertical bar graphs are often referred to as *column* graphs. Bars can be arranged alphabetically, chronologically, numerically, or in descending (generally preferred) or ascending order. Two variations of the bar graph are the multiple bar and the bilateral bar.

Most charting software will produce bar graphs in "3-D" format, which may have greater impact than a standard two-dimensional graph. If you select a 3-D form, however, sort your data so that the smaller figures are in the foreground of the graph where they are visible. Also, be careful to avoid "chart junk"—graphs that are so fancy that the meaningful data become lost. Figure 7-1 illustrates a horizontal bar graph.

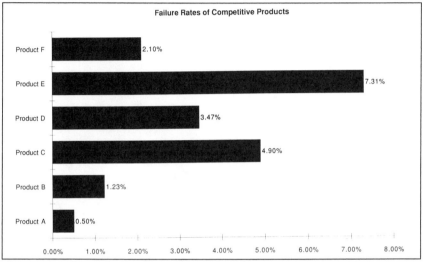

Figure 7-1. Sample Horizontal Bar Graph.

Multiple Bar Graphs

Multiple bar graphs compare two or three variables within a single bar chart. The multiple bars are distinguished from each other by color, shading, or crosshatching. A legend or key identifies the bars. The largest component is placed at the bottom of the vertical bar and to the left of a horizontal bar unless alphabetical or chronological order would be more logical.

Bilateral Bar Graphs

Bilateral bar graphs show increases on one side of a zero line and decreases on the other side of the zero line. When the zero line runs horizontally, place the positive numerical values above it. When the zero line runs vertically, place the positive numerical values to the right. Figures 7-2, 7-3, 7-4, 7-5, and 7-6, illustrate a variety of multiple and bilateral bar graphs. Note that the same information can be presented in a variety of ways and that depending on the size of the graph and quality of reproduction, not all forms may be equally effective. Some forms, for example, are best reserved for color slides or overhead transparencies, as they do not reproduce well in black and white.

Also, note that the 3-D graph in Figure 7-4 places the smallest category ("poor") in the foreground where it is visible. Most charting programs will not automatically place a smaller figure in the foreground, so you will need to sort your data to ensure a readable chart before producing it.

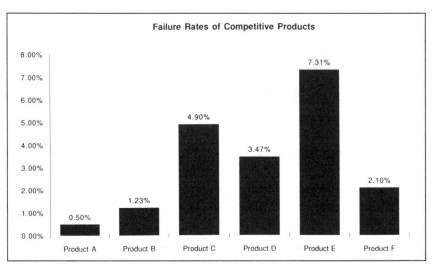

Figure 7-2. Sample Vertical Bar (Column) Graph.

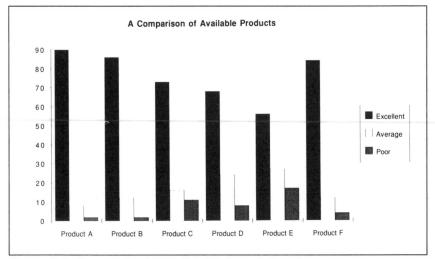

Figure 7-3. Sample Multiple Bar (Column) Graph.

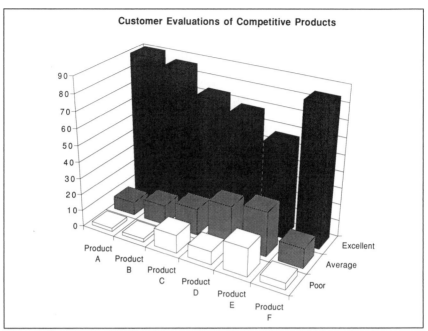

Figure 7-4. Sample Multiple Column Graph in 3-D Form.

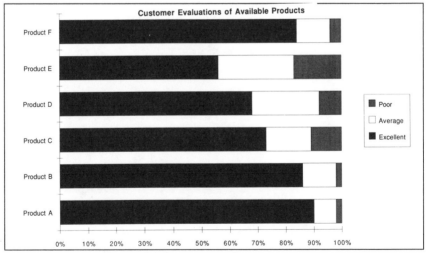

Figure 7-5. Sample Multiple Bar Graph.

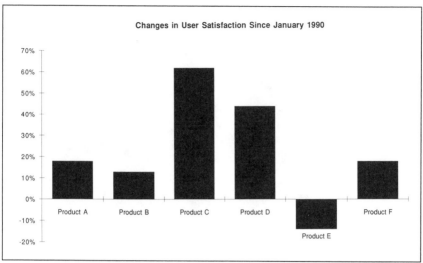

Figure 7-6. Sample Bilateral Column Graph.

Line Graphs

Line graphs are best used to depict trends or changes over time. Plot lines represent the data. A solid line represents the main idea; dots and dashes can represent other lines. Different symbols can also be used to distinguish the lines, as is illustrated in Figure 7-7.

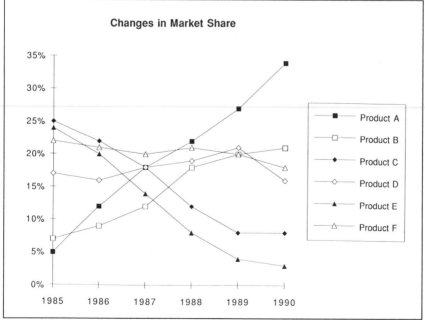

Figure 7-7. Sample Line Graph.

The plot lines should be kept to a minimum, especially if they intersect each other, because as the number of lines increases, the chart becomes more difficult to read and interpret. Figure 7-7 plots the changes in market share for the six hypothetical products we have used in many of the sample graphs, and you can see that while it is relatively easy to follow the plot lines for the best and the worst products, it is not so easy to follow those for the others. When you wish to show changes over time for a number of items, you may need to present the data in a table. While multiple line graphs may be used to show similar data, it is difficult for readers to draw comparisons based on separate line graphs.

Most charting programs can also present line graphs in three dimensions. We recommend that you use three-dimensional line graphs for presentation purposes only, when the lines are distinguished by colors. Note that the 3-D line graph illustrated in Figure 7-8 is more difficult to read and interpret than the sample line graph shown in Figure 7-7.

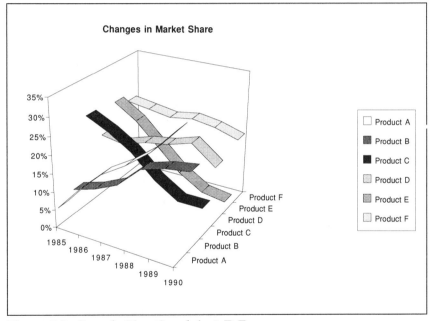

Figure 7-8. Sample Line Graph in 3-D Form.

To avoid distorting the data presented in line graphs, make sure that the grid lines form squares. If the units of measurement on either the X or Y axis are longer than the measurement in the other direction, the meaning of the data appears to change. Most charting programs will not automatically produce square grids, and different programs require different operations to correct for distortions. If you are using a charting program, check your user manual for the appropriate procedure. Figure 7-9 illustrates the way in which the same data can be distorted to convey different impressions.

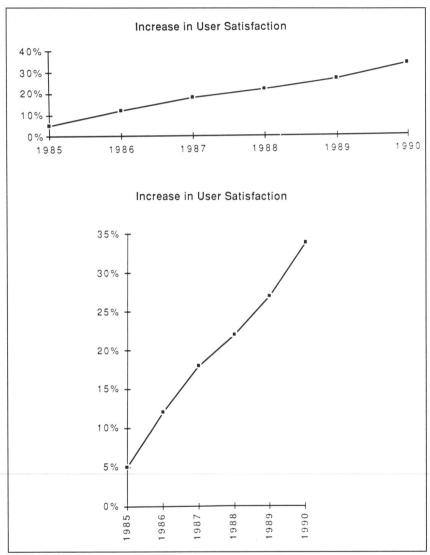

Figure 7-9. Distorted Line Graphs.

The issue here is more than simply the need to develop skill with whatever charting program you are using. Presenting data in a way that communicates accurately is essentially a question of ethics: If your graphs and charts are distorted, your reader may well question your ethics regardless of whether the distortion was deliberate. The classic study of this kind of distortion remains Darrell Huff's *How to Lie with Statistics* (W.W Norton, NY: 1954), which makes a useful addition to any proposal writer's library.

Pie Graphs

Pie graphs are used to depict parts of a whole, which always equals 100 percent. When designing a pie graph, start at the twelve o'clock position with the largest percentage, and continue clockwise in descending order. Reserve the last slice of the pie for "other" or "miscellaneous," even though it may be larger than the preceding slice. When possible, avoid having more than seven slices, and avoid 3-D, "exploded" pie graphs unless the number of divisions is small, and the percentage for each is shown. In the 3-D view, the part of the pie in the "foreground" appears larger than the rest of the graph. Also, avoid using two pie graphs to compare two wholes, as the differences may be difficult to see.

Most charting software will *not* automatically produce a correctly configured pie graph. Most programs produce the chart according to the order in which the data are entered, so you may need to sort the data before creating the chart. Sort the data in descending order, and then move the miscellaneous or "other" category to the end position. Figures 7-10 and 7-11 show sample pie graphs.

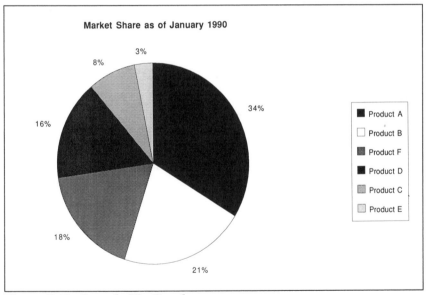

Figure 7-10. Sample Pie Graph.

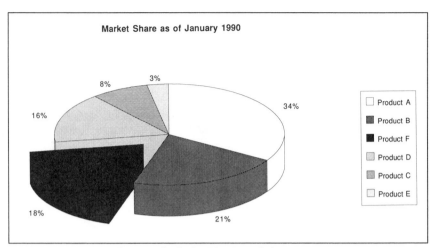

Figure 7-11. Sample "Exploded" Pie Graph in 3-D Form.

Pictographs

A pictograph is a visual representation of plotted data using pictures to represent the data. Pictographs are common in newspapers and newsweeklies because readers quickly grasp the main idea. Pictographs may be misleading, however, because they typically don't present differences with a high degree of accuracy. One common mistake is to attempt to show differences by using pictures of different sizes to illustrate the difference. If you double the height and width of a barrel, for example, what actually happens to the volume? Because size is difficult to judge, the size of the pictures should remain constant, and the number of pictures should be changed to indicate changes in amount.

For most proposal audiences, traditional bar graphs would be preferred, although pictographs may be useful as a visual aid in an oral presentation. Note that when the height of the graphic aid becomes awkward, the vertical line should be broken between zero and the lowest value to indicate an omission, as is illustrated in Figure 7-12.

Scatter Graph

A scatter graph presents statistical or mathematical data plotted on an X and Y axis, with each item of data represented by a dot. Such graphs are useful for showing trends, clustering, and dispersion of data. Figure 7-13 illustrates a scatter graph.

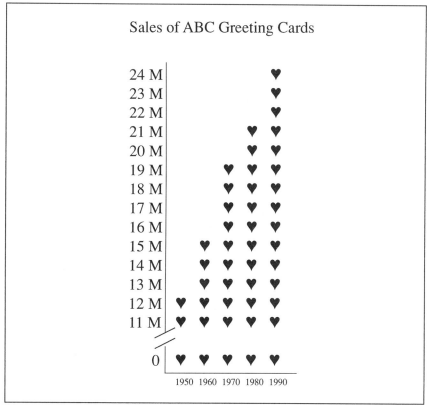

Figure 7-12. Sample Pictograph.

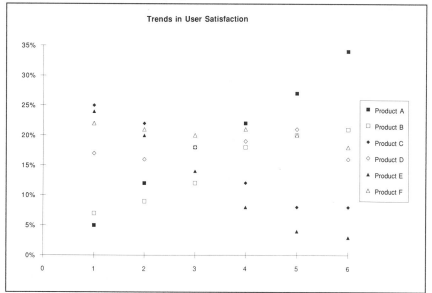

Figure 7-13. Sample Scatter Graph.

CHARTS

Virtually any unplotted graphic aid is a chart. Among the most common are PERT charts, Gantt charts, flow charts, diagrams, organizational charts, maps, blueprints, printouts, and drawings.

PERT Charts

Program Evaluation and Review Techniques (PERT) were originally developed in the late 1950s as part of the U.S. Navy's project to develop the *Polaris*, the first nuclear-powered submarine. Since then, PERT charts, which graphically represent the components of the project and their relationships with one another, have become a common management tool for planning, scheduling, and controlling large, complex projects. Virtually all proposals for complex projects include either a PERT or Gantt chart to provide the required evidence that those planning the project have carefully considered how the project will be completed.

PERT charts will show whether any required tasks have been omitted, whether the tasks are sequenced logically, and whether sufficient time has been allocated to ensure the completion of the project. PERT charts show which tasks depend on or require the completion of a previous task, and which tasks can be performed at the same time. Tasks that can be performed simultaneously are usually referred to as *parallel* activities. PERT charts also typically show the *critical path* for completion, which consists of the longest line of dependency from start to finish as measured by the time of completion of steps dependent on preceding tasks. The critical path provides an estimate of the total time required to complete the project. To develop a PERT chart, the project manager

1. Specifies a goal—the exact purpose of the project. Does "building a better computer" mean building a computer that will do more things more quickly or one that costs less to manufacture?
2. Identifies all the major steps or tasks that need to be performed.
3. Determines which tasks should be accomplished when and by whom.
4. Estimates the completion time for each task, allowing time for the unexpected.
5. Prepares a network to show the order in which the tasks are to be completed.
6. Controls the project by reviewing the difference between the time schedule and the time it actually takes to complete a task.

All of these steps can, of course, be performed by hand. Currently, however, managers typically use a variety of computer software to help. A spreadsheet program may be used to list and order the required steps and their estimated time for completion. Spreadsheets can also be used to track required resources, responsibilities, and estimated and actual costs.

Spreadsheet information may be imported into a project management program or charted by hand or with graphics software. Figure 7-14 illustrates the use of a spreadsheet for listing tasks, their order of completion, and the estimated time (measured in weeks in this case) for their completion.

Task	Description	Predecessor	Best	Likely	Worst	Resource	Est. Costs
1	Activity A	N/A	3	4	5	Smith	$650
2	Activity B	N/A	3	4	5	Jones	$1,015
3	Activity C	A	2	3	4	Johnson	$425
4	Activity D	B	4	5	6	Belmundo	$23,000
5	Activity E	C	1	2	3	Mu	$150
6	Activity F	D	1	2	3	Eberly	$1,750

Figure 7-14. PERT Data in Spreadsheet Format.

Project management software typically provides for both listing of task responsibilities and charting. In traditional PERT charts, the task or activities are represented by solid lines, with circled numbers indicating the *events* that mark the beginning and ending points of the activities. Figure 7-15 illustrates a simplified PERT chart in traditional form. Activities C and D are parallel activities, and the critical path follows the event sequence of 1, 3, 5, and 6.

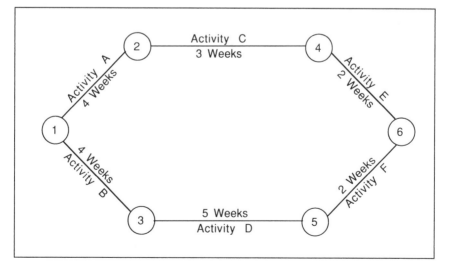

Figure 7-15. Simplified PERT Chart.

Since the inception of project management software, a more sophisticated form of the PERT chart has evolved. Most current project management software depicts tasks as labeled boxes, with the lines between them indicating dependencies. The beginning, end, and major goals along the way are frequently termed *milestones*, which are indicated by circles, ovals, or boxes with rounded corners to distinguish them from ordinary tasks. Some tasks may be designated "supertasks" or "subprojects" because they are sufficiently large and complex to require separate PERT charts for themselves. When a project is sufficiently large to require charts for the main or master project and a variety of subprojects, the group may be called a *project family*.

PERT charts, especially for complex projects, may require several pages to display. This is not critical for planning, as the various sheets may be posted on a wall or storyboard for easy visibility. It may pose a problem, however, for the purposes of inclusion in a proposal. The following options are possible:

1. **Photoreduce.** The entire chart may be photographically reduced so that it will fit comfortably on one page. Make sure that the smallest print included on the chart remains legible.
2. **Print reduce.** Most laser printers are able to reduce the size of the printed chart so that it will fit on one page. In general, charts that have been reduced in the printing process are less clear than those reduced photographically.
3. **Fold out.** The chart may be printed on a larger sized sheet designed to fold out as the proposal is read. Printing on such paper typically requires special equipment.
4. **Section.** The chart may be printed in sections, with each section clearly labeled and identified.

Figure 7-16 illustrates a sample PERT chart.

Gantt Charts

A Gantt chart is another common management tool that allows the proposal writer to identify the steps or major tasks and to assign specific starting and ending dates. The Gantt chart is also a control tool because a person can easily assess the progress of the work. The Gantt chart displays time on the horizontal axis and tasks on the vertical axis. Gantt charts are typically easier to read and understand than PERT charts and may make a better choice for displaying project activities to those not already familiar with project management concepts. Figure 7-17 illustrates a typical Gantt chart.

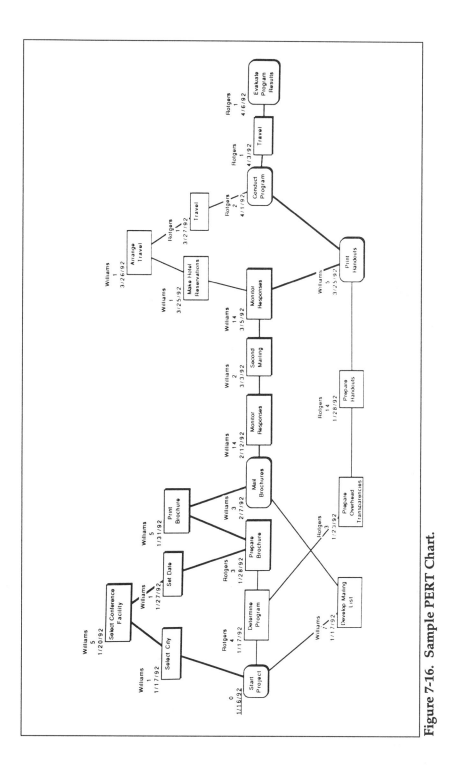

Figure 7-16. Sample PERT Chart.

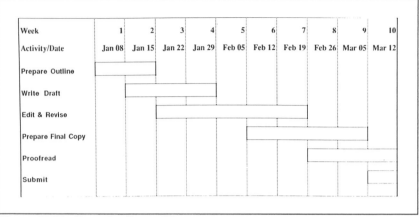

Figure 7-17. Sample Gantt Chart.

Flow Charts

A flow chart is a schematic representation of a sequence of steps; it traces the movement of a product, process, or procedure from beginning to end. Flow charts depict a series of actions graphically so the reader can have a quick overview of the entire procedure. Steps in the procedure are described in boxes or pictograms, with arrows indicating the decision and the flow of direction.

In conventional flow charts, circles (or ovals or rectangles with rounded corners) typically indicate beginning and ending points, rectangles indicate processes or procedures, diamonds indicate decision or branching points, and parallelograms indicate input or output. Arrows are used to indicate directional flow other than the normal or expected flow, which is downward, from the top to the bottom of the chart. When pictograms are used, arrows are required regardless of the directional flow. Figure 7-18 illustrates a conventional flow chart, and Figure 7-19 illustrates a pictorial flow chart.

COMPUTER GRAPHICS

Computer graphics can save the proposal writer hours of design work. The proposal writer selects the appropriate design for presenting the data and then employs the computer to create the graphic aid. As mentioned previously, however, you cannot assume that all computer graphics programs create accurate graphics—pie graphs will not automatically begin at noon, for example, and not all vertical and horizontal gradations on line charts will equal automatically. To make sure that your reader interprets your graphic aids correctly, be careful to follow the guidelines for creating graphic aids.

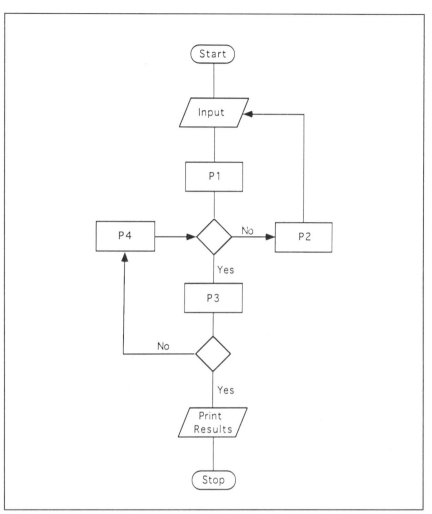

Figure 7-18. Sample Flow Chart.

Computers can take complicated data and quickly, easily, and attractively present that data in a well-designed graphic aid. Computer programs can print the title, provide the legend or key, draw the lines, and "slice the pie." Computer programs will allow you to use shading, screening, shadows, and borders. They will allow you to enrich your graphic aids with various typefaces, type styles, and type sizes. Most programs can now produce charts and graphs in 3-D, and, if the right printer is available, in color. Further, computer programs can quickly and easily produce aids in two versions, one suitable for inclusion in the proposal and one suitable for use as a visual aid during the sales presentation. With the right equipment, graphs produced on the computer can be converted directly into 35 mm slides.

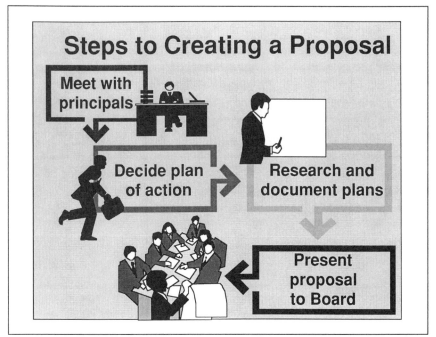

Figure 7-19. Sample Flow Chart with Pictograms.*

Project management and presentation software and the equipment necessary to take full advantage of them are good investments for those who spend much of their time writing proposals and preparing related materials for presentations. The software and equipment will not only save time but also increase the competitiveness of the proposal and presentation.

In addition to the kinds of charting programs we've already discussed, special programs are available to help produce organizational charts. If you need to produce drawings for your proposal and are not already equipped to do so, you may find computer-aided-design (CAD) software helpful.

CONSTRUCTION GUIDELINES

The following guidelines apply to all graphic aids.
1. Give each figure a title and an Arabic number. Number figures consecutively. Place titles above a graphic aid.
2. Identify every column and row in formal tables.

---

* "Steps to Creating a Proposal" was supplied courtesy of The Aldus Corporation, which developed the slide with Aldus Persuasion, a comprehensive presentation program.

3. Align digits from the right. Figures with decimals are aligned on the decimal point.
   For example

1	.05
278	5.5
4,560	3.98
12,680	235.50

4. Round off numbers when appropriate.
5. Place dollar signs and other symbols before the first entry at the top of the column and with the totals.
6. Add legends, keys, and footnotes for clarification. Legends and keys are generally typed within the graphic aid; footnotes, at the bottom.
7. Use horizontal and vertical lines sparingly.
8. Frame the graphic aid with rules above and below or all around it.
9. Do not extend the graphic aid beyond the margins of the page.
10. Try to keep the graphic aid to one vertical page. The size of a graphic aid depends on its complexity. Simple graphic aids can be a quarter or a third of a page; complex ones may use a half or full page.
11. Introduce the graphic aid before the reader encounters it. In most cases, the reference to the aid should emphasize its benefit to the reader rather than simply stating that the aid is there. What do you want the reader to notice in the aid? How will the reader benefit from the information? The following wording automatically places the emphasis on the benefit rather than on the existence of the aid:
    - As Figure 1 indicates, . . .
    - As Table 9 shows, . . .
    - As Chart 5 illustrates, . . .
    - . . ., while Figure 3 proves . . . .

    Parenthetical references to graphic aids may be brief reminders of the existence of the aid: (see Figure 2) or (Figure 2, Section 4).

12. Position the top of a two-page wide graphic aid next to the left margin.
13. Break the vertical line between zero and the lowest value when the height becomes too unwieldily. Clearly indicate the deletion.
14. Place lengthy graphic aids in an appendix, especially when they contain only supporting information or information that disrupts the flow of the text. Extensive graphic aids can be photographically reduced as long as legibility is maintained.
15. Arrange data in a logical order—chronologically, alphabetically, geographically, descending, or ascending.
16. Make graphic aids attractive, inviting, readable, clear, and uncluttered.

KEY POINTS FROM CHAPTER 7

The key points from Chapter 7 are the following:

1. Any graphic aid that is not a table is a figure. Common figures include bar graphs, line graphs, pie graphs, pictographs, scatter graphs, PERT charts, Gantt charts, and flow charts.
2. Bar graphs illustrate comparisons by showing horizontal or vertical bars in one or two quadrants of an X and Y axis grid. Vertical bar graphs are often called column graphs.
3. Line graphs show trends and present one or more variables plotted on an X and Y axis.
4. Pie graphs illustrate the division of a whole into component parts representing percentages of the whole.
5. Pictographs illustrate comparisons by showing a pictorial representation of data.
6. Scatter graphs show the clustering of diversity of data as plotted on an X and Y axis.
7. PERT charts provide a visual representation of the times and resources required for the completion a project.
8. Gantt charts provide a visual representation of the times and resources required for the completion of a project.
9. Flow charts show the relationship among processes or components.
10. Computer programs are available to help generate the common charts. The programs will not, however, automatically generate the charts correctly, so the writer will need to sort data appropriately and check the chart to ensure that all the appropriate construction guidelines have been followed.

CHAPTER 8

Format and Appearance

While the appearance of a proposal will not typically be the main criterion by which it is evaluated, appearance does count. In many cases, competing companies will submit similar proposals and offer many of the same advantages. In such cases, the appearance of the proposal may well be the deciding factor. If two proposals are nearly identical in every respect except appearance, readers are psychologically predisposed to favor the proposal with the better, more professional appearance.

The format and appearance of proposals do, of course, vary greatly from industry to industry. Even when produced with modern word processing equipment and software, technical proposals, for example, typically follow formatting guidelines developed for typewritten documents. As microcomputers, laser printers, and appropriate software become commonplace, however, the standards for acceptable appearance for proposals and other business documents will increase. Today's microcomputers, in combination with a modern word processing or page layout program and a laser printer (or one of the newer ink jet or even many of the 24-pin dot matrix printers), are capable of producing work that rivals that produced by a professional printer. For this reason, using such equipment to produce business documents is usually referred to as *desktop publishing* (DTP).

While DTP equipment and software produce documents that look much more professional than those produced by typewriters and older computers and printers, most current equipment is not an effective substitute for professional printing. Some documents need to be designed and printed by a professional to be effective. Sales brochures, product fliers, other sales support documents, and most documents that will be widely distributed without change over an extended time are generally more effective when typeset and printed.

Proposals and their related documents, however, rarely need the additional expenses of professional design and typesetting. Because it is capable of producing more readable documents, DTP equipment and software will typically give organizations using it an advantage over those using typewriters or word processors and older-style impact printers. Impact printers often have just two or three typefaces and sizes available, and changing print elements to achieve special effects can be awkward. The type produced by such equipment is typically *monospaced*, with each letter being allocated the same amount of space regardless of its actual width. DTP equipment and software, on the other hand, allows for a greater variety of typefaces and sizes and typically employs *proportional spacing,* in which letters receive space according to their actual width, with an *i* receiving less space than an *m,* for example. Proportional spacing is easier to read and looks more professional.

Figures 8-1 and 8-2 illustrate the differences between a page produced by typewriter or standard word processor using the monofont Courier and one produced by DTP equipment and software using two proportional fonts, Helvetica for the headings and Bookman for the body copy.

MAJOR HEADING

Typewriters and word processing equipment using impact

printers are limited in what they can do to make the text appear

interesting. It is difficult to change typefaces using older

equipment, and it is difficult to incorporate graphics.

Subheading

When boldface is available, it is generally better to use

boldface for the headings than to use the underscore because words

in boldface are both more visible and easier to read than those

that are underscored. If you boldface one heading, be sure to

boldface them all, including those in solid capital letters, which

are never underscored.

Sub-subheading

There's nothing wrong with this format, and you can use it

to prepare successful proposals. Because the cost of equipment

and software capable of a wider range of options has dropped sig-

nificantly in the last several years, however, organizations still

using this format may be at a disadvantage when competing with

firms using a more sophisticated design.

Compare the appearance of the sample page from a document

prepared using desktop publishing equipment, and decide for your-

self.

Figure 8-1. Typical Typewritten Format.

Main Heading

This is an example of a page produced using desktop publishing equipment and software. Note that the headings are in a different typeface than that which is used for the text. The headings are also different sizes, based on their relative importance.

Subheading

Note that the proportional spacing of the characters is easier to read than the uniform spacing of the monofont used in Figure 8-1. Note also that the headings are more visible. If appropriate for the kind of proposal we were preparing, we could use **REVERSE** print to make headings even more visible.

Sub-subheading

With desktop publishing equipment and software, it is also relatively easy to incorporate graphics so that the text flows around them and they appear an integral part of the document. The graphic placed here, for example, could be a

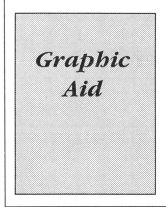

any kind of graph or chart or even a scanned photograph of a product or construction site. Having the text explaining the graphic aid adjacent to the aid itself is an aid to readability. Of course, even with desktop publishing equipment, many graphic aids require a half page or even a full page to be easily readable. With DTP equipment and software, you have that choice.

Figure 8-2. Sample Page Using Desktop Publishing Equipment.

This new technology presents both advantages and disadvantages. The advantages are that those responsible for document production have much greater control over the appearance of the documents they produce and that professional-looking documents can be produced at much lower cost than would be possible if they were typeset and printed. The principal disadvantage is that those responsible for producing the documents need to understand the fundamental concepts of graphic design. If you have a document design specialist on your proposal writing team, this will not pose a problem for you. If you don't, someone on your team will need to assume that responsibility.

While this chapter will cover some of the fundamentals of the design process, you may wish to invest in one or more of the books written especially to help those responsible for document design. See the list of suggested readings at the end of the book for examples. A number of books covering specific software and specific brands of computers are also available and helpful to those with design responsibilities.

THE FUNDAMENTALS OF DESIGN

Effective document design begins with an understanding of the audience for and the purpose of the document. Many large organizations have established specific guidelines and standards for document design, and you should be sure to check those guidelines before preparing the final copy of your proposal. Although the basic design concepts remain the same regardless of the kind of document, magazine and newspaper advertisements, brochures, flyers, letters, and reports all need different design strategies based on the use to which the readers will put them and the conditions under which they will be read. Neatness, proportion, direction, unity, and simplicity are the fundamental guiding principles of effective document design.

Neatness

The first rule of document production is that neatness counts. The final copy (or *copies*, when multiple copies of the proposal are required) should be neat and clean. Ink corrections, stray marks, stains (from thumb prints to coffee rings), irregular photocopying (crooked paper feed or faded print), and similar problems detract from the sense of professionalism a proposal should convey.

Regardless of the kind of equipment you have, the final document should be prepared with as much attention to detail and design as possible. The principal considerations of the design for most documents and especially for proposals center on the readers and their expectations. Readers of technical proposals, for example, will expect a serviceable document that allows the technical considerations to speak for themselves. Readers of proposals for a public relations or advertising campaign, on the other hand, would expect the documents to demonstrate the features being proffered. Readers' expectations should be exceeded but not violated. If a technical proposal were *too* fancy, the readers might well be as offended as they would be by a proposal prepared with too little attention to design.

Proportion

The size of an element, whether a heading or a graphic, should be proportional to its importance. The most important element on a page should be the most visible. The size of an element also needs to correspond with the space available for it. Headings too large for the space that contain them appear crowded. Those too small fail to catch attention. The thickness of rules (lines) should be determined by the adjacent type and the available space. Figures 8-3 and 8-4 illustrate the influence of proportion on the appearance of a document.

Figure 8-3. Improper Proportion.

Figure 8-4. Proper Proportion.

Direction

A document should be designed so that readers can tell at a glance where they should look first and in what order the material should be read. In Western culture, readers have been taught to begin reading a document in the upper-left corner, and most documents should be designed to take advantage of that natural starting point. In general, proposals should read from front to back, from left to right, and from top to bottom.

Regardless of its placement on the page, readers will read large print before they will read small print, and difference in type size can help guide readers through a document in an atypical sequence. Readers will also tend to look at graphic elements (charts, graphs, drawings, and other illustrations) before they will read the accompanying text. For this reason, it is important that graphic elements be self-explanatory. (See Chapter 7.) Figure 8-5 illustrates the use of type size to control the order in which the information is read.

Unity

Effective documents are consistent and unified. Visual unity is every bit as important as grammatical and stylistic unity. (See Chapters 5 and 6.) Just as lists need to use parallel grammatical structure, the visual components of a document need to follow an organized system of presentation. The same size type and font, for example, should always be used to indicate headings or elements of equal importance. If page 1 has one-inch margins, page 2 should have one-inch margins. In general, it's best for all the documents produced by an organization to have a certain degree of consistency. On the other hand, some variation in appearance—usually referred to as *contrast*—helps maintain reader interest. If patterns are too predictable, readers tend to ignore them.

Simplicity

When it comes to document design, the most important rule is the old and well-known rule of communication: keep it simple. Because every change in typeface and size slows the reader, keep such changes to a minimum. Use boldface and italics sparingly, and be consistent in the way you use them. Avoid a cluttered appearance. White space is an important component of document design. The contrast it provides with the print is what makes the print stand out. Remember that if you try to emphasize everything, you end up emphasizing nothing.

DESIGNS FOR BRIEF DOCUMENTS

In addition to preparing the proposal, you may be responsible for preparing a number of related documents, including brochures, letters, memos, and masters for overhead and slide transparencies. When prepared as part of a presentation package, the related materials should maintain the same general appearance as that used for the proposal.

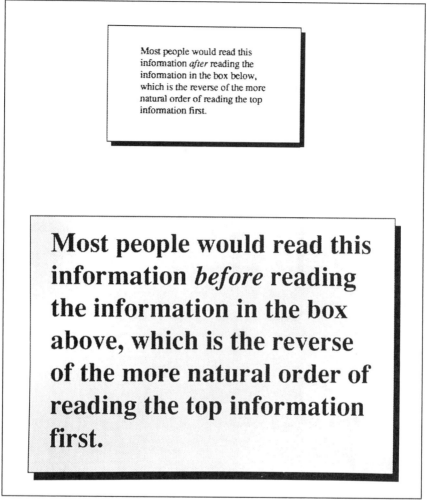

Figure 8-5. Use of Type Size to Control Reading Order.

Brochures

Most brochures are primarily informational and are used to convey that information to a specific audience for a specific purpose. A brochure may make a useful addition to a proposal, especially when the proposal is brief, in letter or memo format, and is offering relatively low-cost products or services (such as a bid on a single product or a training program). Many organizations prefer to have brochures prepared and printed professionally because of the greater flexibility in paper size and quality, use of color, and other design advantages. When time or costs are important considerations, effective brochures can be produced using a microcomputer, page layout software, and a laser printer.

The most common type of brochure produced on a microcomputer is a bifold (folded twice) printed on 8½ X 11-inch paper in the horizontal or "landscape" mode. That results in three panels for text and graphics on each side. Because brochures are typically printed front-to-back, the panels need to be arranged so that the "cover" of the folded brochure is opposite the first inside panel. Figure 8-6 illustrates the panel layout for the front and back of a typical brochure.

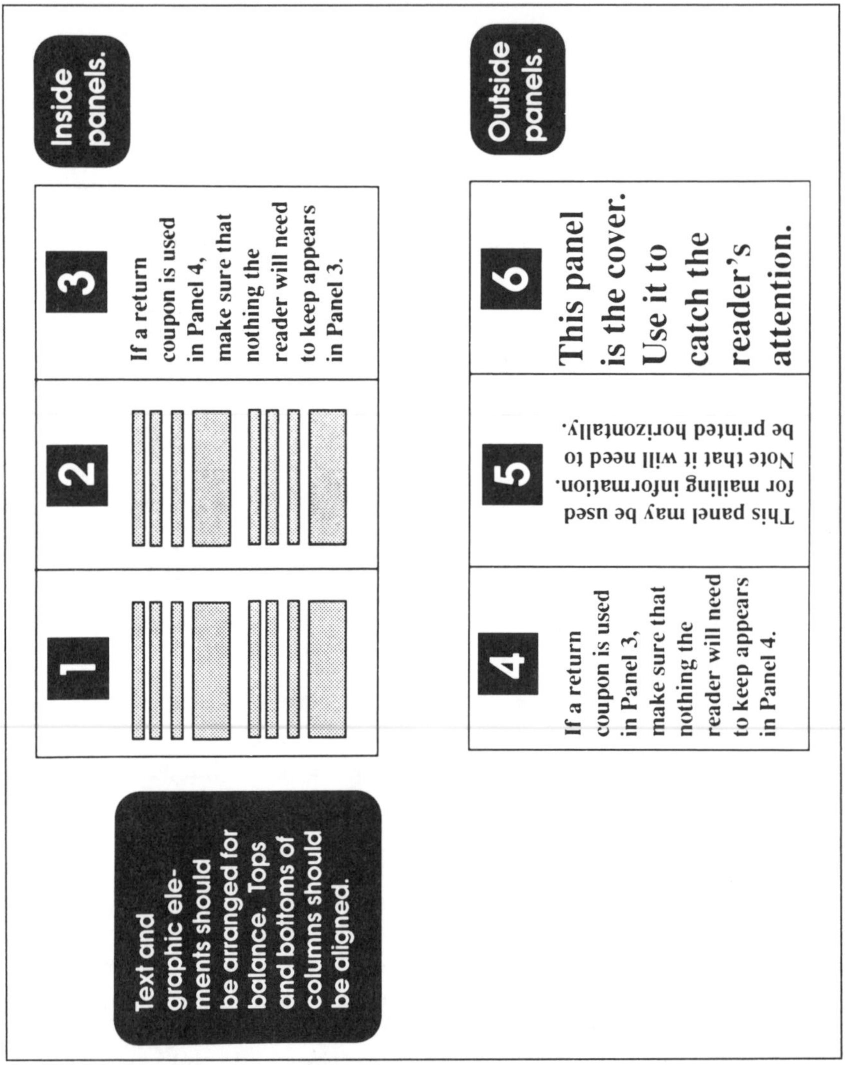

Inside panels.

3 If a return coupon is used in Panel 4, make sure that nothing the reader will need to keep appears in Panel 3.

2

1

Text and graphic elements should be arranged for balance. Tops and bottoms of columns should be aligned.

Outside panels.

6 This panel is the cover. Use it to catch the reader's attention.

5 This panel may be used for mailing information. Note that it will need to be printed horizontally.

4 If a return coupon is used in Panel 3, make sure that nothing the reader will need to keep appears in Panel 4.

Figure 8-6. Brochure Layout.

Letters and Memos

In general, proposals in letter or memo format and letters and memos accompanying proposals follow the traditional guidelines for document design with two exceptions. First, desktop publishing equipment and software permit the inclusion of graphic elements (charts and drawings) into correspondence. Second, italics should be used rather than the underscore for type that would normally be set in italics.

If a graphic element is incorporated, avoid placing it in a location where the reader is forced to read around it. Rather, place the element on a margin or between columns so that the text ends at the edges of the graphic aid, as is shown in Figure 8-7. To increase the readability of informal letters and memos,

If you put a graphic ele- reader must look past the reading, the graphic actu- to the reader's understand- Note the way this material compared with the ex- the graphic is placed more ment in a place where the graphic to continue ally becomes a hindrance ing rather than an aid. is difficult to read, as amples below, in which appropriately.

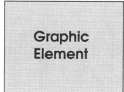 Note how much easier the text is to read when it appears adjacent to the graphic element, and you don't have to read around the graphic to make sense of the text. The graphic element can appear on either the left or the right margin, based on your own sense of balance between it, headings, and other graphic elements on the same page (and facing pages, if the document is printed on both sides of the page).

When you are using a two-column format, the graphic element may be placed in the middle of the page, with one column of print being adjacent to the left side of the graphic, and the other column being adjacent to the right. 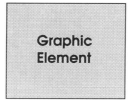 To ensure that your document remains visually interesting, provide some variation in the placement of the graphics. If your document is brief and contains only two graphics, both may appear in essentially the same location (right or left margin or

Most page layout programs allow you to match the adjacent edge of type to irregular shapes, should your graphic have an irregular shape. Most page layout programs also allow you to select the amount of "standoff" (distance) between the text and the graphic. centered), but if you have a longer document with a number of graphics, try to arrange them so that their appearance will not be too predictable. Try to arrange them for balance, taking their size and relative importance into account. Note that the lines in adjacent columns should be even.

Figure 8-7. Placement of Graphic Aids.

you may wish to consider using the caption format, which places the headings in a column to the left of the text. (See Figure 6-5.) Figure 8-8 illustrates a letter proposal, and Figure 8-9 illustrates a memo in caption format.

Masters for Overhead and Slide Transparencies

In many cases, the two or three organizations submitting the best proposals will be invited to present their ideas in person. (See Chapter 11.) Such presentations generally require visual aids to support information

---

Dynamic Sales Inc　　　　　　　*Sales Training That Works*
1000 Mandell Avenue
Malibu, California 90265
Voice: 1-800-555-1297 • FAX: 213-555-1200

24 July 19xx

Mr. David Johnston, Director
Corporate Training
Kirszner Pharmeceuticals
One Kirszner Place
Fairfax, VA 22030

Dear Mr. Johnston:

The enclosed brochure and fliers will explain the fundamentals of our training procedures and provide you with information about our trainers and the results we have achieved with other companies. Thank you for calling and inviting us to submit our ideas for your sales training program.

We suspect that the reason your new sales representatives are having difficulty with the sales aspect of their training is that they are concentrating on mastering product knowledge. Because selling your products requires such specialized knowledge of both the product and the audience, we recommend that your sales training be separated from the specific training you provide about your products and the doctors responsible for ordering and prescribing them.

We recommend that you conduct in-house training on your products and markets before the basic sales training begins. Once your new sales representatives are comfortable with the product information and understand how your products are marketed, they will be ready to learn more about basic sales procedures.

We would be glad to assume responsibility for the basic sales training and could comfortably adapt our program to your current training schedule. In the three weeks you have available for the sales portion of your training program, we would cover the following topics:

❑ Interpersonal Relations
❑ Customer Service, Customer Relations
❑ Persuasive Communication
❑ The Ethics of Persuasion
❑ Practical Applications
　• Role playing/rehearsal
　• Video analysis

Our fee for conducting the three-week training (15 six-hour days) for 20 to 30 participants would be $12,500. We would provide each participant with a copy of our 225-page text/workbook; a 30-minute videotape, "Selling the Dynamic Way"; a pen; and notepaper. The fee also includes pre- and posttesting to ensure that the participants have learned the course concepts.

Please review the enclosed materials and check your current costs for administering the program. We believe you'll find that Dynamic Sales Inc. can improve your results and reduce your expenses at the same time. Please call me when you have completed your review. I'll be looking forward to hearing from you.

Sincerely,

Sondra J. Spielman
President

enc

Figure 8-8. Proposal in Letter Format.

NEWHOUSE, GROVE, AND ASSOCIATES

INTEROFFICE CORRESPONDENCE Only

19xx 09 02

To: Chris Weston, VP Operations

From: Seiki Inazu, Data Processing

DATA STORAGE PROBLEM AND PROPOSED SOLUTION

Problem	Our two file servers are rapidly running out of free disk space. In spite of the current freeze on new purchases, we will need to take some action to ensure uninterrupted progress on the projects we currently have underway.
Background	We currently have two 660 MB Pivotal Digital file servers used for all shared applications and files. In addition, each of the personal computers used by our engineers has 80 MB for individual files, and those used by our graphic designers have 100 MB each. The file server used for applications and the principal customer database is full, with approximately 600 MB used. The remaining 60 MB of file space on that server is required for file transfers and other necessary disk operations. The other file server is now at two-thirds capacity.
	In addition, 5 of our 15 engineers and all 4 of our graphic designers have reported that they are running low on disk space. It is only a matter of time until a shortage of disk space begins causing us major problems.
Alternatives	One possible solution would be to have each employee go through all his or her files, cull those that are outdated or otherwise unessential, and optimize the disks.
• **Unnecessary Files**	While we continue to encourage everyone to eliminate unnecessary files, we have avoided making a major project of disk optimizing because the time the entire process would take would delay critical projects. This is still true, and it is unlikely to change in the near future.

Figure 8-9. Memo Proposal in Caption Format.

delivered orally. The most important rule for effective transparencies is to keep them simple. The typeface needs to be large enough to be readable by those sitting at a distance (usually 18 point or larger). Also, transparencies are more readable when they are printed horizontally and contain a title or headline separated from the body of the information by a rule (line). Keep the number of elements in each transparency small. If the information is complex, use more than one transparency to present the data.

If done well, color transparencies look more professional and can be more memorable and persuasive. Color transparencies, however, are not easy to do or to do well. Transparencies that automatically print in reverse

---

- **File Compression**   Even if we were able to delete all outdated files and optimize the file servers and individual hard drives, however, this would buy us only a small amount of time. With each new project the firm undertakes, demands on disk space increase. Another possible solution would be to install a data compression utility. Some compression utilities can reduce the amount of disk space for a given file by 50 percent.

  Compressing and decompressing files each time they are used would slow computer operations and would also be a short-term solution. We may wish to combine a compression utility with another solution and compress older files and those accessed less frequently.

- **New File Server**   Assuming we continue our current rate of growth, and with an improved program of file management, a new 660 MB file server would meet our needs for approximately another year. The total investment for a new server, controller, and installation would be approximately $12,000.

  Regardless of our efforts to improve file management, our storage needs are going to continue to grow as the company grows. For this reason, I propose that we invest in an optical storage device that would meet our needs for many years to come. For $15,500, we could install a read/write optical drive capable of storing a gigabyte of data on each optical disk. Additional disks (currently priced at around $250) would provide us with virtually unlimited storage.

Recommended Solution   Read/write technology is well-tested and reliable and would eliminate worry about disk space for a long time to come. I would appreciate meeting with you to discuss the possibility of asking our usual vendors to provide us with more specific information and price quotes. Please call me to let me know your thinking on this.

Figure 8-9. Memo Proposal in Caption Format (continued).

(white lettering on a black or blue background) or in preselected contrasting colors (yellow lettering on a blue background, for example) are also available and may be used to good effect. The production of color slides other than photographs (of sites, products, or activities) requires special equipment and expertise. Figure 8-10 illustrates typical layout for a transparency. See Chapter 11 for additional information.

PROPOSAL FORMATS

Proposal formats suitable for DTP equipment and software do not differ significantly from those used with older word processing equipment. The three principal differences are that the size and style of type can be used

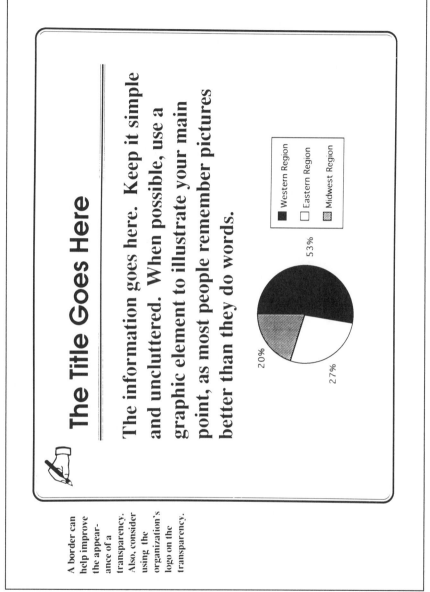

Figure 8-10. Typical Layout for a Transparency.

effectively to indicate the relative importance of the components of the report, graphic elements can be incorporated quickly and easily, and the document may be prepared in two or three columns, if appropriate.

In designing the proposal, remember to leave sufficient gutter margin (the margin on the bound side) for binding and that the odd numbered pages (1, 3, 5, etc.) will be on the right (*recto*) side, and even numbered pages

(2, 4, 6, etc.) will be on the left (*verso*) side. The gutter margins are on the *left* side of recto pages and the *right* side of verso pages. Most modern word processors allow for different settings for recto and verso pages, so be sure to check the user's manual accompanying your software.

Figure 8-11 shows the format for recto and verso pages from a proposal using a two-column presentation for the body copy. Figure 8-12 illustrates a three-column format, more suitable for product or service informational sheets accompanying a proposal than for the proposal itself.

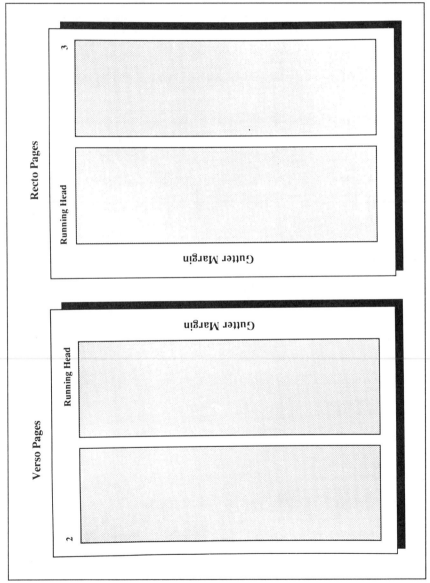

Figure 8-11. Recto and Verso Page Layout.

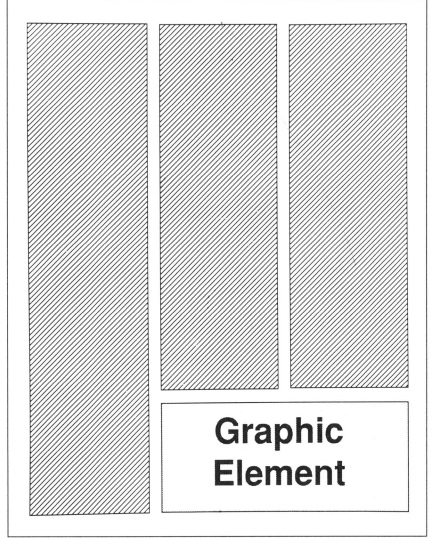

Graphic Element

Figure 8-12. Three-column Format.

TYPOGRAPHY

The most common failings of those new to document design are that they use too many typefaces and sizes in one document. Typefaces should be selected and used because they facilitate communication rather than because they are "there." The following are the basic rules for using typefaces:

1. Use no more than two *typefamilies* (consisting of all the typefaces of a particular design, such as Times Roman) in a single document.

Also, keep changes in size and style to a minimum. Every change in typeface slows the reader down, so each change should serve a specific purpose.

2. Use a *serif* typeface for body copy because it is easier to read, especially when the font is small and the lines are relatively long. The serifs, the small lines used to finish the main stroke of letters, help guide the reader's eye along the line of type, as is illustrated in Figure 8-13.

Figure 8-13. Serif and Sans Serif Typefaces.

3. A *sans serif* typeface (those without the extra "finishing" lines) can be used for headlines and headings to provide contrast with the typeface used in the body copy as shown in Figure 8-14.

4. A *sans serif* typeface is easier to read when the print is reversed (white print on a black or solid color background), as can be seen in Figure 8-14.

Sans Serif Type is Good for Headings

Because headings should stand out and attract attention to the text that follows, it is often useful to use a different typeface for them. Changes in typeface slow the reader down, and headings are a good place to do that.

Sans serif type is easier to read when the print is reversed. Note how much easier it is to read this, than it is to read similar material in a serif typeface. The sans serif type face has a cleaner appearance when the print is reversed.

MATERIAL WRITTEN IN SOLID CAPITAL LETTERS IS MORE DIFFICULT TO READ THAN MATERIAL WRITTEN WITH A COMBINATION OF CAPITAL AND LOWER-CASE LETTERS. NOTE HOW DIFICULT THIS MATERIAL IS TO READ. ALSO, THE MATERIAL WOULD BECOME INCREASINGLY DIFFICULT TO READ THE LONGER THE PARAGRAPH.

Material written in a combination of capital and lower-case letters (using normal capitalization) is easier to read than material written in solid capital letters. Note that the greater variation in letter shapes and sizes offered by the combination of capital and lower-case letters helps you read quickly and easily.

Figure 8-14. Uses of Serif and Sans Serif Type.

5. A combination of capital and lowercase letters is generally easier to read than solid capital letters, so keep the use of solid capital letters to a minimum. (See Figure 8-14.)

6. Use the typefamilies preferred by professionals. Many of the typefamilies available on microcomputer are carefully crafted designs that have been used by printers for hundreds of years. Others, of more recent origin, are useful primarily for novelty pieces. For documents with a professional appearance, use the typefaces you see in professionally prepared materials.

Figures 8-15 and 8-16 illustrate a variety of serif and sans serif typefaces commonly available for desktop publishing equipment. Specialty typefaces and display typefaces may be useful in special circumstances, but keep their use to a minimun. The typefaces shown in Figures 8-15 and 8-16 are the PostScript® versions developed by Adobe Systems Incorporated.

10-Point Bookman
12-Point Bookman
12-Point Bookman Italic
12-Point Bookman Bold
12-Point Bookman Bold Italic
14-Point Bookman

24-Point Bookman

10-Point Century Schoolbook
12-Point Century Schoolbook
12-Point Century Schoolbook Italic
12-Point Century Schoolbook Bold
12-Point Century Schoolbook Bold Italic
14-Point Century Schoolbook

24-Point Century Schoolbook

10-Point Palatino
12-Point Palatino
12-Point Palatino Italic
12-Point Palatino Bold
12-Point Palatino Bold Italic
14-Point Palatino

24-Point Palatino

10-Point Times
12-Point Times
12-Point Times Italic
12-Point Times Bold
12-Point Times Bold Italic
14-Point Times

24-Point Times

Figure 8-15. Common Serif Typefaces.

10-Point Avant Garde
12-Point Avant Garde
12-Point Avant Garde Italic
12-Point Avant Garde Bold
12-Point Avant Garde Bold Italic
14-Point Avant Garde

24-Point Avant Garde

10-Point Helvetica Narrow
12-Point Helvetica Narrow
12-Point Helvetica Narrow Italic
12-Point Helvetica Narrow Bold
12-Point Helvetica Narrow Bold Italic
14-Point Helvetica Narrow

24-Point Helvetica Narrow

10-Point Lucida Sans
12-Point Lucida Sans
12-Point Lucida Sans Italic
12-Point Lucida Sans Bold
12-Point Lucida Sans Bold Italic
14-Point Lucida Sans

24-Point Lucida Sans

10-Point Helvetica
12-Point Helvetica
12-Point Helvetica Italic
12-Point Helvetica Bold
12-Point Helvetica Bold Italic
14-Point Helvetica

24-Point Helvetica

Figure 8-16. Common Sans Serif Typefaces.

KEY POINTS FROM CHAPTER 8

The key points from Chapter 8 are the following:

1. When competing companies submit similar proposals, the appearance of the document may well prove the deciding factor.
2. The format and appearance of proposals will vary from industry to industry, but as microcomputers, laser printers, and modern word processing and page layout proliferate, the expectations of readers increase.
3. Organizations that use desktop publishing equipment to produce proposals and related documents typically have a competitive advantage over those that don't.
4. Proportionally spaced material looks more professional than that which is monospaced.
5. A proposal team needs someone willing to assume the responsibility for document design.
6. Effective document design begins with an understanding of the audience for and the purpose of the document.
7. Neatness counts.
8. A document should be designed so that readers can tell at a glance where they should look first and in what order the material should be read.
9. Visual unity is as important as grammatical and stylistic unity.
10. Keep it simple.
11. Related documents—including brochures, letters, memos, and masters for overhead and slide transparencies—should maintain the same general appearance as that used for the proposal.
12. Proposal formats prepared on desktop publishing equipment can take advantage of different type sizes and faces, the incorporation of graphic elements, and multiple-column presentations.

CHAPTER 9

The Finished Document

As the process of writing and revising progresses, those responsible for preparing the proposal need to consider the form and function of the final document. Proposals have a variety of formats and components, depending on their length, degree of formality, and expectations established in a particular industry. Some proposals are informal, one-paragraph memos or one-page letters; others are formal, multivolume documents. While proposals differ in appearance and size, their basic components are similar.

Figure 9-1 lists the various categories and types of information typically found in proposals. Lengthy, formal proposals may include all the major categories and subcategories; shorter, informal proposals may contain just a few. Also, depending on your business or industry, the names used for the categories may vary. Be sure to check the RFP carefully to see whether specific terminology is preferred for the components, and, if so, use that terminology.

Front Matter	Body	Supplemental Parts
Cover	Introduction	Appendix
Title page	Statement of the problem	Bibliography
Letter of transmittal	Recommend solution	Index
Table of contents	Scope of services	
List of illustrations	Principal qualifications for work	
Abstract	Technical Section	
Conformance checklist	Problem statement	
	Scope of work	
	Project Management	
	Description of work	
	Schedule for work	
	Responsibilities for work	
	Project organization	
	Evaluation	
	Set objectives	
	Establish standards	
	Monitor progress	
	Costs	
	Direct	
	Indirect	
	Budget	
	Qualifications	
	Experience and past performance	
	Personnel	

Figure 9-1. Possible Proposal Components.

The formats shown for the components illustrated in this chapter are traditional and will be acceptable for most proposal audiences. If you work for a business or industry in which graphic design plays an important role, however, a nontraditional format may prove more successful for you. Regardless of the format you use, however, the *content* of the components will remain essentially the same.

FRONT MATTER

Unless directed otherwise by the RFP, use the following order for the front matter for your proposal:

1. Cover
2. Title page
3. Letter of transmittal
4. Table of contents
5. List of illustrations
6. Abstract or executive summary
7. Conformance checklist

Cover

The kind of cover used for a proposal depends on the binding used. Cover sheets are necessary when plastic comb or spiral (either wire or plastic) is used. The purpose of a cover sheet is to identify and protect the proposal. For that reason cover sheets are often heavy paper, typically card stock. Short, informal proposals (those that can be stapled) may omit the cover sheet, as can proposals submitted in three-ring binders.

The cover sheet carries the title of the proposal, usually in large print, and the author's name, the name of his or her organization, and the address of the organization. The cover sheet may also include additional identifying information, such as the RFP number and, if it is not clear from the title of the proposal itself, the title of the RFP. The RFP number and title are most commonly placed either in the upper-left corner of the cover or below the title, although occasionally an RFP will request that the additional identifying information appear in the lower-right corner. Check the RFP to see whether specific directions are provided.

The title of the proposal should be clear, concise, and complete. When possible, it should answer the questions *who, what, when where, why,* and *how.* When the title of the proposal is longer than one line, type it in *inverted pyramid* style, with the longest line on top and the shortest line on the bottom:

A Proposal to Determine the Cost Effectiveness of Flextime in the Division of Human Resources and Development at American Computer Company Inc.

Figure 9-2 illustrates a cover sheet, and Figure 9-3 shows a nontraditional design.

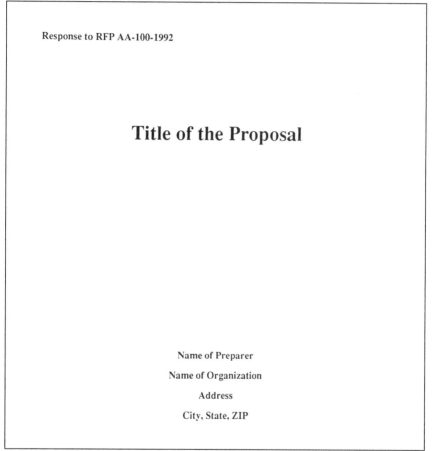

Figure 9-2. Sample Cover Sheet.

Title Page

The title page contains (1) the title of the proposal; (2) the name, title, and address of the person, group, or organization to whom the proposal is submitted; (3) the name, title, and address of the person, group, or organization submitting the proposal; (4) proprietary information, when appropriate; (5) the date of submission; (6) a copyright date when appropriate; and (7) the RFP number and title. The words "Prepared for" precede the second block of information, and the words "Prepared by" precede the third block of information. The RFP identifying information should appear in the same location on the title page as it does on the cover unless the RFP specifies otherwise.

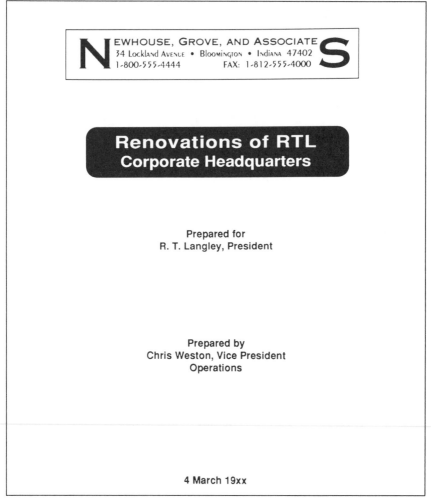

Figure 9-3. Sample Cover for a Formal Proposal.

When proprietary information is appropriate, use the wording suggested by the governmental agency or your organization's legal department. Also, if you wish, you may copyright your proposal. As original written material is automatically covered by copyright, it is not necessary to register with the Copyright Office of the U. S. Library of Congress unless you are involved in a litigation, at which time you would register it. Figure 9-4 illustrates a title page.

Response to RFP AA-100-1992

Title of the Proposal

Prepared for

Name and Title of Individual

Name of Organization

Address

City, State, ZIP

Prepared by

Name and Title of Individual

Name of Organization

Address

City, State, ZIP

Date Prepared

Figure 9-4. Sample Title Page.

Letter of Transmittal

Except for those proposals short enough to prepare as a letter or memo, completed proposals are typically accompanied by a letter or memo of transmittal, depending primarily on whether the proposal is external (letter) or internal (memo). The letter or memo of transmittal includes (1) the title of the proposal, (2) an identifying number if one were provided, (3) reference to the RFP or to the situation where the proposal was initiated or suggested, (4) a summary of the major features of the proposal (including proposed research methodology, costs, procedures, and other important details), and (5) the time period for the offer, if appropriate. If the authority of the person signing the letter is not clear from the letterhead or signature block, the letter of transmittal should also contain a statement indicating that the signer has the authority to make the offer on behalf of the organization. If the proposal is being submitted by a division of a larger organization, the letter of transmittal should also indicate whether the entire organization supports the project.

Letters and memos of transmittal usually begin with a statement transmitting the proposal, often with the words "here is" followed by a reference to the RFP, IFB, or other request leading to the development of the proposal. The central portion of the letter or memo provides a brief overview or summary of the proposal with emphasis on the major reader benefits. Letters and memos of transmittal should close on a positive note, usually with a statement of interest in performing the work or service and offering to provide additional information in writing or in a meeting or oral presentation. Figure 9-5 illustrates a letter of transmittal.

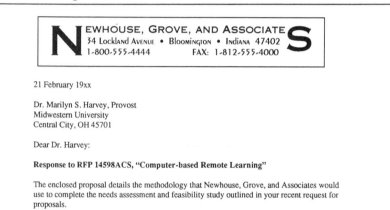

NEWHOUSE, GROVE, AND ASSOCIATES
34 Lockland Avenue • Bloomington • Indiana 47402
1-800-555-4444   FAX: 1-812-555-4000

21 February 19xx

Dr. Marilyn S. Harvey, Provost
Midwestern University
Central City, OH 45701

Dear Dr. Harvey:

Response to RFP 14598ACS, "Computer-based Remote Learning"

The enclosed proposal details the methodology that Newhouse, Grove, and Associates would use to complete the needs assessment and feasibility study outlined in your recent request for proposals.

Based on our extensive previous experience in designing and implementing computer-based educational delivery systems, we recommend a three-phase survey, including mail questionnaires, telephone interviews, and focus groups to assess the needs of your potential client base. The questionnaires would be sent to a random sampling of 1,000 households and 100 businesses within a 100-mile radius of Central City. We would conduct follow-up telephone calls from 10 percent of the responders and 10 percent of the nonresponders, and we would select 10 focus groups of 10 individuals each based on the results of the telephone interviews.

While those surveys are being completed, we would evaluate your current equipment, software, and personnel so that we would be able to determine whether your existing equipment and software will be sufficient to meet the needs of your potential clients and whether your personnel will be able to design and maintain any additional hardware and software that might be required.

We have recently completed similar studies for Western University, in Surf's Edge, Oregon, and Eastern University, in Clam Cove, Maine. Based on those studies, we anticipate that your study can be completed for under $200,000, of which our fee for organizing the study, developing and administering the survey instruments, documenting the results, and preparing a comprehensive recommendation report, will be $94,500.

Please give me a call when you have had the opportunity to evaluate the enclosed proposal and to discuss it with the members of your computing staff. I will be glad to answer any questions you might have about the proposal.

Sincerely,

Gregg Newhouse

enc

Figure 9-5. Sample Letter of Transmittal.

Table of Contents

The table of contents is prepared once the proposal is complete and page numbers have been assigned. The purpose of the table of contents is to show the organization of the proposal and assist the reader in locating information or sections of the proposal readily. Proposals of five or fewer pages do not require a table of contents.

The table of contents lists the headings exactly as they appear in the proposal. Because the front matter—cover, title page, letter of transmittal—precede the table of contents, they are not included in the table of contents. Begin the table of contents with the list of illustrations and the executive summary followed by listings for the elements of the proposal proper and the appendixes and other supplemental parts. Figure 9-6 illustrates a sample table of contents, and 9-7 shows a nontraditional table

---

Contents

iv

Figure 9-6. Sample Table of Contents.

of contents. Note that the words "table of" are not necessary, as it is obvious that the page is a table. Occasionally, however, an RFP will specify that the table of contents be labeled *Table of Contents*, in which case use the wording specified in the RFP. Note also that Figure 9-6 uses the generic names for the components of the proposal, and that actual proposals should use specific headings, as discussed in Chapter 6.

Contents

2 *Part One: Current Status*

30 *Part Two: Proposed Design*

60 *Part Three: Costs*

90 *Appendixes*

Figure 9-7. Sample Table of Contents—Nontraditional.

List of Illustrations

When a proposal more than five pages long contains at least three graphic aids—tables, charts, graphs, maps, drawings, photographs—it should include a list of illustrations. Like the table of contents, the list of illustrations is prepared after the proposal is complete and page and figure numbers have been assigned. The purpose of the list of illustrations is to help the reader locate illustrations in the proposal quickly. When the table of contents and list of illustrations are short, they can appear on the same page, with the list of illustrations following the table of contents. Otherwise the list of illustrations appears on a page by itself following the table of contents. Figure 9-8 is an example of a list of illustrations.

Abstract or Executive Summary

When a proposal contains six or more pages, prepare an abstract or executive summary. An abstract is a brief summary of the entire proposal, and an executive summary is a longer, more thorough overview especially helpful when the proposal itself is long. Abstracts or executive summaries

---

Illustrations

	Page
Schedule of Work	4
Organizational Chart	52
Support Services	56
Evaluation Schedule	68
Costs	80

v

Figure 9-8. Sample List of Illustrations.

are also prepared after the proposal is complete. Their purpose is to provide the reader with a condensed version of the proposal. Busy executives may not have the time or the technical expertise to read the entire proposal, especially if it is highly technical and lengthy. If the summary shows promise, then those individuals with the appropriate technical expertise will evaluate the entire proposal and make recommendations to management.

An abstract or executive summary should be short, approximately 10 percent the length of the entire document. Regardless of the length of a proposal, however, an abstract should be no longer than one complete page, and an executive summary should not exceed five pages. When an RFP imposes a length limit on the abstract, for example 250 or 500 words, you need to abide by those limitations. Other requests for proposal may provide a certain number of lines or a ruled box in which to provide a summary. When that is the case, be sure that you do not exceed the allotted space. Some RFPs may want a short abstract as part of an informational cover sheet accompanying a lengthy proposal. In that case, you may need to provide both the abstract and a more detailed executive summary.

An executive summary is the proposal in miniature; it identifies and explains the problem, purpose, proposed plan or procedures, staffing and personnel, costs, evaluation criteria, and the proposed solution. Executive summaries may contain headings and graphic aids.

Although abstracts and executive summaries are generally prepared last, neither should be done as an afterthought. The abstract or executive summary is an essential element of the proposal because it will be one of the first sections looked for and read by everyone. If it does what it is supposed to do— persuade the reader to consider the entire proposal— your proposal will have made it past the first hurdle. If the abstract or executive summary does not provide the essential elements, the reader may ignore the rest of the proposal. Figure 9-9 illustrates an abstract.

Conformance Checklist

Another essential element of the front matter is the "conformance checklist" or matrix of proposal requirements. The conformance checklist lists all the customer requirements to which you must respond. A matrix lists similar information in table format. The purpose of the checklist or matrix is to permit the client to observe at a glance that you have met or exceeded all the requirements stated in the RFP. Many RFPs will provide a checklist or matrix for you to complete, and others will simply request that you provide them. Even when one is not requested in the RFP, including one is frequently a good idea as long as you don't allow the checklist to subordinate material that was specifically requested. See Chapter 4 and Appendix B for more information about conformance checklists.

Abstract

Newhouse, Grove, and Associates is well-qualified to complete the needs assessment and feasibility study outlined in RFP 14598ACS, "Computer-based Remote Learning."

Based on our extensive previous experience in designing and implementing computer-based educational delivery systems, we recommend a three-phase survey, including mail questionnaires, telephone interviews, and focus groups to assess the needs of your potential client base. The questionnaires would be sent to a random sampling of 1,000 households and 100 businesses within a 100-mile radius of Central City. We would conduct follow-up telephone calls from 10 percent of the responders and 10 percent of the nonresponders, and we would select 10 focus groups of 10 individuals each based on the results of the telephone interviews.

While those surveys are being completed, we would evaluate your current equipment, software, and personnel so that we would be able to determine whether your existing equipment and software will be sufficient to meet the needs of your potential clients and whether your personnel will be able to design and maintain any additional hardware and software that might be required.

The questionnaires would be developed by a joint committee of senior faculty and key administrators from Midwestern University, which would be headed by Karla Grove, who has a Ph.D. in statistics from Stanford University and over 25 years' experience in designing and conducting field research. Our key research assistants would conduct the telephone interviews and focus groups.

With a contract date of 1 August, as was specified in the RFP, we would be ready to begin the process of questionnaire design by 1 September and would be available to meet with the appointed committee members on a weekly basis throughout your fall semester. The questionnaires would be ready for distribution no later than 15 November. Telephone interviews would begin in January, and the focus groups would begin meeting in March. Complete documentation would be provided at the completion of each phase of the needs assessment process. We would complete our evaluation of your computer center by mid-April and submit our final report by 1 June 19xx.

We have recently completed similar studies for Western University, in Surf's Edge, Oregon, and Eastern University, in Clam Cove, Maine. Based on those studies, we anticipate that your study can be completed for under $200,000, of which our fee for organizing the study, developing and administering the survey instruments, documenting the results, and preparing a comprehensive recommendation report, will be $94,500. Our fee is based on a materials cost of $6,500, $10,000 for required travel, and $78,000 for professional services.

The remainder of the costs will be partially within your control and will include such items as printing, postage, telephone, reimbursement for the participants in the focus groups, computer time, and office space and secretarial assistance for Dr. Grove and three research assistants.

vi

Figure 9-9. Sample Abstract.

BODY

The body of the proposal provides the details that support and clarify the general statements and claims presented in the preliminary sections. The body covers the following topics, although the names and order may not always be the same as those we show here.

1. Introduction (Overview).
2. Technical Section (Technical Proposal, Problem Statement, Discussion, Proposed Project, Methodology and Objectives).
3. Project Management (Administration, Work Plan).
4. Evaluation.

5. Costs (Cost Proposal, Budget).
6. Qualifications (Personnel, Previous Experience).

Introduction

The introduction follows the front matter and is the beginning of the body of the proposal proper. Unless the RFP specifically requests it, the introduction follows the title of the proposal and, unless the proposal is especially long, does not require a separate heading. Like the abstract or executive summary, the introduction should be approximately 10 percent the length of the entire report. It needs to be long enough to (1) demonstrate an understanding of the problem, (2) introduce yourself and your organization, and (3) establish yourself as an important contender for the contract. In a multivolume proposal, the introduction may require the entire first volume.

The introduction actually covers the same basic elements that the reader will have already encountered in the letter or memo of transmittal and the abstract or executive summary. The reader will also soon be seeing these elements in greater detail in subsequent sections of the proposal, so you should watch for and avoid excessive repetition. The language used in each of these sections should be similar but not identical, with each section adding detail and perspective not present in the previous section. The overview provided in the transmittal should be extremely brief; that in the abstract or executive summary should focus on the major concepts in summary form. The introduction should concentrate on introducing the reader to the rest of the proposal, as it establishes the context by which the reader will interpret and evaluate the entire proposal.

The introduction should also play an important role in the persuasive process by catching the reader's attention. What makes your proposal different from (superior to) the others the reader will receive? Be sure to include something that makes your offer special:

An innovative approach to solving the problem.
Special insight or knowledge.
Special background or qualifications.
Superior facilities or resources.
Superior technical skill.

A good introduction compels the reader to continue to read the more technical components of the proposal. The introduction typically contains the following elements: statement of the problem, the recommended solution, the scope of services, and the principal qualifications of the writer or writer's organization to undertake the project.

Statement of the Problem

Everything flows from the problem statement; it's the foundation and starting point of the proposal. The statement of the problem defines or describes the problem, identifies a task to be accomplished, or presents a need. When writing an unsolicited proposal, you will need to explain what the problem is and its significance. Your first task is to convince the reader that a problem exists. Then, show your reader or client that you understand the problem by presenting its background or history. Indicate that you have a complete understanding of the problem by providing answers to such questions as "When and how did the problem occur?" "What circumstances brought it about?" "Who is affected by the problem?" You can also indicate what the outcome is likely to be if the problem is not solved as compared with the probable results of following your proposed course of action. A review of related literature may be helpful in showing how others may have solved similar problems and the results they achieved.

When responding to a request for a proposal, you may find that the problem is well-defined in the RFP, in which case you need to assure your client that you have a thorough understanding of that problem. The language used here is critical. Echo the *value* words used in the RFP (see Chapter 2), but do not simply copy or paraphrase the problem description in the RFP. Copying or paraphrasing does not demonstrate understanding. You need to show the reader that you understand the problem by providing an accurate analysis. What is the *core* of the problem that must be addressed for the other elements to fall into place? Identify that central issue, and show how the other problems are subordinate to it.

In some cases, a client will know that a problem exists but needs help in defining it. For example, a client may solicit proposals to help his or her organization "improve employee morale." Before proposing a solution, you would need to discover why the client believed that morale needed improving, how he or she was measuring morale, and how he or she would measure an improvement in morale. A phone call or preproposal letter of inquiry may provide you with the information you need to persuade the client that you understand and can solve the problem.

Recommended Solution

In the recommended solution section of the introduction, tell your client what you will do, *not* what you would *like* to do. Focus on the ways in which your solution is unique or superior. Emphasize the principal benefits of your proposed solution: cost, quality, speed of completion, convenience, or whatever advantage you have over your competitors. Show your reader that you have thought the problem out, considered several alternatives, and have the best solution for solving the problem. The introduction should contain the highlights only, as the technical section will include the specific details.

Scope of Services

In addition to the statement of the problem, the introduction contains an overview of what will be covered—*the scope*—and what will not be covered—*the limits* of what you are proposing. Your introduction should include the most important elements of the services you propose so that the reader can see that you understand and have covered the essentials. Amplify material already presented in the abstract or executive summary, focusing on the *what* rather than on the *how*, which will be addressed in the technical section of the proposal.

Note that the limits of what you are proposing should not be confused with *limitations*. Limitations are factors beyond your control that might prevent you from conducting research in the way you had planned. If you were submitting a request for continuation on an approved proposal to conduct research on a new drought-resistant strain of corn, for example, and the location where you were conducting the study had an unusually wet spring and summer, your data might not provide the evidence of success required. In such a case, the weather would constitute a limitation that you would need to overcome before your research could be considered complete.

Principal Qualifications

The introduction should also state your organization's major qualifications for undertaking the proposed project. The information about your background and experience in dealing with the kind of problem in question will vary depending on the formality of the proposal, how well your reader knows you, and whether the proposal is solicited or unsolicited. Because this material will be covered in greater detail later, focus on the one or two qualifications that best demonstrate your competence to perform the proposed work.

Technical Section

The technical section is sometimes referred to as the *problem statement, discussion section,* or *objectives and methodology.* When this section is submitted separately, it is typically called the *technical proposal* (as opposed to the *managerial proposal* or the *cost proposal,* which perform the same functions as their respective sections). In most cases, the technical section is the most important part—the heart—of the proposal. It tells how, when, and sometimes why, the work will be performed. The technical proposal provides specific evidence that the proposal writer clearly understands the client's problem and is responsive to his or her needs. This section provides the client with a statement of the problem and the scope of work required to solve it.

Problem Statement

Depending on the nature of the problem and the completeness with which it was described in the introduction, this component of the technical section may be omitted or abbreviated to avoid redundancy. When the technical section is submitted separately, it will, of course, need to contain a complete analysis of the problem. Complex problems may require that the main problem be divided into its component parts, with each part receiving separate attention in the technical section.

The purpose of the problem statement in the technical section also differs from the purpose of the problem statement in the introduction. In the introduction, the purpose of the problem statement is to show the reader that you understand the problem. The statement of the problem in the technical section is primarily to demonstrate your understanding of the procedures required to solve it. What kinds of drawings will be required? What specifications need to be met? To whom will you need to submit what report when? Show your reader that you understand the relationship between the problem and the work required to solve it.

Scope of Work

The scope of work section of the technical proposal details the procedure for solving the problem. It is the plan of action. It defines what work will be done, and what work will not be done. This is an important section of the proposal because it is essentially a contract or promise, and you will typically be held accountable for what you have promised. If you say that you will base your data on a survey of a thousand people, you will need to ensure that you actually survey a thousand—any fewer would constitute a violation of your contract with the reader.

When providing the scope of your services, you may need to clarify the limits of your services to explicitly exclude products or services that you do not wish to provide as part of the proposal. If you are bidding on supplying computer support services, for example, will those services cover the organization's mainframe computer system, its workstations, and its microcomputers, or do you intend to provide service for the workstations only? If you base your proposal on the 100 workstations you know about without considering the client's other computers, you may inadvertently word your proposal in a way that seems to include the client's mainframe and microcomputers as well. Be explicit about the limits of your services whenever the scope of what you are proposing may be subject to interpretation and assumptions on the part of the reader.

In the scope of work section, you may also discuss alternatives to the recommended plan and clarify the reasons they were rejected. Some procedures may be too costly or have insufficient quality to meet the client's long-term objectives. This section may also include acceptable alternatives for achieving the same objective. A client may desire a technical training program, for example, and the information may require two days of training. Those two days can, of course, be divided a number of ways: two full, consecutive days; one day one week, the second day a week later; four half-days; 8 two-hour training sessions; or 16 one-hour sessions. What format would be the most effective from an educational standpoint? What format would be most convenient for the client? Which format would be the most economical? How would the different formats affect your fees? Make the reader's options clear.

Project Management

The project management section of the proposal details *how* you are going to accomplish the work specified in the technical section. Readers typically want to know all the details about the actual completion of the project. In almost all cases, comprehensive plans are more persuasive than sketchy overviews. This is particularly true when the project is complex and will require a substantial financial investment. The project management section typically includes a description of the work, a schedule of when the work will be accomplished, and an organizational chart showing the project management structure and indicating who will be responsible for which task.

Description of Work

The scope of work is the plan of action, and the description of work is the blueprint for that action. The description section provides the details of how and when the plan will be put into action. The client wants to know what methods will be used to solve the problem. In most cases, the only way to convey this is by providing a comprehensive, chronological, step-by-step description of the work to be performed. This section may also list materials, supplies, or parts that will be required or supplied, or refer to an appendix containing such lists.

Part of this section will be devoted to the specifications for the work requirements, which are given in most RFPs. The specifications may include certain qualifications and product performance standards. The specifications may also stipulate procedures for designing, manufacturing, or assembling a product. When proposal writers are not able to meet those work requirements, they need to provide explanations and make arrangements for waivers or compromises. Not being able to meet the stated requirements is not always a weakness; it can be a strength. In providing an explanation of why a requirement cannot be met, a proposal writer may alert the client to a possible difficulty—something that the client may not have thought of. For example, after preliminary testing, the proposal writer might determine that the specifications given by the client cannot be met.

The writer explains the testing results and requests permission to change the specifications. He or she would gain credibility by having detected the error or flaw.

This section typically includes graphic aids to help explain and illustrate materials and methods that will be used in solving the client's problem. Graphic aids are covered in Chapter 7.

Schedule for Work

To accomplish the work on time, the proposal writer develops a time schedule that will ensure meeting the client's deadline. When no deadline is specified in the proposal, the writer may develop the schedule in conjunction with the client. The purpose of the detailed time schedule is to specify all the required steps and to provide the start and end dates for each of these steps. Depending on the nature of the proposal, some elements to be considered in developing the work schedule are (1) system analysis and engineering; (2) design; (3) logistics and procurement of materials; (4) manufacturing; (5) assembly; (6) development, acceptance, and field testing; (8) evaluating; (9) transportation; (10) training; and (11) operation. Each of these elements could have subcategories.

Two techniques used to develop a graphic time schedule are the Gantt chart and the program evaluation and review techniques (PERT) chart. Many requests for proposals stipulate that the proposal writer submit one or both of these charts, which are explained and illustrated in Chapter 7. Whether you use a Gantt chart, PERT chart, or both, in developing time schedules be sure to allow for unexpected delays and to develop and explain contingency plans for meeting the client's deadlines in spite of unavoidable delays.

Responsibilities for Work

Once the schedule of work has been prepared, the proposal writer needs to identify the personnel who will be responsible for that work. An organizational chart showing the relationships among those who will do the work (rather than the company's organizational chart) may help identify the functions and work responsibilities of each member of the team. Each member of the team should also receive a copy of this chart and any other lists of responsibilities (such as the Gantt or PERT charts) so that everyone can see at a glance who is responsible for which tasks and the deadlines for each. The organizational chart for the project is important to the client because it shows who is responsible for the overall success of the project and who will be reporting to whom. The client can see who will be supervising which tasks and can evaluate each person's background and expertise for his or her area of responsibility.

Project Organization

The project organization section of the proposal typically presents an introduction to and an overview of the company, its personnel, its resources, and its facilities. It shows how the project fits into the overall structure and purpose of the writer's organization. As with the other sections of the proposal, the size, format, and contents of the project organizational section will depend on the guidelines given in the RFP and materials presented elsewhere in the proposal.

The function of the project organization section is to describe how your organization will manage the project. It shows that the organization has both the personnel qualified to do the work and the required resources and facilities. It may also provide evidence that the organization has experience in conducting similar research or completing similar projects. Clients typically want to know such things as how organizational resources can be allocated to ensure that the project receives the required attention and who will be responsible for ensuring that critical objectives are met.

This section may also discuss the way in which project-related information will be managed. Who will be in charge of documentation? What informational services will be provided? How and when will they be provided? Will computers and fax machines be required and available? Additional areas that the proposal writer may need to address are such things as administrative duties, staffing, conflicts and disagreements among workers or between managers, office support, utilities, equipment, supplies, procurement, manufacturing, packaging, inventory, transportation, repair and maintenance, evaluation, and safety.

Evaluation

The evaluation section of the proposal is designed to show the client that you understand the need for establishing and meeting standards and objectives. At what points in the project development will you monitor your progress? Will you provide the client with an appropriate procedure for ensuring that standards and performance objectives continue once the project is complete?

Complex projects typically require regular monitoring of the budget to show any discrepancies between the proposed budget and actual expenditures. The type and extent of ongoing evaluations will vary widely from project to project, but almost all proposals should include an awareness of the need to set specific objectives and to monitor progress toward those objectives on a regular basis. If the client desires an "effective" training program, for example, how will you measure effectiveness? How will you know when you are meeting that objective? You may need to test for effectiveness at several stages and modify the training program based on the feedback you receive from participants.

Costs

A budget or other statement of costs is typically included in a proposal. Because some organizations, especially government agencies, may want evaluators to make their recommendations based on the technical proposal, without being influenced by the cost, the budget may be submitted as a separate cost proposal. The cost section or cost proposal spells out the costs for the client. Like other sections of the proposal, the cost proposal will vary in size, scope, and format based on the complexity of the project or the products or services required. Cost proposals can be short, giving brief explanations on how the writer arrived at the cost figures, or they can be long and detailed, depending on the amount of justification required to support certain charges.

Depending on the nature of the proposal and the stipulations of the RFP, the proposal itself may contain only an overview of the budget, showing major expenses and total costs, with the details being relegated to an appendix. In a multivolume proposal, one volume may contain only the cost proposal. Regardless of its length and complexity, budget information needs to be formatted for readability. When the information is complex, use summary sheets to clarify totals and subtotals for the itemized entries. Cost information should be presented so that every reader, regardless of his or her degree of interest in that aspect of the proposal, can find as much information as he or she desires.

Itemize all costs, both direct and indirect. Direct costs are those associated directly with the project: labor, equipment, supplies, travel, telephone calls, printing, postage, and any other tangibles for which you can keep separate and complete accounting. Indirect costs are those you cannot associate specifically with the client's project but without which you could not remain in business: facilities, lighting, heating, air conditioning, employee fringe benefits, taxes, insurance, telephone service, office furniture and equipment, and other such administrative costs. When actual figures are unavailable, provide estimates. When figures are estimated, the proposal writer needs to be able to predict costs not knowing what future economic conditions will be. If the proposal writer overestimates costs, he or she may lose the contract to someone who submits a lower bid. If the figures are underestimated, the proposal writer can not only lose the profit but also incur liabilities. In estimating costs, the proposal writer or the person on the team with responsibilities for the budget must consider the problem or product in detail. Resources required to accomplish the tasks or activities need to be estimated.

Although costs will vary depending on the problem being solved or the product being produced, common costs might include equipment (office equipment, machinery, cars, trucks), labor, salaries, operating expenses (office supplies, mail, telephone and fax use, photocopying or printing), overhead (heat, electricity, water, waste disposal, rent, insurance) fringe benefits, materials, taxes (city, state, federal), safety and security, patents and copyrights, travel, transportation, computer time, computer software and hardware, testing, office support, consultants, administrative expenses, and finally the fee or profit.

Proposal readers and evaluators will want to know not only the bottom-line price but also how that price was derived. What will be the purchasing procedure for supplies, equipment, and other resources? Will the organization issue competitive bids for tasks or activities or jobs or equipment that it was not able to perform or produce itself? Be prepared to give a detailed accounting of how you arrived at figures and the ways in which you will control or minimize costs.

When all other factors are judged equally attractive, cost may be the deciding factor in awarding contracts or funds, so the proposal writer or appropriate member of the writing team should take time to prepare the cost estimates carefully, justifying the cost of each item. Finally, the proposal writer may wish to include the time frame in which the quotes are valid and also the terms and conditions of payment. Construction costs, for example, tend to fluctuate with the costs of materials and with interest rates, and for this reason, bids are typically valid for a limited period only.

Qualifications

The qualifications section of the proposal is concerned with two kinds of qualifications: those of the organization and those of the individuals who will be responsible for the client's project.

This section typically begins with an overview of the company and a summary of its history of success with similar projects. To show the organization of the company, submit an organizational chart showing the corporate structure and lines of authority. Your client will want to know how the project fits within the structure of your organization. Who will manage the project? To whom will that person report? When appropriate, also note in this section of the proposal that the company is in compliance with Equal Employment Opportunity Commission, Civil Rights Act, Affirmative Action, Occupational Safety and Health Administration, and Environmental Protection Agency requirements, and if conducting research using human subjects, that you will comply with the Department of Health and Human Services regulations for the Protection of Human Research Subjects.

Experiences and Past Performances

In some ways, the background, qualifications, competence, and experiences of the organization are more important than the qualifications of the individuals who will manage the project. An organization with a number of successful projects over the past several years can provide the kind of structure that will assist inexperienced managers at completing complex projects. The credibility of the organization and its reputation for quality and reliability are critical deciding factors.

The experiences and past performances section of the proposal identifies similar or identical projects that the organization has successfully completed. For example, an organization submitting a proposal to construct a manufacturing plant should describe other manufacturing plants it has constructed. When an organization has not had the specific experience called for in the request for proposal, then the proposal writer can discuss how the organization completed similar projects. Be careful not to talk about experiences that are irrelevant to the project. Other topics that may provide the reader with information about the organization would be financial status, growth rate, labor relations, and minority or small business record.

This section is written persuasively, stating that the organization has the facilities, equipment, and resources to complete the project. To be more persuasive, the proposal writer should prepare lists of the facilities, equipment, and resources, and demonstrate how these items will aid in the completion of the work. If the organization has won awards or received citations for outstanding performances or excellent workmanship, then these achievements would be noted here. Letters, certifications, and endorsements from recognized authorities or previous customers are excellent validations of the organization's capabilities. An organizational experience matrix, as illustrated in Figure 9-10, is an effective way to illustrate an organization's previous experience with the areas of expertise required by the proposed project.

Previous Clients	Required Areas of Expertise						
Client 1	Skill 1	Skill 2	Skill 3	Skill 4	Skill 5	Skill 6	Skill 7
Client 2	X		X	X	X	X	
Client 3	X	X	X		X	X	X
Client 4	X	X	X	X	X	X	X
Client 5		X	X	X	X		X
Client 6		X	X		X	X	X
Client 7	X	X	X		X	X	X
Client 8	X	X	X	X	X	X	X
Client 9			X	X	X	X	X

Figure 9-10. Sample Experience Matrix.

Personnel

The personnel section contains the names of all individuals who will be working on the project. It includes (1) the credentials, such as educational background and technical, professional, and managerial qualifications, experience, and accomplishments of key personnel ; (2) the qualifications of the support staff; (3) the relationships among and project responsibilities of individuals; and (4) direct and indirect reporting procedures for all personnel.

Unless complete vitas are requested, one-page resumes of key personnel, such as the project sponsor, project leader, project manager, principal investigator, and division managers, are provided in this section. Brief resumes of office and staff personnel, part-time specialty workers, outside consultants, or subcontractors may be included in an appendix. When names of some individuals, such as consultants or subcontractors, are not known at the time of preparing the proposal or when resumes are not available for those individuals, you can prepare a job description with appropriate qualifications or skills for those positions and include it in the personnel section of the proposal.

SUPPLEMENTAL PARTS

The supplemental parts are literally *supplemental*. Information is supplemental when it amplifies or supports the proposal, is not central to the development of your main idea, and may be of interest to those readers who want more detailed information about a particular aspect of the proposal. Nothing important should be put into a supplemental part as many readers do not bother reading the supporting materials. The most common supplemental parts are appendixes, a bibliography, and an index.

Appendix

Most supplemental information belongs in an appendix. Readers with technical backgrounds, for example, will appreciate seeing the technical details of your proposal that would bore many other readers. The appendixes can also contain complete resumes of key personnel, supplemental graphic aids, summary questionnaires, formulas, a glossary of terms, sample forms, statistical computations, computer printouts, cost itemizations, and any other items not essential for the body of the proposal.

Bibliography

When your research has included a search of secondary sources, provide a bibliography. Scientific proposals, for example, often need to demonstrate familiarity with the body of research that has led to the proposed project, and business and engineering proposals may need to show that certain solutions to problems have been used successfully in similar circumstances previously. See Chapter 12 for more information on documentation and bibliographic form.

Index

Long proposals may require a separate index of key terms. Where in the proposal can a person find all the references to a specific product or procedure? The index is typically prepared after the proposal is complete, and indexing software (or the indexing function of word processing software) may help. If indexing software is not available, you can use a spreadsheet or database. Identify the key terms and names a user might wish to locate along with their page references, entering terms in one column or field and the page references in an adjacent column. When complete, sort the terms alphabetically and export the file to a word processor for formatting.

BINDING

Long proposals are almost always bound. Common bindings include plastic comb, wire or plastic spiral binding, and three-ring binder. Although most proposals are submitted on 8½ x 11 inch paper and bound at the side, some proposals are bound at the top. Side binding requires extra gutter margin (see Chapter 8), and top binding requires additional top margin. Allow for these margins in all drafts of the report.

Most RFPs for complex projects will anticipate the need for binding and specify a particular form and number of copies. Remember that the appearance of the binding influences the reader's perception of the entire proposal, so the binder is not a good place to economize. A research proposal on which you and your organization have spent dozens—or perhaps hundreds—of hours does not belong in a cheap-looking binder. Whatever form of binding you select, use materials that convey the image you wish your organization to have. Binding doesn't have to be expensive to convey quality. Plastic comb binding can be used effectively as long as the covers are of high grade card stock; three-ring binders don't need to be leather to convey integrity and substance.

If your proposal is bound in more than one volume, consider color coding the volumes for easy identification. If multiple copies are required, ensure that the same color coding is used consistently for all copies.

KEY POINTS FROM CHAPTER 9

The key points from Chapter 9 are the following:

1. Proposals have a variety of formats and components, depending on their length, degree of formality, and expectations established with a particular industry.
2. The front matter for a proposal may include one or more of the following components: the cover, title page, letter of transmittal, table of contents, list of illustrations, abstract or executive summary, and conformance checklists.
3. The body of the proposal may include one or more of the following components: introduction, technical section, project management evaluation, costs, qualifications.
4. The supplemental parts of a proposal may include one or more of the following components: the appendixes, bibliography, and index.
5. Long proposals are typically bound. The common types of binders are plastic comb, wire or plastic spiral, and three-ring.

CHAPTER 10

Proposal Evaluations

Proposals are evaluated at least twice: once by the proposal writer and once by the client. The internal evaluation by the proposal writer or writing team and perhaps by other members of the submitting organization includes checks for content, organization, format, and appearance. The external evaluation is concerned primarily with whether the proposal fulfills all the requirements of the RFP. The external areas of analysis typically include the analysis of the problem, approach or methodology, project management and organization, costs, and qualifications and experience of personnel. The proposal planning and evaluation checklists presented in Appendix B can help with evaluation as well as with planning.

PROPOSAL WRITER

Many RFPs provide a detailed evaluation form that lists the major criteria with subdivisions for each and provides a scale of values for each of the criteria by which the proposals will be evaluated. Knowing how the client is going to evaluate the proposal and knowing the assigned weight, points, or minimum-maximum point range for each of the criteria will help you with both the preparation of the proposal and its evaluation. If most of the items are worth 10 points, while one item is worth 30, you would know that the 30-point item requires close attention and thorough coverage. Figures 10-1 and 10-2 illustrate sample criteria and point values.

Some RFPs merely state a few criteria for how the proposal will be judged and do not provide point values. For example, a request for proposal might say that the proposal will be evaluated on the analysis of the problem, the organizational plan, and the qualifications of personnel. Not all RFPs, however, provide criteria for evaluation. When the RFP does not state the evaluation procedures and does not require an evaluation section, the proposal writer may choose to include an evaluation section in the proposal to show that the project has achieved its goals and objectives as stated in the request for proposal.

Evaluation Criteria	Points
Analysis of Problem	25
Approach	10
Credibility	10
Project Organization	10
Costs	20
Qualifications of Personnel	25
Total	**100**

Figure 10-1. List of Criteria and Points.

Evaluation Criteria	Points
Statement of the Problem	
Objectives and Goals	10
Scope and Limitations	5
Completeness	10
Methodology	
Practicality	5
Probability of success	5
Credibility	10
Project Organization	10
Costs	20
Qualifications of Personnel	
Education, experience, accomplishments	25
Total	100

Figure 10-2. List of Detailed Criteria and Points.

RFP Requirements

The first and most important thing to check is, of course, conformance to the RFP. The conformance checklist discussed in Chapter 4 will be your principal tool for ensuring compliance. Although the proposal will be the central means by which the clients will award the contract, they may obtain additional information from other sources, such as on-site visits, calls to references, or additional written or oral presentations. Check the RFP carefully for explicit or implied statements about the procedures that will be used in evaluating the proposal. If none are present in the RFP, call the contact person listed on the RFP to see whether criteria are available separately.

Content

To evaluate the content of the proposal, you may wish to enlist the aid of content specialists who were not members of the proposal team. If you are proposing a new construction, for example, you might wish to have the engineering calculations developed by the engineers on your team checked by other engineers. Other technical, financial, and legal considerations may benefit from outside review as well. Because it is easy to overlook one's own errors in spelling, grammar, and mechanics, it is often advisable to have an outside proofreader check for errors of that variety. Are the headings and all lists, for example, parallel grammatically? Also, all figures and mathematical calculations should be checked to ensure their accuracy. A misplaced decimal point in one figure, for example, could make a big difference in the estimated cost of the project. By all means, take advantage of the resources available to you, and be sure to include time for a thorough evaluation of the proposal in your schedule.

Organization

While you are completing your internal evaluation, check the organization of the proposal against the requirements of the RFP. Check also to ensure that individual paragraphs are clear and that the transitions from idea to idea are clear and logical. Have you provided sufficient support for your claims? Do the conclusions flow logically out of the data presented, and are the recommendations based logically on the conclusions?

Your internal evaluation of the organization of the proposal will best be performed by someone who was not part of the development team. You and the other members of the team are, after all, already comfortable with the way in which you have organized the materials, and at this point you need to ensure that an outside reader will be comfortable with it as well. If possible, have two or three members of your organization who were not members of the proposal writing team read the completed document. Their reviews and suggestions will be especially helpful if their backgrounds and interests are similar to those of the people who will be reviewing the proposal for the client organization.

Format and Appearance

Because the appearance of the final document will play an important psychological role in the way the audience views it, the format and appearance also deserve special attention as part of your internal evaluation. Is the overall design appropriate for the purpose of and audience for the proposal? Have headings been used appropriately and consistently? Are the graphic aids correct and placed for greatest effectiveness? Are the typefaces appropriate for their function? (See Chapter 8.)

CLIENT

After receiving the proposal, the client or a designated team of evaluators will check to see that the proposal demonstrates a thorough understanding of the problem, an appropriate approach to solving the problem, and evidence of credibility. The evaluators will compare the overall project-management plan, costs, and the qualifications of personnel with those presented in other proposals.

For complex projects requiring lengthy and complex proposals, the client will typically employ an evaluation team. Each member of the team will have a specific area of responsibility—technical, managerial, cost, and so on—and will probably not read the entire proposal. Those responsible for reading the technical sections of the proposals, for example, will develop a specific evaluation sheet to allow for an objective assessment of that section. The scores of each evaluator will be averaged, and then the average scores for each section will be weighted. The proposal with the best overall score may be selected, or a limited number of proposals with the best scores will be reevaluated, and perhaps the organizations submitting the best proposals will be invited to present their ideas in person.

Analysis of the Problem

Typically two of the most important criteria for evaluation will be your analysis of the problem and approach to solving it. The evaluators will consider whether your understanding seems complete and realistic. What needs to be done? How long will it take? What materials and equipment will be needed? Will consultants with special expertise be needed, or will subcontractors be hired for some of the tasks? The clients will want to see whether you have under- or overestimated the complexity of the problem. They will feel most comfortable if your view of the problem matches theirs, and if you suspect that it does not, you will need to provide additional support for your perspective.

Credibility

Unless the clients have done business with you before, one of their chief concerns will be with your credibility. The client wants to be assured that those who are awarded the contract will do what they have promised and that the proposed solution to the problem will actually work. Will scheduled commitments be met in a timely and efficient manner? Will the products or services you are supplying meet or exceed the expectation of quality created by the proposal?

In the absence of direct previous experience with the client organization, your record of success with similar projects completed for other companies is the best indicator of your credibility. The logic of your analysis of the problem and approach to solving it and the established expertise of those who will be performing the work will also add to your credibility and increase the client's confidence in your organization's ability to satisfy the components of the contract.

Project Management

In the project management section, the client looks to see how well the proposal writer has anticipated and planned for the overall management of the project. Answers to the five Ws will help the client evaluate the organization of the project. *What* work will be performed? *Who* will be doing the work? *When* will the work be accomplished? *Where* will the work be performed? *How* will the work be performed? Detailed Gantt and PERT charts help the client see whether your plan seems adequate.

Costs

Selecting the best proposal—the one that best meets the needs of the client—is not an easy decision, especially when it involves costs. Although costs are typically not the principal factor in determining which proposal receives the contract, they are certainly important. If your costs are considerably higher than those submitted by others, you will need to be especially careful to explain the additional charges and the need for them.

If, on the other hand, your costs are considerably lower than those in the other proposals, you may well need to explain how you can perform the same quality work as others in your industry for a lower cost.

In evaluating your proposed budget, the evaluators will consider both your direct and indirect costs. Clients will want to know whether the direct and indirect costs for which you intend to bill their organization are legitimate and fair. Recently, for example, several major universities were charged with excessive and unethical billing of the government for indirect costs associated with a number of research projects. As a result, many funding organizations are paying much closer attention to evaluating proposed budgets and cost overruns. Ensure that all charges are clear and that they have been adequately explained or justified.

Qualifications

As mentioned in Chapter 9, clients will be concerned with the background and experience of the organization as a whole and with the individual qualifications of those responsible for the proposed project. Conformance checklists and experience matrices are the best ways of illustrating the organization's ability to meet the client's requirements.

Clients will also want to see the resumes of key personnel to help them determine whether the people are qualified and capable of doing the work. RFPs typically state whether resumes should be attached and whether there is a length restriction. In the absence of specific directions, a one-page summary sheet of each team member's major accomplishments should suffice for most proposals. Longer proposals for complex projects, especially when scientific research is a major component of the project, may require complete vitas of the principal investigator and other key members of the project team.

In some circumstances, you may also need to indicate that you have made appropriate contingency plans in the event that key personnel are not able to perform their duties. When the work is hazardous or otherwise presents circumstances that might interfere with individuals being able to complete their assignments, the RFP will typically request explicit contingency plans in the case of problems with either equipment or personnel. While equipment can usually be replaced with something similar if not identical, you may need to make special allowances when the backgrounds and skills of members of your substitute team don't match those of your primary project team.

REASONS FOR REJECTION

Although proposals are submitted to an extremely wide variety of companies and governmental agencies, and although the reasons for acceptance also vary widely, the reasons proposals are rejected are comparatively few. The following reasons are the most often cited:

1. The proposer did not demonstrate a clear understanding of the problem.
2. The proposal did not arrive by the submission deadline.
3. The information requested in the RFP was not provided.
4. The objectives were not well-defined.
5. The wrong audience was addressed.
6. The procedures and methodology were not specific.
7. The overall design was questionable.
8. The proposal lacked evidence of intent to meet all terms and conditions specified in the RFP.
9. Cost estimates were not realistic—either too high or too low.
10. Resumes of key personnel were inadequate.
11. Personnel lacked experience or the required qualifications.
12. The proposal was poorly written and not well-organized. Writing was not clear or concise. The proposal rambled.
13. The proposal did not follow the organizational pattern specified in the RFP.
14. The completed proposal was not attractive.
15. The proposal did not provide adequate assurance that completion deadlines would be met.
16. Essential data were not included in the proposal.
17. The proposed facilities were inadequate.
18. The proposal failed to show that essential equipment and facilities were available.
19. The proposed time schedule was unrealistic.
20. The proposal failed to include the qualifications of the submitting organization.

The items in this list can, of course, be used as an additional checklist in both the preparation of the proposal and in its final evaluation. By avoiding these common problems, you will already be a step ahead of much of your competition.

KEY POINTS FROM CHAPTER 10

The key points from Chapter 10 are the following:

1. Proposals are evaluated by both the proposal writer and the client.

2. Experts who are not part of the proposal writing team can help the proposal writer evaluate the proposal in critical areas: technical, financial, managerial, legal, and editorial.
3. Specialists can also help with the organization, format, and appearance of the document, paying particular attention to such things as heading use and graphic aids.
4. The proposal writer needs to check the completed document against the original conformance checklist to ensure compliance with the RFP.
5. The client will evaluate the proposal to ensure that the proposal presents a thorough understanding of the problem and that the approach is feasible.
6. The client will evaluate the proposal writer's credibility and that of the submitting organization.
7. The client will evaluate the proposed management plan, the budget, and the qualifications of key personnel to see whether the submitting organization will be able to perform quality work on schedule in a cost-effective way.
8. Proposal writers should be especially careful to avoid the faults that most often result in the rejection of proposals.

CHAPTER 11

Oral Presentations

In addition to preparing a written proposal, you may also need to prepare an oral presentation as part of the proposal process. Readers of the written proposal may desire additional information about the product, service, idea, or solution that was provided—or rightfully not contained—in the written proposal. Readers may also wish to ask questions for clarification of statements made in the proposal or to discuss the ramifications of your recommended approach. Whatever the reason for the oral presentation, you need to be prepared.

When you are requested to make an oral presentation on your written proposal, ask for a list of concerns, issues, or questions that need to be addressed. Ask what issues concern the audience the most—management data, technical data, or budget and costs? Ask not only *who* and *how many* will be in the audience, but also *why* the audience will be attending the presentation. Ask if there will be a time limit on your presentation. Ask, too, where your presentation will be held, and what audiovisual equipment will be available to you. The more you know about your audience's attitude toward your proposal, background, experience, education, and position within the company, and the more you know about the environment in which you will present, the better.

When preparing for an oral presentation, you need to analyze your audience, define your purpose, organize your message, prepare appropriate visual aids, and rehearse your delivery.

ANALYZE YOUR AUDIENCE

Just as you need to consider your audience in writing the proposal (see Chapter 2), you need to know something about the people who will be listening to you. Most members of your audience will be attending your presentation because they genuinely want more information about what you are proposing. They also want to get to know the person behind the proposal. What is the person like? Will we be able to work with this individual? Does he or she exude enthusiasm for the project? Does he or she display confidence and credibility?

While the majority of your listeners will be sincere in attending and asking questions, some may well be skeptical of—or even hostile to—what you are proposing. Does your proposal present a threat to any members of your client's organization? Will your recommended solution eliminate jobs or alter lines of authority? If so, proceed carefully, emphasizing the benefits to the organization as a whole. Some people may attend the presentation so that they can ask questions merely to look good in the eyes of their peers or those of higher rank in the organization. Plan your presentation so that you can remain on track regardless of lack of full cooperation from all members of the audience.

When asked to give an oral presentation in conjunction with your written proposal, consider the audience's size, attitude and interests, and knowledge. Being prepared and knowledgeable will help convince the audience that you are someone with whom they will want to work.

Audience Size

Generally, when making an oral presentation of your proposal, your audience size will be small—ten or fewer people—and the presentation will be fairly informal. You are at an advantage when speaking to a small group because you can relate more easily to each individual than you could to members of a large group. Also, you can more easily keep an audience's attention in a small group. When speaking to a small group, maintain eye contact with the individuals and speak to their concerns. Be prepared to answer their specific questions. Come prepared with facts and figures. Support all your claims with evidence.

No matter what the size of the audience, be sure that each person can hear you. Adapt your message for everyone in the group by explaining all technical terms. Some people in your audience may be your professional colleagues and understand the technical terminology; others may not. Your audience may also include company executives who will decide whether to accept or reject your proposal but who may not have the expertise and technical background that you possess. Their needs, interests, and concerns may differ from those of your professional colleagues. You will need to adjust your vocabulary and the content of your presentation to meet their needs. Such an audience may be more interested in the financial rather than the technical aspects of the document. Be prepared to explain and document all costs.

Because an audience likes to be involved in a presentation, ask questions and encourage audience responses and participation when the group is small. When possible, involve everyone in the audience. Maintain eye contact. Move around the room so that all can see and hear you. When presenting in a small group, you are apt to be informal and personal. Learn the names of the individuals in the group, and use them. People appreciate being called by their names. In a small group, it's best to answer questions when they arise, although you may also wish to allow time at the end of your presentation for specific questions about issues not covered in your presentation.

When the occasion calls for you to speak to a large group of people, you will still follow the guidelines for speaking to a small group, but you have a more difficult task of maintaining eye contact and relating informally to your group. You will want to be more formal with the group, but you still need to be sure that the audience can see and hear you. Because the audience is more likely to be diverse, you will need to provide more examples and illustrations and, unless the group consists entirely of technical specialists, avoid technical jargon and vocabulary as much as possible. Emphasize the principal benefits of accepting your proposal.

Audience Attitude and Interests

The attitude of the audience toward you and your topic can vary in several ways. The audience may be positive and welcome you and your presentation; they may be essentially neutral to you and your presentation; or they may resent and resist you and your presentation. If you have already made it through a screening of the written proposals, you at least know that the evaluators liked your proposal better than most of the others they received. That does not automatically mean, however, that your presentation will be well-received by everyone or that everyone already agrees with your recommendations. You may still encounter differences of opinion and vested interests in one or more alternative courses of action.

When you know that the audience is positive toward you and your subject, use deductive structure and begin by stating your principal recommendation, and then show how and why you arrived at that conclusion or recommendation. When you have reason to suspect that the audience is negative toward you or your subject, it is better to be indirect. When the audience resents or is inclined to resist your proposal, inductive structure, which builds to a conclusion, will be more persuasive. Begin by stating individual facts leading to your principal recommendation, stressing the reasons and benefits of your proposal. Try to learn why individuals are against your ideas. What are their concerns? Why do they seem to be resisting the proposal? Even when you cannot determine why an audience is negative to you or your subject, present your proposal with confidence. Show how and why the proposal should be accepted. Provide all the benefits of what you plan to do and show how it will help solve a problem or provide a needed service.

Convince the audience with examples, illustrations, facts, and figures that what you are proposing will solve the problem. Be positive, stressing what you *will* be doing rather than emphasizing what you *won't* be doing.

Show how cost-effective your proposal is. Just as you overcame objections in the written report, do the same in your oral presentation. When appropriate, be willing to modify your proposal to met those needs expressed during the presentation that were not included in the RFP.

Audience Knowledge

Before the presentation, try to discover what your audience already knows about your proposal and what they need to know. In a written proposal, readers have the opportunity to read slowly or reread complex or technical parts. The audience for an oral presentation, however, may find it difficult to grasp your message as you present complex ideas and topics. To help your audience understand and follow you, use a vocabulary that all will comprehend. Be highly organized. Speak slowly and distinctly. Explain all technical terms. Repeat and emphasize key ideas. Give the audience an opportunity to ask questions.

After you have identified your audience, you can focus on the purpose of your presentation.

DEFINE YOUR PURPOSE

Your purpose is determined by what you want your audience to do after you have made your presentation. Do you want your audience to have more information so that they will be more knowledgeable about your subject, or do you want to persuade your audience to act on, accept, or approve the information you present? The two main purposes of oral presentations delivered as part of the proposal process are to inform and to persuade.

To Inform

If your proposal has essentially been accepted, the purpose of your presentation will be to inform. If you attempt to be too persuasive in such circumstances, you could easily "unsell" your proposal. You will want to reinforce the positive opinion your audience already has without appearing overconfident or pushy. At this point, you are basically demonstrating that you and the other members of your team will be good business partners, and the presentation is performing the same general role as a job interview—the client liked what you presented on paper and now wants to see if you live up to that image in person. Sell yourself more than you sell your proposal. Show the audience that you are the kind of person who will work with members of their organization to achieve the objective.

To Persuade

On the other hand, if the presentation is the final stage of the competitive process, you will need to take advantage of the presentation as an additional opportunity to sell your proposal. In such a case, you are still trying to show that your proposal is somehow superior to the others. Can you add anything to what you presented in the written proposal? If additional research and planning have suggested new benefits and advantages, by all means include them in your presentation. Use standard sales techniques to overcome possible objections the audience might have to certain aspects of your proposal. If you know that your products or services are more expensive than some of the others with which yours are competing, stress their high-quality, long-term value, or the service and support you provide.

Even when the presentation is competitive, one of the central issues will be your desirability as a business partner. Are you reasonable and cooperative? Do you have confidence in your products or services? Do you have integrity? One of the reasons clients sometimes request oral presentations is to develop a feeling for these and related factors that are not easy to determine from the written proposal.

ORGANIZE YOUR MESSAGE

After you have analyzed your audience and defined your purpose, you are ready to organize your message. As you probably learned in a speech class, an oral presentation has three parts: (1) the introduction or opening, (2) the body or middle, and (3) the conclusion or closing. In other words, you state your purpose, provide the information, and then summarize the information for the audience. The cliché of public speaking is essentially true: First, you tell them what you are going to tell them; then you tell them; and then you tell them what you told them.

Remember that information delivered orally is more difficult to understand and follow than that presented in writing, so you need to be more explicit with transitions from point to point and to emphasize key points by repeating them, specifically mentioning their importance, or using an appropriate visual aid.

Opening

In your opening, identify who you are, your affiliations, your experiences, and your qualifications so that you provide credibility for what you are about to present. In your beginning provide the necessary background for your topic and then present the purpose of your presentation. Explain what you will cover and what you will not cover. This is the preview of what is to follow. Your opening attracts the audience's attention and sets the tone for the entire presentation.

The way you begin helps establish your audience's attitude toward you and your presentation. Smile, and do your best to appear relaxed and confident. If you are comfortable and relaxed, you help your audience relax and enjoy your presentation. Avoid exhibiting a negative attitude by criticizing, condemning, and complaining. Regardless of what happens, make the best of it. If the sound system fails, whether it's yours or the client's, don't complain about it. If the overhead projector quits on you, improvise. If your luggage went to Fairbanks, Alaska, and your presentation is in Orlando, Florida, don't criticize the airline. Don't apologize for what you perceive as your own nervousness or lack of experience as a public speaker. Thank the audience for having provided you with the opportunity to present your ideas in person, and do your best.

Middle

The middle portion of your presentation includes the supporting evidence and details for the purpose, main idea, or thesis that you announced in your introduction. This is the heart of your presentation. It is the equivalent of the technical, managerial, cost, and perhaps the evaluation sections of the written proposal.

When possible, progress from simple concepts to the more complex so that your audience can easily follow the presentation. So that you don't lose your audience, use explicit transitional phrases and use appropriate visual aids, examples, demonstrations, definitions, descriptions, statistics, testimonials, quotations, explanations, illustrations, analogies, and whatever else may be necessary to convey your meaning and to convince your audience of the value of your proposal.

Closing

The closing may be the most important part of your presentation. Make it strong. Summarize your major points and ideas. Tell the audience what you told them; it's the review of what you have previewed in your opening. In most cases, you will need to allow time for questions and answers. If your question-and-answer period is extensive, you may wish to offer an additional brief summary, emphasizing points of agreement, following the last question. At the close of the presentation, you should also make clear who is responsible for taking the next step. Will you prepare the contract, or will the client? Do you need to resubmit your proposal according to new agreements following your presentation? What do you want the audience to do after the presentation? Before you leave, make sure that you and the client understand who will be responsible for the next action.

Avoid ending with expressions that imply that you did not deserve the attention of those present or that you have run out of material, such as "That's it, folks," which is both casual and abrupt; or "That's all I have to say." A vague, nonspecific "thank you" as your conclusion suggests that you are amazed that the audience remained attentive for your presentation. If you invite questions and no one has any, you may thank the appropriate individuals for having invited you and express your appreciation for having the opportunity to present your information.

Questions and Answers

As mentioned earlier, when you are speaking to a small group, you will want to encourage the audience to ask questions and make comments throughout your presentation. When speaking to a large group, however, you may want to discourage questions during your presentation because they can be disruptive. Questions about side issues or about topics you will cover later in the presentation tend to distract both the presenter and the audience. If you have too many questions about a particular point, your audience may lose interest in the presentation, and you may lose your continuity of thought. Also, you may not be able to control the time element. Answering questions may not leave you enough time to cover the topics you have prepared to present. For large audiences, it's usually best to save the question-and-answer period until after you have summarized your major points and concluded your presentation.

When an individual in a large group asks a question, others in the audience may not hear it, so it is a good practice to repeat the question before answering it. This also helps to avoid having the same question repeated, because the second questioner may not have heard the question when it was asked the first time. If you are asked the same question twice, try to rephrase your answer or to provide additional detail to help the individual save face. Never offend a member of the audience even though the person may not be fully attentive or otherwise be obnoxious.

When questions from members of your audience are not forthcoming, you might begin the process by saying, "One question that I am frequently asked is" or "You might be interested in knowing more about . . ." Be sure to allow time for the audience to think of questions. When you don't know an answer to a particular question, say so. Offer to obtain the information, and say that you will call the individual with the answer later. Sometimes an individual is too timid to ask a question in front of his or her peers or administrators but will come to you after the presentation and ask questions. Allow time after the question-and-answer period to further discuss your presentation with these individuals.

PREPARE VISUAL AIDS

Visual aids are important in oral presentations because they attract an audience's attention, maintain their interest, clarify important and complex concepts, convince the decision makers, prove points, display data, reinforce what you say, and increase retention. Visual aids are supplements to your presentation; they are not substitutes for it. As you might suspect from the information presented in Chapter 2, most people remember more of what they see than of what they hear. When they receive the same information both orally and visually, using two of the major representational systems, they will understand and retain more. The visual aid serves as an anchor for the information being presented.

Visual aids vary widely. An object of any kind that helps your audience remember can be classified as a visual aid. Select the visual aid that will best present your ideas based on your purpose, audience, equipment, physical arrangements, and time constraints. When preparing visual aids, make certain that they are large enough for the audience to see and simple enough for the audience to grasp. The most common visual aids are transparencies and handouts. Visual aids also include boards, models, and videotapes.

Transparencies

Overhead and slide transparencies are used in the vast majority of professional presentations. Transparencies for an overhead projector are typically easier to produce and faster to produce than are slides for slide projectors. They show text and simple graphics well, and they do so in a well-lit room.

With the right equipment for producing slides, you can use slides to show everything that can be shown with an overhead transparency plus photographs of sites, products, or other complex graphic information not easily transferred to an overhead transparency. The room usually needs to be dimmed for slides to be easily seen, however. Which form of transparency you use depends more on the equipment and time available, as both methods of displaying visual information can be fully professional.

Although overhead transparencies can still be hand drawn or prepared on a typewriter, most transparencies today are prepared on a computer or by graphic design professionals using special equipment. Presentation software and desktop publishing programs have made the preparation of transparencies easier and faster than was preparation by hand or typewriter. The results are also superior, as computer preparation allows for a typesize large enough for everyone to see. Borders, boldface, and color can also be used to help attract the audience's attention.

Present the material horizontally rather than vertically, and display only one idea with plenty of white space in a single visual. Basic design considerations are presented in Chapter 7. Figures 11-1 and 11-2 illustrate variations and provide additional suggestions.

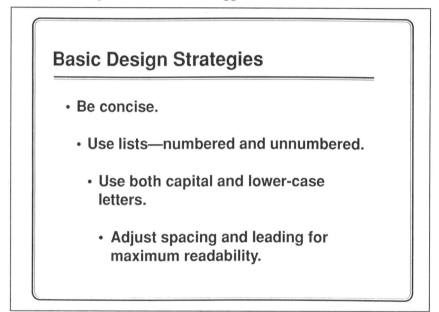

Figure 11-1. Basic Design Strategies for Transparencies.

Handouts

People appreciate receiving handouts. The handout will serve as a reminder of your principal points and provide the audience with something on which they can take additional notes. Deciding whether to distribute handouts at the beginning or at the end of your presentation depends on their purpose. If you want the audience to use the handouts as worksheets, where people fill in information as you present, then distribute the handout package at the beginning of your presentation. When the handouts are a summary of what you have presented, then distribute them after your presentation, otherwise people will be looking over the handouts rather than listening to you.

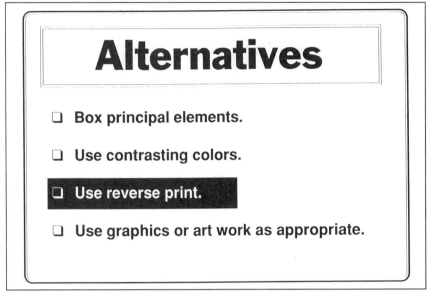

Figure 11-2. Variations in Design Strategies for Transparencies.

Handouts can be prepared as a packet or as individual sheets that you distribute as you refer to them throughout your presentation. Handouts are useful for providing complex and statistical data and for providing the audience with something they can keep.

Boards, Models, and Videotapes

Chalkboards and flip charts are useful for noting issues raised during the presentation or for providing information not available on a transparency or in the handout material. A chalkboard or flip chart is a welcome addition to any presentation room, especially when the audience and the room are relatively small. As handy as these devices are, however, it is difficult to use them well. Few people write large enough on them for everyone to read what is written, and chalkboards need to be erased and the pages on flip charts need to be turned on a regular basis to avoid having the board or sheet become cluttered.

In some cases, the only way you will be able to display something is by using a model. Very few people, for example, can look at a blueprint and envision the building it represents. If you want to convince an audience that your design is the one that will most satisfy them, you will need to provide a model and drawings of the finished building, complete with appropriate landscaping, for the audience to see what a trained architect or engineer can see by looking at the blueprint. If each of your products is unique, and if the client needs to be able to visualize it to appreciate it, use a model if at all possible. Allow time before and after your presentation for members of the audience to examine the model and ask questions about it.

If you are proposing a service, a videotape might make a useful addition to your presentation. The videotape, like other visual aids, should be designed to supplement your oral presentation and not serve as a substitute. If you are proposing a training program, for example, showing a videotape of a similar program delivered for another client would provide your audience with a clear impression of the skills of your training staff. A professional-quality videotape is not easy to produce, however, and a bad videotape will work against you rather than for you. If you regularly submit proposals for the kind of service that would be well-displayed by videotape, consider investing in professional help producing a tape that you can submit with your written proposals or bring with you to oral presentations.

Guidelines for Preparing Visual Aids

Here are a few guidelines to help you prepare and use your visual aids.

1. Prepare visual aids well in advance of your presentation so that you can practice your delivery with them.
2. Keep your visual aids organized so that you don't waste time during the presentation looking for them. Overhead transparencies should be numbered by writing on the frame or on a backing sheet so they can be put back in order quickly if an accident should happen.
3. Keep visual aids simple, focusing on the main idea or point.
4. Remove the visual aid after it has served its purpose, or members of your audience may continue to focus on the visual aid when they should be listening to you.
5. Use a pointer to direct the audience's attention to the point you are emphasizing. When using an overhead projector, use the pointer on the transparency and not on the screen.
6. Do not turn your back to the audience because your voice will not carry to the audience. If you need to refer to a point on the transparency, read from the copy on the overhead projector or from a printed copy (rather than from the screen).
7. Test all equipment before your presentation to be sure that everything is working perfectly.

REHEARSE YOUR DELIVERY

Now that you have everything prepared for your presentation, you are ready to rehearse your delivery. Rehearsal is a critical step. Everyone needs practice. Those who have a few hundred successful presentations behind them may not need much rehearsal to do well, but those who are just beginning should practice until they are confident of their knowledge of the product or services being offered and the structure and content of the presentation.

Three common errors are attempting to memorize the entire presentation, reading from your notes, and hiding behind the lectern. If you memorize, you will sound stilted and artificial. When you read from your notes, you lose contact with the audience. You also lose contact with the audience if you hide behind the lectern. Remember that at this point your audience is as interested in you as they are in your proposal, which they have read for themselves already. Know your material well enough that you can get out from behind the lectern and present most of your material without relying on notes. Rather than prepare a complete copy of the text of your presentation, make an outline of the key ideas on note cards, or you can make transparencies of the key points you want to cover. Note cards are less obtrusive than transparencies, but transparencies allow the audience to see at a glance what you are going to cover and where you are in your presentation.

If you are new to oral presentations, rehearse your delivery in front of a mirror so you can observe yourself, speak into a tape recorder so you can hear what your voice sounds like, and have someone videotape you so that you can observe your own presentation, including your appearance, body movements, and voice. As painful as it may be, practice your delivery in front of other members of your organization. In addition to making sure that you know your material well enough to deliver it with confidence, make sure that your appearance is appropriate for the image you wish to convey.

Appearance

You are, after all, your most important visual aid, and you should present yourself as a well-organized, well-prepared, well-informed, and well-mannered individual. But no matter how well-prepared you are, you still need to project a professional image to your audience. First impressions count. If your appearance shows signs of neglect or your mannerisms are distractive, your audience will be watching you rather than listening to you. And you want the audience to focus on what you have to say. You want, therefore, to pay particular attention to your appearance.

Be conservative in your dress. Neatness and cleanliness are essential. Consider your total grooming—hair, nails, clothing, shoes, accessories, lotions, and perfumes. Hair should be clean and styled, nails should be manicured, clothing should be conservative, clean, and pressed. Shoes should be shined and in good repair. Trained interviewers, in fact, often use the condition of the applicant's shoes to gauge the care they will take of any object entrusted to them. Your shoes, and the rest of your attire, should convey the impression that you take good care of everything in your possession. Accessories should complement your attire, and lotions and perfumes should be used sparingly.

Body Movements

You can be well-dressed in expensive clothing, but if your body movements are distracting, your audience will be focusing on your mannerisms and not on what you are saying. Learn to control your posture, facial expressions, and gestures.

Posture

Your nonverbal behavior should command attention, show vitality and enthusiasm, and project confidence and forcefulness. Good posture is the best way to convey a positive image. Poor posture, on the other hand, can indicate insecurity, low self-esteem, laziness, and an uninterested attitude. With shoulders back and head erect, stand straight with both feet flat on the floor. Face your audience, and don't hide behind the lectern. Learn to move naturally while standing erect. If you have developed a habit of poor posture, perhaps from spending too many hours hunched over a drawing table or seated at a computer, stand and practice your delivery in front of a full-length mirror. When the body adjusts to a slump, you will *feel* as though you are standing up straight when you are actually slumped. Force yourself to stand straight until it feels natural.

Facial Expressions

Your facial expressions reveal your emotions—nervousness, confidence, anxiety, happiness, and so forth. You want your audience to know that you are interested in them and are enthusiastic about what you are about to present, so smile and maintain eye contact with them. Maintaining eye contact with the audience helps you to observe their facial expressions and to note the way in which they are responding to you. If the audience looks bored, you can increase the pace of your presentation; if the audience looks bewildered, you can provide an analogy, an example, or an illustration; and if the audience looks sleepy, you can call for a stretch break.

Gestures

Gestures are body movements that help us express our thoughts. Learn how to use gestures appropriately. Too much hand gesturing can be distracting, and an absence of gestures can be boring. Use gestures to emphasize a point and to maintain your audience's attention. You may wish to practice your presentation in front of a mirror or to have someone videotape it so that you can observe your own gestures and evaluate their effectiveness.

Voice

Your voice also says a lot about you. Consider your vocal qualities— volume, rate, and pitch—when giving oral presentations. Your diction— the way in which you use and pronounce words—and other aspects of paralanguage will also influence the impression you make on your audience.

Volume

Volume is the degree of sound intensity or loudness of your voice. Project your voice. You want everyone in your audience to hear you, but you don't want to shout. If the audience is large, use a sound system. Your volume should rise and fall naturally, depending on the kind of information you are conveying. It is natural to increase your volume when making an important point.

Rate of Speech

The rate or pace at which you speak should not be so fast that you lose your audience or so slow that you put the audience to sleep. Practice increasing and decreasing your rate of speech. You can increase your rate when the material may be familiar to the audience; decrease your rate when you are presenting information that is complex and information that may be unfamiliar to your audience. Learn how to use pauses effectively. Pauses can help to emphasize a point you are trying to make.

Pitch

Pitch or tone refers to the highs and lows in your voice. Vary your pitch to avoid monotony. Nothing puts an audience to sleep faster than a presenter who speaks (or reads) in a monotone. Be enthusiastic, excited, and energetic about what you are telling your audience, and they will be too.

Diction

Diction—your choice of words and how you enunciate and pronounce them—reveals your command of the English language. An audience likes to hear a good speaker, one who has control of his or her vocabulary and one who can speak clearly and distinctly. When a speaker mispronounces words or makes grammatical mistakes, he or she loses credibility. Review your material to make sure that you are familiar with and know how to pronounce all the words. Check your lists and series for parallel construction, subjects and verbs for agreement, and your pronoun usage.

Paralanguage

Paralanguage refers to vocalizations, such as throat clearing, coughing, and laughing. Untrained speakers often fill gaps between ideas with *ums* and *uhs*. Avoid this kind of paralanguage and other kinds of "verbal tics" that speakers use when they are nervous. For example, speakers may unconsciously and frequently say, "you know," "you see what I mean," or "okay." When you listen to yourself on a tape recorder or when a friend listens to your presentation, be alert to how often you employ these nervous mannerisms and work to eliminate them.

KEY POINTS FROM CHAPTER 11

The key points from Chapter 11 are the following:

1. Proposal writers may be asked to make an oral presentation in addition to submitting the written proposal.
2. Presenters will want to analyze their audience and consider the audience's size, attitude, interests, and knowledge so that they can anticipate their needs and concerns.
3. The purpose of an oral presentation is to inform or to persuade.
4. The organization of an oral presentation has an opening, a middle, and a closing.
5. Presenters should know how to handle questions and answers in an oral presentation.
6. Visual aids attract an audience's attention, maintain their interest, clarify important and complex concepts, convince the decision makers, prove points, display data, reinforce what the speaker says, and increase retention.
7. Transparencies and handouts are the two common visual aids used in proposal presentations.
8. Presenters need to rehearse their delivery and be conscious of their appearance, body movements, and voice.

CHAPTER 12

Documentation

As a proposal writer, you may need to gather information from various sources to show that you understand the problem and that you have consulted other experts. Readers of your proposal do not expect you to know everything about a situation, condition, or problem, but they do expect you to investigate other sources to see if the same or a similar problem existed previously, how it was solved, and which techniques were useful and which weren't. They will expect you to base your conclusions and recommendations on what you have been able to learn from others as well as on what you know based on your own experience.

Readers will expect you to have undertaken the appropriate research, and they will expect you to acknowledge your sources of information. The acknowledgement of sources is typically called *documentation*.

DEFINITION

Documentation is essentially the use of documentary evidence—the use of documents as a source of evidence or information. For the purposes of proposals and other common reports in business and industry, documentation refers to the identification of the sources of information used in the proposal or report.

Whenever you use secondary sources—words, ideas, or information that did not originate with you—whether directly (verbatim) or indirectly (paraphrased or summarized), you should document your work by acknowledging the source of the information and giving credit to the originator of the idea. Documentation serves several purposes:

1. It identifies the sources of information.
2. It acknowledges indebtedness to others for their ideas and information.
3. It allows readers to check your sources to see whether they agree with your interpretation of the data.
4. It allows readers who wish to investigate the topic further to pursue your sources of information.
5. It helps establish your credibility by showing your use of outside experts.

6. It helps convince your readers that you have thoroughly researched the topic.
7. It precludes the accusation of plagiarism.

PLAGIARISM AND COPYRIGHT LAWS

The presentation of someone else's information as though it were your own is *plagiarism*. Plagiarism is the use of another person's words, ideas, or information—whether verbatim, paraphrased, or abstracted—as your own. When you use material from a another source, regardless of the form of that source—books, magazines, newspapers, radio or TV broadcasts, public speeches, or even a business report written by someone else—you are obligated to acknowledge the source. Failing to do so is not only a violation of commonly accepted ethical practices but also a crime punishable by law.

While the chances that a proposal writer would face criminal prosecution for failing to document his or her sources are slim, the absence of appropriate documentation could easily result in the loss of a contract. The chances are good that those who will be evaluating the proposals will have examined a variety of secondary sources in developing the RFP, and they will be suspicious of undocumented language that sounds similar to that used in their reference material.

U.S. copyright laws protect people from having their published words and ideas "stolen" by another. The U.S. Copyright Law (effective 1 January 1978) protects copyrighted material from being copied without permission of the copyright holder. The Copyright Law protects all written documents, regardless of whether the author has applied for a copyright. Virtually all published material is covered by specific copyright, which requires a formal application and a fee.

Whenever you cite an authority in your proposal, be sure to give credit to that source. For short quotations, you have met your ethical obligations to the author by providing a citation to the original source so that readers can verify the accuracy and context of the original. When you wish to make more extensive use of copyrighted material, as we have done in Appendix B, you must secure the permission of the copyright holder. Typically, the request and permission must both be in writing. Sometimes the copyright holder will charge you a fee for doing so. Fifty years after the death of the copyright holder, the information becomes public domain. You no longer need permission from the copyright holder to publish the information, but you are still obligated to acknowledge the source.

When material and information is known by the general public or cannot be attributed to one specific source, you are not required to provide a source. You are required to document the following kinds of information: (1) direct quotations—material taken verbatim from another source and placed in quotation marks; (2) a paraphrase—material from another source that you rephrase in your own words; (3) a summary—material from another source that you summarize; (4) quantifiable data—facts and statistics taken from another source; (5) graphic aids—graphs, charts, photographs, slides, diagrams, or maps taken from another source; and (6) art work (cartoons, drawings, photographs, and the like) developed by someone else.

When you are using information provided by another individual who is employed at the same company as you, the company may be the copyright holder because the individual is paid by the company to conduct experiments or to design new products. In that case, you do not need to cite the source, although you may wish to indicate intellectual indebtedness if appropriate.

PLACEMENT OF REFERENCES

Different businesses and industries typically employ different methods of documentation. One of the ways in which styles of documentation differ is in the placement of the reference note. The three most common placements are within the body of the text set off by parentheses, at the bottom—the foot—of the page, and at the end of chapters, divisions, or the entire proposal or report.

Parenthetical References

The parenthetical reference method is the preferred one for proposal writing for three reasons: (1) most proposals do not usually contain many citations, (2) parenthetical citations are easy to prepare, and (3) parenthetical citations are convenient for the reader. In the parenthetical reference method, the documentation is contained within the text immediately following the quoted or paraphrased material. The three formats for the parenthetical reference method are (1) complete citation, (2) author and year of publication, and (3) number.

Complete Citation

The complete citation format includes the author's full name, the title of the work, the place of publication, the publisher, the date of publication, and the page number.

According to William Hanover (Project Management [Chicago: Piller Press, 19xx] 25), "scientists recommended a diameter of .055 for the T-rings."

Author and Year

The author and year of publication format includes just the author's last name and the year of publication of the work in parentheses after the quoted material. The complete citation is provided in the bibliography at the end of the proposal in a section entitled *Bibliography, References, Sources,* or *Works Cited,* depending on the style of documentation selected.

Scientists were able to specify sizes for the T-rings (Hanover, 19xx).

Number

The number format gives the number of the reference listing in the bibliography, which lists the entries of all the references serially or alphabetically and then numbers the entries sequentially. In the text of the proposal immediately after the quoted material, place in parentheses the number of the bibliographic entry followed by the page number. In the following example, 4 refers to the bibliographic listing, and 32 refers to the page number on which the citation appears in the original document.

T-rings should have a diameter of .055. (4, 32).

Footnotes

Footnotes are so called because they are placed at the foot or bottom of the page where the reference is first mentioned. They are separated from the text by an inch and a half line beginning at the left margin. If the proposal or report includes several footnotes, they are numbered consecutively throughout the document using raised Arabic numbers. If there are only a few, they may be indicated by an asterisk (*) or other symbol, such as a dagger (†), with subsequent footnotes receiving additional symbols (** or †††, for example).

Although the order and method of presentation may vary according to the style manual you are following, footnotes typically contain the author's full name, the title of the article, the name of the book or periodical, the place of publication, the publisher, and the date of publication. Page numbers are given for periodicals.

Endnotes

When all the references are gathered at the ends of chapters, divisions, or documents, they are typically referred to as *endnotes* or simply as *notes.* In recent years, the trend has been to use endnotes rather than footnotes for two principal reasons. First, placing the references at the ends of the document (or major divisions in long documents) was easier when word processing software was not capable of automatically numbering and placing footnotes correctly at the bottom of the appropriate page.

Second, page lengths of typewritten or word processed material rarely correspond with those of printed material, so typesetters were required to reposition all the footnotes, and text and notes were typically set on different proofs. Repositioning the text to allow for the notes was time consuming and costly. For these reasons, most modern style manuals recommend endnotes rather than footnotes.

Endnotes follow the same form as that used for footnotes. The only difference is their placement.

INFORMATION IN REFERENCES

The term *references* applies to two separate ways of citing sources: notes (footnotes or endnotes) and bibliographic entries. Style manuals differ in the way they enter information for each. Because different businesses, industries, and academic disciplines employ different style manuals, you need to discover and use the style manual preferred in your organization. It would also be useful to know which style manual is preferred by the client organizations to which you will be submitting proposals. The information presented here provides general introduction to some of the choices available to you.

The information in references for books and periodicals usually includes the following:

Books
1. Author's name
2. Title of the book
3. Edition
4. Place of publication
5. Name of publisher
6. Date of publication

Periodicals
1. Author's name
2. Title of the article
3. Name of the periodical
4. Series number
5. Volume number
6. Date of publication
7. Page numbers

FORM FOR REFERENCES

Entries for notes and the bibliography contain similar information, but the format for the entries differs. The format will also differ depending on which style manual you are following, the type of source, and the number of authors.

Style Manuals

A style manual is a reference tool that tells how something is done— conventions or rules for capitalizing letters, using numbers, addressing people, dividing words, spelling words, using words, and documenting sources. Different style manuals have been developed to meet the needs of those in various disciplines—science, engineering, government, humanities, and business. For a comprehensive list of style manuals, see John Bruce Howell's *Style Manuals of the English-Speaking World* (Phoenix: Oryx, 1983). Three of the most often used style manuals are

Publication Manual of the American Psychological Association. 3d ed. Washington: American Psychological Association, 1983.
Chicago Manual of Style. 13th ed., rev. and exp. Chicago: The University of Chicago Press, 1982.
Joseph Gilbaldi and Water S. Achtert. *MLA Handbook for Writers of Research Papers*. 2d ed. New York: The Modern Language Association, 1984.

In addition to these fairly standard style manuals, a number of governmental agencies have published their own style manuals. One or more of the following might be useful for you:

American National Standard for Bibliographic References
Guide for Preparation of Air Force Publications
Handbook for Authors of Papers in American Chemical Society Publications
NASA Publication Manual
Style Manual for Engineering Authors and Editors
U. S. Government Printing Office Style Manual

Before you select a style manual, check to see whether your discipline, the RFP, or the editor or publisher with whom you are working has already stipulated one that you must use. If you do not follow the stipulations of the RFP for documenting your sources, for example, your proposal may be rejected.

Sample Reference Styles

As mentioned previously, each of the style manuals requires slightly different entry forms. The brief coverage of the forms of citation provided here is not intended to substitute for the complete instructions in the actual reference manual but is rather designed to illustrate some of the differences among the manuals.

You cannot assume that the style manual recommended by the RFP will employ the same forms for entries as those recommended by the style manual you have used previously. Make sure that you obtain a copy of the recommended style manual and follow its directions. When the RFP does not recommend a specific style manual, use the manual most often employed by others in your business or industry.

Publication Manual of the American Psychological Association

The *Publication Manual of the American Psychological Association* (*APA*) uses the author and year form of citation within the text, with complete source information being provided in a list entitled *References* at the end of the document. *APA* form uses only the initial letters of first and middle names of authors, and it capitalizes only the first letter of articles and books, although it uses standard capitalization for the titles of journals.

APA does not provide for the use of italics in manuscripts, although it does indicate that titles of books, journals, and magazines will be set in italics when printed. In general, italic print is easier to read than print that has been underscored, so if your word processing equipment and software can produce italics, use italics as though the document were printed. Figure 12-1 illustrates sample *APA* entries.

Citations within the Text

Citations within the text are treated the same regardless of the type of source. References to portions of a work are included within the parentheses.

Adams (1991) has reported consistent success with the Brown construction process.

Previous research (Smith & Rodrigues, 1991) has indicated that the Brown construction process is appropriate in these circumstances.

Others have noted that the Brown construction process holds up well under extreme freeze-thaw conditions (Construction Society of America [CSA], 1991, chap. 3).

Citations in References

Books

Adams, J. H. (1990). *Construction methodology for severe weather conditions*. New York: I-Beam Press.

Adams, J. H., & Fraser, C. F. (1991). *Freeze-thaw effects on reinforced concrete*. New York: I-Beam Press.

Construction Society of America (1989). *Standards for the industry* (rev. ed.). Burbank, CA: Author.

Smith, J. M., & Rodrigues, L. H. (1991). *Practical construction techniques for cold-weather climates*. Burbank, CA: Construction Society of America.

Articles

Adams, J. H. (1991). Freeze-thaw effects on exposed steel. *Construction Quarterly, 37*(2), 7-10.

Rodrigues, L. H. (1990). Insulation: The new standards. *The Journal of Fiberglass Technology, 9,* 521-557.

Smith, J. M. (1989, December 4). A history of cold-weather construction. *The Fairbanks Times,* pp. 1, 14.

Figure 12-1. *APA* **Sample Entries.**

Chicago Manual of Style

Like *APA, The Chicago Manual of Style* recommends the use of an author-date system for in-text references, with full documentation being provided in a section entitled *Bibliography, Select Bibliography, Works Cited, Literature Cited,* or *References.* Figure 12-2 illustrates sample entries based on *The Chicago Manual of Style.*

Citations within the Text

Citations within the text are treated the same regardless of the type of source. Note that no punctuation separates the author(s) and the date in this form.

Adams (1991) has reported consistent success with the Brown construction process.

Previous research (Smith and Rodrigues 1991) has indicated that the Brown construction process is appropriate in these circumstances.

Others have noted that the Brown construction process holds up well under extreme freeze-thaw conditions (Rodrigues 1991, 3-7).

Citations in References

Books

Adams, J. H. 1990. *Construction methodology for severe weather conditions.* New York: I-Beam Press.

Adams, J. H., & Fraser, C. F. 1991. *Freeze-thaw effects on reinforced concrete.* New York: I-Beam Press.

Construction Society of America. 1989. *Standards for the industry* (rev. ed.). Burbank, CA: Construction Society of America.

Smith, J. M., & Rodrigues, L. H. 1991. *Practical construction techniques for cold-weather climates.* Burbank, CA: Construction Society of America.

Articles

Adams, J. H. 1991. Freeze-thaw effects on exposed steel. *Construction Quarterly,* 37(2), 7-10.

Rodrigues. L. H. 1990. Insulation: The new standards. *The Journal of Fiberglass Technology,* 9, 521-57.

Smith, J. M. 1989. A history of cold-weather construction. *The Fairbanks Times,* December 4, 1, 14.

Figure 12-2. *Chicago Manual of Style* **Sample Entries.**

MLA Handbook for Writers of Research Papers

The *MLA Handbook for Writers of Research Papers* (*MLA Handbook*) also recommends the use of an author-date system for in-text references, with full documentation being provided in a section entitled *Works Cited.*

Like *APA*, the *MLA Handbook* does not provide for the use of italics in manuscripts, but most readers would prefer italics to underscore for titles of major publications. Figure 12-3 illustrates sample entries based on the *MLA Handbook*.

Citations within the Text

Citations within the text are treated the same regardless of the type of source. Note that the page references are provided within the parentheses.

Adams (167) has reported consistent success with the Brown construction process.

Previous research (Smith and Rodrigues, 214-307) has indicated that the Brown construction process is appropriate in these circumstances.

Others have noted that the Brown construction process holds up well under extreme freeze-thaw conditions (Construction Society of America, 178-221).

Citations in References

Books

Adams, John H. *Construction Methodology for Severe Weather Conditions.* New York: I-Beam Press, 1991.

Adams, John H., and Charles F. Fraser. *Freeze-thaw Effects on Reinforced Concrete.* New York: I-Beam Press, 1991.

Construction Society of America. *Standards for the Industry* (rev. ed.). Burbank, CA: Construction Society of America, 1989.

Smith, Jerry M., and Larry H. Rodrigues. *Practical Construction Techniques for Cold-weather Climates.* Burbank, CA: Construction Society of America.

Articles

Adams, John H. "Freeze-thaw Effects on Exposed Steel." *Construction Quarterly* 37(1991): 7-10.

Rodrigues, Larry H. "Insulation: The New Standards." *The Journal of Fiberglass Technology* 9 (1990): 521-57.

Smith, Jerry M. "A History of Cold-weather Construction." *The Fairbanks Times* 4 December 1989, all ed.: A 1, 14.

Figure 12-3. *MLA* **Sample Entries.**

KEY POINTS FROM CHAPTER 12

The key points from Chapter 12 are the following:

1. Documentation means identifying the source of your information.
2. Plagiarism is using another person's words, ideas, or information— either condensed or abstracted— as your own.

3. Three common methods of documentation are parenthetical references, footnotes, and endnotes.
4. The three formats for the parenthetical reference method are (1) the complete citation, (2) the author and year of publication, and (3) the number.
5. The information in references for books should include the following: author's name, title of the book, edition, place of publication, name of publisher, and date of publication.
6. The information in references for periodicals should include the following: author's name, title of the article, name of the periodical, series number, volume number, date of publication, and page numbers.
7. A style manual is a reference tool that tells how something is done—conventions or rules for capitalizing letters, using numbers, addressing people, dividing words, spelling words, using words, and documenting sources.
8. Use the style manual recommended in the RFP or, if the RFP does not specify a specific manual, use the one most common in your business or industry.

Appendixes

APPENDIX A

Selected Readings

Those who spend much time writing proposals and other income-producing documents should have a well-stocked library of reference materials. The following list is by no means exhaustive. We have included here the books that we have found most useful in forming our own ideas about communication, writing style, report writing, and proposal writing in particular. We believe that you will find these books helpful.

COMMUNICATION

Bettinghaus, E.P. and M.J. Cody, *Persausive Communication*, 4th ed. New York: Holt, Rinehart and Winston: 1987.

Blicq, R.S., *Communicating at Work: Creating Messages that Get Results*. Scarborough, Ontario: Prentice-Hall, 1991.

Covey, S.R., *The 7 Habits of Highly Effective People*. New York: Simon and Schuster, 1989.

————. *Principle-Centered Leadership*. New York: Summit Books, 1991.

Fisher, R. and W. Ury, *Getting to Yes: Negotiating Agreement without Giving In*. New York: Penguin Books, 1981.

King, M., L. Novik, and C. Citrenbaum, *Irresistible Communication: Creative Skills for the Health Professional*. Philadelphia: W.B. Saunders, 1983.

Kostere, K. and L. Malatesta, *Get the Results You Want: A Guide to Communication Excellence for the Helping Professional*. Portland, OR: Metamorphous Press, 1989.

Laborde, G. Z., *Influencing with Integrity: Management Skills for Communication and Negotiation*. Palo Alto, CA: Syntony Publishing, 1987.

McMaster, M. and J. Grinder, *Precision: A New Approach to Communication: How to Get the Information You Need to Get Results*. Bonny Doon, CA: Precision Models, 1980.

Sides, Charles H., *How to Write & Present Technical Information*. Phoenix, AZ: The Oryx Press, 1991.

Wurman, R. S., *Follow the Yellow Brick Road: Learning to Give, Take, and Use Instructions*. New York, Bantam: 1992.

WRITING STYLE

Alred, G. J., W. E. Oliu, and C. T. Brusaw, *The Professional Writer: A Guide for Advanced Technical Writing.* New York: St. Martin's Press, 1992.

Bernstein, T. M., *The Careful Writer: A Modern Guide to English Usage.* New York: Atheneum, 1980.

The Chicago Manual of Style: For Authors, Editors, and Copywriters, 13th ed. Chicago: The University of Chicago Press, 1982.

Eisenberg, A., *Effective Technical Communication.* New York: McGraw-Hill, 1982.

Flower, L., *Problem-Solving Strategies for Writing.* New York: Harcourt Brace Jovanovich, 1981.

Gibaldi, J. and W. S. Achtert, *MLA Handbook for Writers of Research Papers,* 2nd ed. New York: The Modern Language Association of America, 1984.

Publication Manual of the American Psychological Association, 3rd ed. Washington, D.C.: American Psychological Association, 1983.

Reep, D. C., *Technical Writing: Principles, Strategies, and Readings.* Boston: Allyn and Bacon, 1991.

Williams, J. M., *Style: Ten Lessons in Clarity & Grace.* Glenview, IL: Scott, Foresman and Company, 1989.

REPORT WRITING

Bowman, J. P. and B. P. Branchaw, *Business Report Writing,* 2nd ed. New York: The Dryden Press, 1988.

Hager, P. J. and H. J. Scheiber, *Report Writing for Management Decisions.* New York: Macmillan Publishing, 1992.

Mathes, J. C. and D. W. Stevenson, *Designing Technical Reports: Writing for Audiences in Organizations,* 2nd ed. Indianapolis, IN: Macmillan, 1991.

Varner, I. I., *Contemporary Business Report Writing,* 2nd ed. New York: The Dryden Press, 1991.

PROPOSAL WRITING

Belcher, Jane C. and Julia M. Jacobsen, *From Idea to Funded Project: Grant Proposals That Work.* Phoenix, AZ: The Oryx Press, 1992.

Hillman, H. and L. Loring, *The Art of Writing Business Reports and Proposals.* New York: Vanguard, 1981.

Holtz, H. and T. Schmidt, *The Winning Proposal: How to Write It.* New York: McGraw-Hill, 1981.

Holtz, H., *The Consultant's Guide to Proposal Writing: How to Satisfy Your Client and Double Your Income,* 2nd ed., New York: Wiley, 1990.

Porter-Roth, B., *Proposal Development: A Winning Approach.* Milpitas, CA: Oasis Press, 1986.

Stewart, R. D. and A. L. Stewart, *Proposal Preparation*, Wiley, 1984.

Tepper, R., *How to Write Winning Proposals for Your Company or Client*. New York: Wiley, 1989.

DOCUMENT DESIGN

Miles, John. *Design for Desktop Publishing: A Guide to Layout and Typography on the Personal Computer*. San Francisco: Chronicle Books, 1987.

Parker, Robert C. *Looking Good in Print: A Guide to Basic Design for Desktop Publishing*. Chapel Hill, NC: Ventana Press, 1988.

Sullivan, David J., Wesley Sullivan, and William L. Sullivan. *Desktop Publishing: Writing and Publishing in the Computer Age*. Boston: Houghton Mifflin Company, 1989.

White, J. V. *Graphic Design for the Electronic Age: The Manual for Traditional and Desktop Publishing*. New York: Watson-Guptill Publications, 1988.

APPENDIX B

Supplemental Checklists

The following checklists were developed by Paul R. McDonald, Sr. and are reprinted here by permission. Because these checklists are comprehensive, not every item will be appropriate for every business or industry. These checklists are meant to serve as a guide that you can use to prepare your own in-house checklist designed to guide a proposal team through the process from conception to submission. Additional copies of the checklists may be obtained from The American Graduate University, 733 North Dodworth Avenue, Covina, California 91724.*

PROPOSAL PREPARATION CHECKLIST

I. Know the Customer
   A. In attempting to fully understand and appreciate the desires of the customer, the proposing firm should determine the following:
      1. During the preparation of a qualitative operational requirement, what does the using command think it will need in the future (even though this desire may never see the light of a proposal)?
         This is important from two standpoints—it affords an opportunity to influence the customer to include information on equipment or techniques that can be supplied and it provides an opportunity to guide company internal research and development programs. In addition, since the using command probably will be represented on the Source Evaluation Group, this will provide information on the operational orientation of the user.
      2. At the level of operational requirements director, what important military systems are likely to be favored and what factors are considered most important?
      3. At the System/Program Office Level, what operational and technical features are likely to be favored?
      4. At the level of research and engineering director, what engineering and technical approaches and features are favored? Also, what is the company's image as a contractor and what, if necessary, can be done to improve that image?
      5. At the Comptroller level, what money has been, or is likely to be, approved on a major program?

*Paul R. McDonald, Sr. and Procurement Associates, Inc., 733 North Dodworth Avenue, Covina, California 91724. Reproduced by permission of The American Graduate University.

     6. At what level has the Source Selection Authority been designated?

     7. At the Joint Chiefs of Staff level, what elements in the various program areas are receiving most attention and support from an operational viewpoint?

     8. At the Secretarial level (Service and DOD), what political factors may influence the Source Selection Authority?

     9. At Congressional and Department of Commerce level, what political and economic factors may influence the placing of large defense contracts?

    10. Will the President's Scientific Advisor or the President's Scientific Advisory Committee be brought into the decision-making process on a particular program?

II.   Analysis of The Request For Proposal (RFP)

   A. Upon receipt of the RFP, a complete analysis such as the following should be made:

     1. Define program and pertinent instructions.

     2. Specify the basic elements of the proposal.

     3. Detail the manner in which the program should be broken down.

   B. Clearly and unambiguously spell out all unusual directions necessary for proposal preparation:

     1. Are existing tools and facilities to be used?

     2. Are special tooling or facilities required?

     3. Will manufacturing use the company's engineering development capability?

     4. Will sketches be used?

     5. What Government Furnished Equipment (GFE) will be used?

     6. What are the documentation requirements?

     7. What are the reliability requirements?

     8. What are delivery requirements?

     9. Are there any special test or unusual acceptance requirements?

   C. The proposal management team members responsible for these areas should query themselves on the following factors:

     1. What does the contract require for reliability and maintainability? Can we meet these requirements? Can we exceed them, and if so, to what degree?

     2. Are there any unusual specifications for inspection requirements?

     3. Are the means for securing approval clearly defined?

     4. Are the requirements of test and demonstration clearly stated?

     5. What kind of reliability, testing inspection, and acceptance requirements will be placed on vendors and subcontractors?

     6. Are the bases for acceptance of all contract items clearly stated? When final acceptance occurs subsequent to delivery or installation, does the company have a provisional acceptance that protects the company against damage due to acts of God, customer negligence, and so forth?

     7. Compatibility of subcontractor type of pricing with the company's expected contract type with the customer?

     8. Are warranties compatible with program requirements?

     9. Special conditions such as options?

    10. Compatibility of subcontract terms and conditions with expected customer's contract and its provisions?

III. Program Schedule
   A. All proposal management team members should study applicable procurement documents to determine any unknowns or special problems that affect their inputs. The team should determine jointly where it is being fully responsive to the RFP, and if it meets the minimum specification requirements. If not, the team should jointly establish a sound basis for making exceptions and requesting waivers.
   B. The team should list all deliverable contract items and plot the schedule milestones for each item. The following deliverable items should be considered when compiling this schedule:
      1. Monthly or quarterly progress reports, other presentations, films, and so forth.
      2. Engineering study reports.
      3. Movies, models, required lecture aids.
      4. Required mockups.
      5. Applicable specifications for breadboards.
      6. Prototype or engineering models.
      7. Applicable specifications for finished equipment.
      8. Applicable specifications for drawings, including vendor documentation.
      9. Applicable specifications for instruction books, maintenance and operation manuals.
      10. Installation requirements.
      11. Services—Engineering, integrated logistic support, and so forth.
      12. Modified GFE to be delivered.
      13. Training programs.
      14. Test tools and test equipment—stated or implied.
      15. Spare parts and assemblies.
      16. Test reports and qualification test data.
      17. Type and amount of effort associated with each deliverable contract item.
      18. Itemization of all travel required.
      19. Specific packing and shipping requirements.
   C. It is highly desirable that a well-structured milestone type of schedule be established. It should consider the following:
      1. Does the contract require any approvals, formal or otherwise, prior to proceeding to the next step such as preliminary design approval, final design approval, or environmental test approval? Will these cause gaps in the schedule?
      2. Do test specifications have to be submitted for formal approval before testing can be started? Is a special format required?
      3. Do parts or equipment designations have to be obtained?
      4. Is the basis for acceptance clear?
      5. Will additional shifts or premium overtime be required for any part of the program? For example, will environmental testing have to be run around the clock? Do facilities limitations and schedule requirements demand multiple shifts? Is final assembly space available for this program and has it been scheduled and phased in properly?
      6. What is the schedule for receipt of GFE?

7. Have vendor deliveries been scheduled to assure availability and, simultaneously, minimize inventory, storage, and maintenance costs? Have long-lead items been phased in promptly enough?
8. What size organization will be required to handle the proposed program?
9. What are the skills and man-loading required by each company element for such tasks?
10. If we do not have all the specialized skills or capabilities needed, how will we obtain them? (Personnel recruiting, subcontracting, consultants, or team of associate companies)?
11. Will the Government have to supply any personnel or services other than those normally involved in technical and legal contract administration?
12. Have we presented a clear explanation of organization functions and procedures in the proposal presentation?

IV. Facilities
   A. A list of all facilities required to accomplish the proposed program should be compiled by the proposal management team. These should be scheduled and phased-in with other contractual commitments. The following question should be answered:
   1. Are these facilities now company-owned capital equipment or must they be procured?
   2. Will any part of the operation require the use of Government sites, aircraft, test ranges, or whatever?
   3. Are these facilities from 2. above Government-owned? Will their use be allowed on this program? Will additional Government facilities be required? Can these be made available? Rent-free use?
   4. Will any part of the operation require the use of specialized engineering or manufacturing test equipment including capitalized items?
   5. Are company laboratory calibration facilities adequate? If not, what capabilities must be met? Can adequate calibration be accomplished elsewhere; if so, at what cost in money and time?
   6. Do we have adequate engineering and factory space for this program? If not, how much additional space is required? Does it have to be specially air conditioned, dust-free, RF noise free, clean rooms, controlled atmospheric conditions, gas purging system and facilities for explosives?
   7. Do any materials require special handling or storage? Security requirements?
   8. Do we have to subcontract to someone who has specialized facilities?
   9. Does the program require computer time? Can this be phased in properly?

V. Management Section
   A. The following checklist should be used to assure full, complete and objective management proposals. These include the following major sections of the management proposal:
   1. Personnel Survey.
   2. Program/Project Management Organization.
   3. Management Procedures.

4. Facilities.
5. Schedule and Program Plan.
6. Related Experience.
7. General Business Situation.
B. Personnel Survey—Have you:
   1. Shown the applicable experience of the key individual assignees as related to this task?
   2. Shown that the past performance of your assignees indicates a capability to cope with unexpected problems?
   3. Balanced your team between practical experience and theoretical capability?
   4. Indicated the availability of required specialists/consultants?
   5. Left any holes in your aggregate team experience, with reference to the types of technical/manufacturing/sub-contractor management which is key or peculiar to this program?
   6. Shown management resources of sufficient quality, stature, and availability? Do not promise to utilize personnel the customer knows very well will not be made available.
   7. Wrongly assumed customer prior knowledge of our capability?
   8. Shown a program manager who can devote full time to the project?
   9. Carefully avoided making biographies sound like boiler-plate material?
   10. Shown how many new personnel required will be secured? Do not rely on rapid hiring programs—the customer has bogeys for how fast he believes you can hire. Shown realistic plans for intracompany transfers? The customer knows that there are practical limits.
   11. Included key subcontractor personnel in biographies/organization chart?

VI. Program/Project Management Organization
A. Have you:
   1. Shown your willingness to commit resources?
   2. Shown top management interest in and support for this program?
   3. Improperly assumed customer prior knowledge of the company and thus failed to display all our resources?
   4. Aligned our organization with that of the customer to specifically show the points of interface?
   5. Shown enough objectivity/organizational independence of value engineering, quality control and reliability functions?
   6. Shown the interrelationships of the contributing functions to the overall program control?
   7. Shown a management organization that covers the full spectrum of the program requirements? Show requirements to fill each organizational block and what percent of time each individual will be employed on the program?
   8. Shown a Program Manager reporting at a high-enough level to have authority to get the job done and to have top management attention and help if needed to resolve problems? Show this clearly and honestly—don't try to hoodwink the customer. Remember to consider future growth of the program in setting the Program Manager's reporting level.

9. Shown other companies which are potential or recommended sub-contractors? Shown how their program management interfaces with our program management? Shown the specific subcontractor controls within our organization (i.e., who controls funding to the subcontractor? Who controls technical specifications?) Have we played up our major subcontractor's strengths as well as our own?

10. Shown only the program organization assignment of people?

11. Specifically defined the Program Manager's duties, authorities (including limitations), lines of responsibility and review from top management?

12. Shown an organization vertical enough to satisfy the customer? Shown the required degree of one man control?

13. If the proposed team (including subcontractors) is one that has been in place working as a team for a considerable time, have we played up their experience in working together and their availability for immediate application?

VII. Management Procedures
   A. Have you:
   1. Stated where and when you will review decisions with the customer?
   2. Incorrectly assumed customer prior knowledge of our procedures and their value?
   3. Clearly identified which company/industry-wide procedures will specifically be used in each phase of the program and for what purposes?
   4. Taken the boilerplate flavor out of writeups of management techniques to be employed?
   5. Shown a management approach to value engineering which is sufficiently detailed to assure proper and thorough consideration throughout all phases of the program?
   6. Erroneously included management control procedures which will not be used on this program?
   7. Included important policies/instructions of primary interest?
   8. Demonstrated past use of management procedures intended for use on this program?
   9. Clearly indicated internal reporting and communication methods to be used?
   10. Shown an objective attitude toward make or buy by providing a detailed account of the procedures and analysis made prior to decision?
   11. Given direct reference to the use of specific management tools for the solution of anticipated or known problem areas?
   12. Shown special management attention for those program variables tied to incentives? Defined and recommended incentive provisions which are not so complex as to put the customer in the position of being unable to settle a contract within a reasonable period of time?
   13. Specifically shown our provisions for configuration control per the applicable customer document?
   14. Specifically discussed provisions for handling program changes?

15. Shown our understanding of applicable customer approval procedures?
16. Discussed relationships of our customer to our subcontractors?
17. Shown provision for in-plant liaisons?
18. Shown procedures for obtaining information from industry as required? Shown methodology for objective review of this data? Set up a credible and objective system for obtaining and handling data from potential subcontractors who might normally be regarded as competitors?
19. Shown procedures for obtaining materials and assuring their quality?

VIII. Facilities
    A. Have you:
      1. Shown that all computation, test, measuring, recording, reproduction, and other equipment necessary for completion of engineering tasks is adequate and available?
      2. Shown access to all necessary special equipment not normally available?
      3. Shown the production capability and capacity to implement a full-scale production program for the system/equipment involved in this proposal?
      4. Improperly assumed customer prior knowledge of the adequacy/advantages of our facilities?
      5. Specifically indicated any requirements for additional GFE facilities, tooling, or equipment to perform the job? Included plans to retain GFE currently on site for other programs?
      6. Taken the boilerplate flavor out of the writeups by detailing the key program-related facilities and separately listed the routine floor area type of statistics.
      7. Shown a factory floor plan indicating the location of key manufacturing functions for the subject program? Shown the number of square feet required for production and storage? Shown the geographical location of facility proposed for this program?
      8. Shown the relation of other programs/contracts which affect the facilities required for this program? In particular, have we resolved any real or imagined facility conflicts which may concern our customer?

IX. Schedule and Program Plan
    A. Have you:
      1. Supported the schedule by analyses and comparisons with previous known major program schedules (both in-house and other programs)?
      2. Avoided changing the customer's schedule (if you are concerned about meeting it) but shown the risks and cost penalties involved in adhering to his schedule? Have you offered possible alternatives and tradeoffs? A cost/time tradeoff is a very effective way to analyze and present this consideration.
      3. Shown a development plan for the engineering effort to be conducted to insure that the system/equipment produced will meet customer

functional and reliability requirements? Have you shown the methodology for getting the job done (simulations, computations, or tests)? Does your development plan include the data, field support equipment development, test methods, maintainability and reliability analyses as well as hardware?

4. Shown an estimated number of man years for each major task that will clearly accomplish the job? Shown the distinction between management/professional/specialists categories?
5. Shown check and control points to assure the adequate, accurate and timely data submittals as required by the program?
6. Incorporated time for customer approval cycles?
7. Incorporated schedule time and events for customer furnished information?
8. Specifically accounted for all items and services to be supplied to the customer?

X. Related Experience
A. Are there sections on:
  1. Past engineering and manufacturing accomplishments similar to those required by the proposed program? Does this section show that we are a leader in the field and completely abreast of the state of the art? If we are not a leader, have we discussed or concluded a team relationship or located a vendor in order to increase our capability? Have we highlighted the past accomplishments for this customer? Have we shown that the accomplishments were of equal or greater complexity? Have we included past experience of our major subcontractors/vendors? Have we included exploratory or advanced programs already accomplished and indicated their impact on the proposed program relative to risk and alternatives? Have we shown systems experience if this is key? Have we shown our experience in delivering data, training, test equipment, field service, as well as equipment? Have we shown our experience with technical direction agencies if applicable? Have we shown our experience with incentive contracts?
  2. Past schedule performance and our proposed schedule control?
  3. Our demonstrated capability to effectively control the efforts of major subcontractors by direction, coordination, and integration?
  4. Past cost performance and our proposed cost control methods?
B. General Business Situation—Have you included your:
  1. Surplus labor area designation?
  2. Small business, and minority support record and proposed use of small businesses?
  3. Capital situation (where applicable)?

XI. Kickoff Meeting
A. The Proposal Director should prepare for kickoff meetings by checking the following:
  1. Representatives from the following areas:
    a. Proposal Support.
    b. Contract Administration.

    c. Finance/Cost Estimating.
    d. Manufacturing.
        Preplanning
        Assembly Planning
        Metal Parts Manufacturing Planning
        Integrated Electronics Manufacturing
        Quality Control Test Equipment Engineering Materials
        Quality Control Engineering
        Quality Assurance
    e. Engineering.
        Engineering Development Shop
        Systems Engineering
        Design Engineering
        Environmental Engineering
        Reliability Engineering
        Spare Parts Engineering
        Instruction Books
        Logistics
        Technical Publications
        Product Service
        Specialty Design Engineering
        Engineering Design and Drafting Standards

2. Proposal Summary.
    a. Identify proposal by number.
    b. Identify potential customer.
    c. Proposal items—quantities and delivery dates.
    d. Functional description of items involved.
    e. Abridged version of technical requirements.
    f. Highlights and peculiarities of the RFP.

3. Historical Review.
    a. History of the project in the customer's organizations.
    b. History of the project, or of allied programs, in the company.

4. Competition.
    a. Major competitors.
    b. Competitor's strengths—particularly as related to proposed program.
    c. Company versus competitors' capabilities.
    d. Anticipated features of competitors' proposals.

5. Sales Potential.
    a. Sales and growth potential underlying this particular program.
    b. Sales potential in allied or complementary fields.
    c. Additional benefits that may be accrued from winning this competition (i.e., incremental and business considerations).

6. Political Climate.
    a. Does the political climate put any competitor in a preferred position?
    b. Is there a specific political reason why our company would not be considered acceptable?
    c. How can we improve our political position in relation to this program?

    d.   Should we propose alone, or is it politically expedient to submit a team or associate proposal?

7. Pricing.
   a. Contract price envisaged by the customer.
   b. Contract price envisaged by the Proposal Director.
   c. Historical pricing information.
   d. Pricing philosophy: shall major emphasis be placed on price? To what level of detail shall pricing be accomplished? Should pricing considerations be tied in with some kind of milestone planning?

8. Engineering.
   a. Consideration of alternative proposals.
   b. Evaluation of tradeoffs.
   c. Specific steps to be taken, such as hiring consultants or joining forces with an associate company to solve these problems.

9. Manufacturing.
   a. Specific steps to be taken, such as fabricating sample or prototype units and other measures phased-in to solve difficult problems.
   b. Make-or-buy decisions should be coordinated with purchasing.
   c. Based on the type of program involved and the sales potential, determine where the manufacturing will be accomplished—model shop, quick reaction shop, regular manufacturing facilities, or some combination of these facilities.

10. Procurement.
    a. Subcontract complete packages?
    b. Can GFE be used? Do these require modification? What are the overall GFE requirements?

11. Sales.
    a. Sales effort required for presentation.
    b. Sales contacts to be made during the proposal preparation period.
    c. Sales inputs required during proposal preparation.
    d. Sales effort required during interim between proposal submission and contract award.
    e. Management contacts and participation required during pre-proposal and post-proposal periods.

12. Contract Requirements.
    a. Specific contract or technical requirements, including specifications that should be examined for exceptions and waivers.
    b. Type of contract anticipated—fixed-price or cost-reimbursement category.
    c. Contract incentive provisions (if any).

13. Proposal Strategy and Decisions.
    a. Review of the reasons underlying the proposal decision.
    b. Factors to be emphasized (i.e., price, delivery, performance, experience, facilities, or whatever).
    c. Teaming up with key subcontractors or associate companies.
    d. Specific assignments proposed and the reasons underlying them.

14. Customer.
  a. Stress the cooperative attitudes toward working with and for the customer.
  b. Prime considerations for proposal evaluation.
  c. Cost effectiveness philosophy.
  d. Availability and magnitude of funds.
  e. Our rating in relation to competition.
  f. Probability of eventual procurement.

XII. Proposal Hints
  A. The following hints may assist in developing a complete, responsive technical proposal:
    1. Don't half bid.
    2. Don't be stereotyped. Think! It may not be desirable to do it as we always have in the past.
    3. Know the customer—his habits, prejudices, and interpolitics.
    4. Don't mix winning a proposal competition with negotiation.
    5. A last-minute estimate of cost, where cost is a decisive factor, does not make for a winning proposal.
    6. Be frank—technically and otherwise.
    7. Don't deviate from the main strategy for minor or irrelevant reasons.
    8. Avoid a false technical opinion of self-capability. Prove technical capability by illustrating accomplishments in related fields.
    9. All functions of the company may not be required. Weed out the unnecessary ones early in the game.
    10. Complicated organization structures presented in a proposal are not readily understood nor desired by the average customer. Customize the program organization plan so that it's tailored to the job and to the customer.
    11. Give objective thought to the use of subcontractors.
    12. Consider the value of submitting as a subcontractor or associate.
    13. An inventive or novel approach doesn't necessarily make a good or winning proposal. The customer may actually want the tried and proved.
    14. Evaluate several proposal approaches rather than choosing the first one considered. Consider alternatives.
    15. Make sure you know the role of any Government laboratories in subsequent proposal evaluation.
    16. Customer contact, especially in the technical area, is most beneficial before the Government initiates proposal action. But customer contact, especially in the technical areas, is least beneficial after the Government initiates proposal action.
    17. Sell your capabilities to the customer before starting the proposal. A written proposal is a poor place to introduce and sell unknown capabilities to a customer. In such a case, it is better to use an associate already known to the customer.
    18. Don't operate in a vacuum in respect to the customer or to the competition.
    19. Proficiency in research-type efforts does not necessarily prepare an organization for accomplishing a development-type program.

20. Familiarity with a subject through analytical techniques is a poor substitute for experimental efforts.
21. Show willingness to consider other contractors and recognize the fact that no one contractor has the best of everything.
22. Do not touch on possible tradeoffs and fail to pursue them to show why you did or did not consider them.
23. Recognize where flexibility is required to reduce design freeze risk to a minimum.
24. Be sure that scope of test plan is complete in recognizing the role and participation of the many agencies involved.
25. Avoid use of percentages that actually are educated guesses in presenting any cost information to the customer.
26. Follow RFP format and instructions to the letter. Give the customer the information he is looking for.
27. Keep to the facts and minimize the flag waving.
28. Find unique examples to portray the company's technical know-how and resource capability.
29. Recognition for past accomplishments from high level sources may be used, but only with caution to avoid the accusation of "name dropping."
30. Do not develop charts or graphs that are so large and complex that they will be difficult to read after reduction in the proposal document.
31. Review program plan for any extras not necessarily required to meet the RFP or the design and mission requirements prior to final pricing.
32. Avoid presentation of uncertain or unsubstantiated financial data that will generate more requests for financial data.
33. The content of the proposal is more important than the form of presentation.
34. Do not hinder technical understanding and/or technical clarity by using excessive technical elegance and/or meticulous technical detail.

B. Most of the check-items listed are incorporated automatically into a proposal by fulfilling the dictates implicit in the following questions:
1. Have we followed what we genuinely believe is the customer's wish, or have we tried to sell him on our "pet" approach?
2. Have we eliminated all the excess in the proposal—not just in dollars but in design, methods, and so forth? Remember, the more we propose to do, the more it will cost.
3. Have we sufficiently coordinated the proposed design with all company functions concerned to establish that our plan is the best that we can possibly submit within the permitted time?
4. Is it precisely clear what we are proposing to do? Have we stated it concretely and unequivocally?
5. Have we offered realistic alternatives (if still responsive) rather than trying to convince the customer that he doesn't know what he is talking about or what he wants and that he should listen to our ideas instead?
6. Have we taken fullest advantage of our good points in what we have said in the proposal, or have we taken for granted that the customer already appreciates the company's capabilities?

7. Have we told the customer clearly just what we intend to do for him—made it crystal clear precisely what he can expect to get for his money?
8. Have we recognized the problem areas and offered realistic alternative approaches to overcome them?

XIII. Proposal Content
    A. Following is a checklist to further assist in the actual preparation of the proposal:
       1. Cite exploratory and advanced programs already accomplished and their impact relative to risk, alternatives, and schedule performance.
       2. Avoid changing customer schedule (assuming it can't be met) but show risks involved in adhering to his schedule. Offer possible alternatives and tradeoffs.
       3. Show history of analogous type programs to support the position that proposed schedules and decision points are realistic.
       4. Show technical risk versus schedule risk.
       5. Be truthful about risks (especially those already known to the customer).
       6. Solutions to problems should, wherever possible, relate to previous successful applications.
       7. Show highest level of company management participation in the program to convince the customer that this program is receiving necessary attention. It is not enough to have just an expression of initial interest. Show how this interest will permeate the organization and be followed throughout the life of the program.
       8. Tailor the management approach to the specific program and its problem areas.
       9. Identify the management process by which total company resources will be used to maximize the benefits of all talents.
     10. Show company organization in such a way as to provide sufficient understanding of the company.
     11. Show responsibilities of key personnel in the program/project organization—that they have key tasks and functions in an organization with a solid foundation.
     12. Biographies should show accomplishments of the individual, not just the jobs that he has held. Relate these accomplishments and experience to the proposed program.
     13. Show the valuable contributions that the individuals you have selected can make to this program.
     14. Indicate communication channels and interrelationship that will be exercised between co-contractors, subcontractors and vendors to assure complete integration and cooperation.
     15. Show principal management controls that the Program/Project Manager will have to do his job effectively.
     16. Demonstrate responsiveness to program changes, the ability of the Program/Project Manager to control funds, and the impact on the program of both.
     17. Show a working organization with key people in place.
     18. Show manpower projections, program loading and resources capabilities in words and charts.

19. Show specific technical subsystem uncertainties along with plans for solution.
20. Identify total systems management capability.
21. Show specific cost objectives for the efforts of cost improvement and value analyses.
22. Avoid boilerplating generalities and stress what is unique and different. Customer highlighted subjects such as Reliability, Value Engineering, and Integrated Logistic Support require particular attention.
23. Stress techniques to be used to assure that all objectives will be accomplished during the test program.
24. Give coverage in detail and scope for all support requirements. Understanding of the total system and its needs will be assessed by the customer.
25. Stress full capability of field programs. Installation and checkout plans may be of high importance to the customer. Thoroughness, scope, and level of detail will reveal depth of understanding, past experience and effort devoted to this critical phase.
26. Provide curves in support of manpower requirements to demonstrate realism in costs.
27. Show available facilities in detail (photographs, schematics, or whatever).
28. Stress willingness to use company-owned facilities with minimum of Government requirements.
29. Avoid guilt complex and negative attitude. Do not bring up problems, such as limited funds.

XIV. Costing Information Requirements
  A. The following checklist is a guide for the Proposal/Project Manager to ensure that necessary information is disseminated to those responsible for cost estimating.
  B. Customer Requirement Summary.
    1. Type of system or equipment.
    2. Type of anticipated contract—fixed-price or cost-reimbursement category.
    3. Anticipated date of award.
    4. Previous requisitions.
    5. Proposed Item.
       a. Segregated by work scope.
       b. Description of item and specifications.
       c. Quantity.
       d. Unit having task responsibility.
    6. Applicable military and/or customer specifications.
    7. Responsibility for design specifications.
    8. Proposed delivery schedule for all proposed items.
    9. CFE or GFE material.
    10. Technical exceptions.
    11. Special estimating instructions.
    12. Other instructions (i.e., subcontract items).

   C. Design Specification Summary.
1. Release schedule.
2. Equipment content, weight and power.
3. Packaging techniques.
4. Electrical and mechanical description.
5. Parts list.
6. Items subcontracted.
7. Special testing on components and subcontracted items.

XV. Material for Final Management Briefing
   A. In preparation for the final management briefing, the proposal management team should provide the following:
1. Completed technical proposal.
2. Summary of salient technical features.
3. Completed cost estimates.
4. Recommended total selling price.
5. List of assumptions.
6. Itemization of risks.
7. Incremental pricing effect.
8. Summary of selected strategy
   Customer
   Competitor
   Internal
9. Tradeoffs or cost effectiveness calculations.
10. Alternative proposals considered.
11. Investment (i.e., dollars, people and facilities).
12. Recommended negotiation tradeoffs.
13. Eventuality plans.
14. Recommended continuing effort.

XVI. Technical Proposal Evaluation.
   A. The following checklist might be used to evaluate the completeness, accuracy and clarity of presentation of the technical proposal:
1. In summary, have you:
   a. Demonstrated familiarity with the customer's problem?
   b. Presented the crux of the solution in simple direct language?
   c. Indicated unique competence to do the job?
   d. Highlighted your program or hardware and company experience to be applied?
   e. Given the development/producibility status of each major component?
   f. Given a physical description of the system or equipment including a photograph or sketch of all major components? Given a summary table of equipment size, weight, power, reliability, life, mean-time-to-repair, or whatever the need requires?
   g. Specified any major deviations you feel you must take to the specification?
   h. Enumerated any new or important features?
   i. Demonstrated conclusively why the customer should buy from us?
   j. Identified any alternatives to be offered, briefly told why, and indicated where they are covered?

2. Have you analyzed and documented in the proposal the technical risk versus the schedule risk and financial risk for each alternative solution proposed?

3. Have you shown the key technical design tree for the program and substantiated this in detailed sections? Have you indicated preferred results?

4. For each alternative considered (and in the summary or a separate section), have you clearly listed the key technical advantages of the approach compared to others considered?

5. Have you highlighted your responsiveness to the RFP?

6. Have you demonstrated objectivity in key decisions?

7. In what way are tradeoffs utilized and made clear to top level evaluators?

8. Are you sure we have not misread or misinterpreted the customer's statement of desired work? Have we clearly stated all assumptions and interpretations?

9. Does the program we propose solve the problem the customer stated or does it emphasize another problem and another solution?

10. Have we proposed a "pet" idea rather than investigating all possible solutions and picking the best one?

11. Do we have open for investigation several approaches rather than picking one? Is this really necessary?

12. Do we merely state we "will comply" with customer requirements or do we also show how?

13. Will the variations, exceptions and deviations to the customer's desired statement of work benefit the Government or will they prejudice the adequate performance of the program?

14. Have we shown originality in concept in the proposal? Have we made recommendations for program improvement?

15. Have we shown specific theoretical models to be employed in technical tradeoffs? Have we given their current status and summarized how they will be applied?

16. Have we recognized and addressed the military/aerospace problem involved? Have we shown the integration with other systems?

17. Have we recognized, considered and identified the limitations of the state of the art?

18. Have we demonstrated our consideration of the economics involved?

19. Have we demonstrated our understanding of the logical integration of human factors? Have we stated the personnel profiles being considered?

20. Have we correctly identified all required laboratory apparatus, test equipment, and measuring or recording equipment required and available? Have we shown that they [are] sufficiently accurate?

21. Have we demonstrated our ability to conduct the requisite operational analyses?

22. Did we describe the process of solving the technical problems including the alternative approaches rejected and why they were rejected?

23. Have we shown adequate and convincing background for our recommended solution including analytical work and applicable test/operational experience?
24. Have we met all specifications as well as general written or implied instructions?
25. Have we analyzed each military or customer specification for our ability to comply, for its appropriateness to the customer's problem, and for the cost of such compliance?
26. Have we expanded the definition of implied customer requirements?
27. Have we demonstrated how we designed (or will design) for maintainability and reliability and have we described these design features?
28. Have we leaned toward the customer's:
    a. Engineering concepts?
    b. Specially developed components or devices?
    c. General purpose test and handling equipment?
29. Have we demonstrated:
    a. The pertinence of our system to the problem?
    b. The completeness of our system?
    c. The quality of our system?
    d. The integration of the subsystem elements of our system?
    e. The technical competence of our subsystem designs?
30. Have we used too much (or too many):
    a. Propaganda?
    b. Technical jargon?
    c. Inconsistent forms or styles?
    d. Duplication or ambiguity?

XVII. Review of Material and Data
    A. In preparation for the final management review briefing, the program management team should provide the following:

	Pre-RFP	RFP Receipt	Final Proposal	Dept. Staff
1. Sales Plan	X	X	X	
2. Opportunity Information Log	X	X	X	
3. RFP Requirements Including Hardware				
Preliminary	X			
Final		X	X	X
4. Competitive Evaluation	X	X	X	X
5. Customer Climate and Organization	X	X	X	X
6. Assumptions	X	X	X	X
7. Program Organization				
8. Proposal Plan and Schedule				
Preliminary	X			
Final		X	X	X
9. Technical Features		X	X	X
10. Costs				

10. Costs (continued)	Pre-RFP	RFP Receipt	Final Proposal	Dept. Staff
Bogeys	X	X		
Estimates			X	X
11. Recommended Selling Price and Pricing Strategy			X	X
12. Incentive Proposal			X	X
13. Risks	X	X	X	X
14. Tradeoffs or Cost Effectiveness	X	X	X	X
15. Alternative Proposals	X	X	X	X
16. Investment				
Dollars—Proposal Cost	X	X	X	
Dollars—Program Cost	X	X	X	X
People	X	X	X	X
Facilities	X	X	X	X
17. Negotiation Tradeoffs			X	X
18. Alternative Courses of Action		X	X	X
19. Continuing Action Plans			X	X

XVIII. Do's and Don'ts of Oral Presentations

    A. Do not give a general or capability pitch (unless specifically requested). Do not give a laundry list. Do not present a solution looking for a problem.

    B. Make sure that a pitch is specific and that it is something that will solve the customer's problems.

    C. Start oral communication at the Program/Project Engineer level and work yourself up.

    D. At the outset of every presentation, tell the customer why you are there and what you want.

    E. Tailor each presentation to the audience and to the objectives.

    F. Dry-run all presentations.

    G. Make sure the customer knows (beforehand) what you intend to present and that he agrees with it.

    H. Be frank.

    I. Consider problems after delivery and maintain communications.

    J. Present earnestly and confidently. And above all, knowledgeably. Remember that the difference between the right word and the almost-right word is like the difference between lightning and the lightning bug.

EVALUATION CHECKLISTS

Table I
General Quality and Responsiveness of the Proposal

COMPLETENESS AND THOROUGHNESS

Considerations:

    1.   Have all essential data required by the Request for Proposal been included?

2. Is the proposal easily legible, well-organized, clear and concise; or is it an uncoordinated collection of unrelated data, hastily assembled and haphazardly edited?
3. Is all data pertinent and significant, or is much of it irrelevant data collected from past proposals for the purpose of impressing by volume alone?
4. Is the proposal presented in a manner which will simplify evaluation, or does it diffuse and confuse the essentials?

GRASP OF PROBLEM

Considerations:
1. Does the proposal recognize and differentiate between the simpler and the more difficult performance requirements?
2. Does it evidence recognition of inherent maintenance and supply problems?
3. Does it demonstrate an awareness of human and environmental factors affecting the scope of the work?
4. Does it evidence a recognition of relationships with other contractors and agencies, and the coordination and liaison problems involved?
5. Is the estimate of professional, technical, and administrative manpower requirements in consonance with the project requirements? Is there a reasonable balance between professional personnel and technicians?
6. Is there evidence of appropriate utilization of scientific and professional personnel; or conversely, are technicians offered where highly qualified professional specialists are required?

RESPONSIVENESS TO TERMS, CONDITIONS AND TIME OF PERFORMANCE

Considerations
1. Is there adequate evidence of intent to meet all terms and conditions specified in the Request for Proposal with regard to reporting requirements, proprietary rights, documentation disclosures, and any other special technical conditions cited in the RFP?
2. Does the proposed delivery schedule conform with mandatory or target schedule requirements? Where time of performance is of the essence and is a competitive evaluation factor, is the proposed delivery schedule adequately supported by the technical proposal?
3. To what extent is the offerer willing to commit him- or herself on the firm requirements, and on the "best efforts" portions of the Technical Scope of Work?
4. If award is contingent upon the existence of a follow-on production capability, is the proposal responsive to the data requested in the RFP? Does data submitted substantiate production capability and cost estimates?

Table II
Organization, Personnel, and Facilities

EVIDENCE OF GOOD ORGANIZATION AND MANAGEMENT PRACTICES
Considerations:
1. Does the proposal evidence the breadth and depth of management capability appropriate to the project? Is there evidence of stability of job tenure in upper management echelons?

2. How does the proposed task organization integrate into the overall organization in terms of effective lines of authority and communication, and in terms of effective integration of research, development, design, drafting, technical writing, reliability, and test functions?

QUALIFICATIONS OF PERSONNEL

Considerations:
1. Does the proposal include definite plans for the assignment of specific key personnel?
2. Do assigned key personnel possess the experience, educational background, and record of past accomplishments appropriate to the scope of the work?
3. Is the quality of personnel as set forth in the proposal generally supported by the salary scales?
4. Is the proposal dependent upon any substantial recruitment of key personnel? If so, would such recruitment result in high cost of performance, or might it adversely affect other vital contracts in the geographical areas of the offerer?
5. Is the success of the project excessively dependent upon subcontract or temporary consultants? If so, to what extent are subcontract plans firm and reasonably irrevocable?

ADEQUACY OF FACILITIES

Considerations:
1. Are the proposed laboratory, pilot manufacturing, and test facilities adequate for the requirements of the Technical Scope of Work?
2. Are the proposed facilities conveniently available to engineering personnel?
3. Is the proposal contingent upon Government furnished capital equipment beyond that set out in the RFP?

EXPERIENCE IN SIMILAR OR RELATED FIELDS

Considerations:
1. Is the normal commercial or Government business of the offerer closely related to the proposed work?
2. Is the offerer experienced with practices and procedures of the contracting agency to an extent which would increase the effectiveness of his or her performance?
3. Does the company enjoy a respected reputation in the field to which the proposal relates?

RECORD OF PAST PERFORMANCE

Considerations:
1. Has the offerer held previous contracts with the agency or other Government establishment?
2. Were schedule commitments generally met?
3. Did the contractor solve his own technical problems, or did he or she rely heavily upon the technical staff of the agency?

4. Was there an unusually high number of contractual problems which might be attributed to inflexibility, naivete, or lack of cooperation on the part of the contractor?
5. If there were significant cost over-runs, were they due to an incompetently low initial cost estimate, or to valid problems which could not have been anticipated?

POTENTIAL AS A PRODUCTION FACILITY

Considerations:
1. Does the proposal present adequate evidence of the existence of physical plant, personnel, and financial resources to permit transition from development to production?
2. Do other mobilization planning commitments of the offerer preclude proposed production of the item under mobilization conditions?
3. Does the proximity of a production facility reflect in valuable feedback to development engineers? If so, is the production-orientation of development engineers of significance to the successful completion of the proposed work?

GEOGRAPHIC LOCATION

Considerations:
1. Will the location of the facility result in excessive inconvenience, expense, and lot time in the conduct of liaison and supervision?
2. Is the plan located in a critical defense area? If so, is it significant to future production plans?

PLANT SECURITY

Considerations:
1. Will extensive alterations be required to physical facilities to meet security requirements of the contract?

TABLE III
TECHNICAL APPROACH

PROJECT PLANNING

Considerations:
1. Does the proposal demonstrate detailed and realistic scheduling of the various technical phases of the project?
2. Does the proposal demonstrate effective review, evaluation, and control and specific check points?
3. Are proposed schedules in line with available personnel resources?
4. Are parallel investigations proposed on critical problems and avoided on more routine problems?
5. Are breadboard tests planned early in the program in vital design areas?

RELIABILITY

Considerations:
1. Is proposal based on proven components and techniques?
2. Is redundancy provided in critical functional features?
3. Will design be based upon "worst-case" analysis?
4. How are theoretical reliability analyses and reliability testing integrated into the design program?

MAINTAINABILITY

Considerations:
1. Have self-checking features been considered in the proposal?
2. Are high mortality components intended to be easily accessible and fully interchangeable?
3. Are requirements for special tools, fixtures, and test equipment expected to be minimal?
4. Has adequate consideration been given to "throwaway" of low-cost modules and field repair of high-cost modules?
5. Has consideration been given to field modification for probable future changes?
6. Does the proposal avoid excessive dependence upon periodic field adjustment or calibration?

PRODUCTION AND ECONOMY

Considerations:
1. Does proposal evidence maximum design simplicity?
2. Does proposal evidence the elimination of special precision components, selection of fits, matched pairs, etc.?
3. Is proposed design overly dependent upon special capital production equipment, critical process controls, and critical materials?
4. Does the proposal adequately consider maximum use of standard components and indicate procedures for screening of selected components and indicate procedures for screening of selected components against standard items?
5. If production cost estimates were requested, are these reasonable, and are they adequately supported by the technical proposal?

TECHNICAL DATA AND DOCUMENTATION

Considerations:
1. Does the proposal contain assurances that drawings, specifications, and other technical data to be supplied under terms of the Request For Proposal will be complete, thoroughly checked for accuracy, and generally suitable for competitive procurement purposes?
2. Does the proposal contain any reservations on full technical disclosure, or restrictions on the use of such data?

3. Are proposed work-hours for drafting and technical writing consistent with requirements for adequate documentation?

TABLE IV
RELATIVE WEIGHTS

EVALUATION FACTORS	WEIGHT
I. General Quality and Responsiveness of Proposal	
A. Completeness and Thoroughness	5
B. Grasp of Problem	10
C. Responsiveness to Terms. Conditions and Time of Performance	3
II. Organization, Personnel, and Facilities	
A. Evidence of Good Organizational and Management Practices	5
B. Qualifications of Personnel	10
C. Adequacy of Facilities	8
D. Experience in Similar or Related Fields	5
E. Record of Past Experience	5
F. Geographic Location	5
III. Technical Approach	
A. Reliability	10
B. Maintainability	5
C. Producibility and Economy	5
D. Technical Data and Documentation	5
E. Overall Size and Weight	10
F. Power Consumption	10
G. Environmental Range	3
H. Shielding Techniques	8
IV. Final Technical Evaluation	
(I) General Quality and Responsiveness of Proposal	1
(II) Organization, Personnel, and Facilities	2
(III) Technical Approach	3

Index

by Linda Webster